Mike McGrath

Windows 10

in easy steps

special edition

Third Edition

In easy steps is an imprint of In Easy Steps Limited
16 Hamilton Terrace · Holly Walk · Leamington Spa
Warwickshire · United Kingdom · CV32 4LY
www.ineasysteps.com

Third Edition

Notice of Liability

Every effort has been made to ensure that this book contains accurate
and current information. However, In Easy Steps Limited and the
author shall not be liable for any loss or damage suffered by readers
as a result of any information contained herein.

Trademarks

Microsoft® and Windows® are registered trademarks of Microsoft
Corporation. All other trademarks are acknowledged as belonging to
their respective companies.

In Easy Steps Limited supports The Forest Stewardship Council (FSC),
the leading international forest certification organization. All our titles
that are printed on Greenpeace approved FSC certified paper carry the
FSC logo.

MIX
Paper from
responsible sources
FSC® C020837

Printed and bound in the United Kingdom

ISBN 978-1-84078-807-5

Contents

5   Windows 10 apps   79

6   Desktop and Taskbar   95

7   Built-in programs   117

19   Protection and Ease of Access   321

20   Troubleshooting   335

21   Backup and recovery   353

1 Introducing Windows 10

This chapter introduces Microsoft's latest operating system by describing its new features, explaining what editions are available, and exploring some free Microsoft downloads.

Windows releases

There have been many versions of Microsoft Windows. The operating system was initially designed for IBM-compatible PCs, but was later extended to support larger computers such as servers and workstations. A derivative version, Windows CE, was also developed for smaller devices such as PDAs and cell phones.

The main versions of Windows that have been released include:

Date	PC Versions	Server Versions
1985	Windows 1.0	
1987	Windows 2.0	
1990	Windows 3.0	
1993		Windows NT 3.1 Server
1995	Windows 95	
1996		Windows NT 4.0 Server
1998	Windows 98	
2000	Windows ME	Windows 2000 Server
2001	Windows XP	
2003		Windows Server 2003
2006	Windows Vista	Windows Server 2003 R2
2008		Windows Server 2008
2009	Windows 7	Windows Server 2008 R2
2012	Windows 8	Windows Server 2012
2013		Windows Server 2012 R2
2015	Windows 10	
2016		Windows Server 2016

The first three versions of Windows listed above were designed for the 16-bit processor featured in the PCs of the day. Windows 95, 98 and ME added support for 32-bit processors. Windows NT was for 32-bit only, while XP and 2000 added 64-bit support. Windows Vista, Windows 7, Windows 8, Windows 10, and the newer server editions support both 32-bit or 64-bit processors. Each version of Windows builds on the functions and features included in the previous versions, so that the knowledge and experience you have gained will still be valuable, even though the appearance and the specifics of the operations may have changed.

Windows 10 receives regular updates from Microsoft. This book describes a "snapshot" of the operating system at the time of writing. Some features may change as Microsoft continues to develop and improve the operating system.

Hot tip

The original IBM PC was supported by **PC-DOS** and **MS-DOS** operating systems, developed for IBM-compatible PCs.

Hot tip

Windows 10 for PCs and larger tablets comes in four main editions:
· **Home**
· **Pro**
· **Enterprise**
· **Education**

Windows 10 compatibility

With Windows 10, Microsoft has created an operating system designed to be compatible with a range of different devices. To make this possible, Windows 10 has a new feature called "Continuum" that helps the operating system work better with devices that support both a mouse and keyboard, and touch input – for example: Microsoft's Surface tablet or Lenovo's Yoga laptops. Continuum offers two operating modes for each type of device:

Tablet mode

When a device is in Tablet mode, the layout of the operating system is appropriate for touchscreen input. This means that the Start screen has tiles that you can tap to launch apps, the apps appear full-screen, and you can navigate using touch gestures. When you connect a mouse and keyboard, or flip your laptop around, you are prompted to change into Desktop mode.

Desktop mode

When a device is in Desktop mode, the layout of the operating system is appropriate for mouse and keyboard input. This means that the Start menu has an A-Z list that you can click to launch apps, the apps appear in windows, and you can navigate using the mouse buttons or keyboard shortcuts. When you disconnect a mouse and keyboard, or flip your laptop around, you are prompted to change into Tablet mode.

Tablet mode is less demanding of system resources, and its introduction in Windows 10 clearly indicates that Microsoft recognizes the importance of mobile devices for the future.

Windows 10 shares its styling and kernel code with many platforms including desktop PCs, laptops, tablets, and even the Xbox games console. This move towards cross-compatibility is one that is intended to establish Microsoft on multiple devices.

A key element in this is the OneDrive app, which is described in detail later. OneDrive enables users to store all their data and apps online, and synchronize that data across all their devices. As a result, they will be able to log in to OneDrive on any Windows 10 device and immediately access their documents, pictures, media, and preference settings. Whatever or whoever's device they are using, it will be as though they are using their own.

The New icon pictured above indicates a new or enhanced feature introduced in Windows 10. For example, the **Continuum** feature is new in Windows 10.

OneDrive is the original "SkyDrive" facility. It was renamed for copyright reasons. Its features and functions remain unchanged.

New features in Windows 10

Each new version of Windows adds new features and facilities. In Windows 10, these include:

Familiar and improved

Windows 10 provides free semi-annual **feature updates** that download automatically to add new features as they become available.

- **Customizable Start menu** – a welcome return after the controversial removal of the Start menu in Windows 8.

- **Windows Defender & Windows Firewall** – integral anti-virus defense against malware and spyware.

- **Fast Startup** – rapid system startup and ready to instantly resume from Sleep mode.

- **Task View** – enhanced with Timeline to quickly resume activities you were working on in the past.

The customizable **Start menu** is a new and welcome feature in Windows 10.

- **Battery Saver** – limits background activity to make the most of your battery.

- **Windows Update** – automatically helps keep your device safer and running smoothly.

- **Bluetooth** – automatically detects nearby devices that can be easily paired for file sharing.

Cortana Personal Digital Assistant

Cortana is a new feature in Windows 10 and requires you to have a Microsoft account. Performance may vary by region and device.

- **Talk or type naturally** – lets you ask for assistance by typing into a text box or by speaking into a microphone.

- **Personal proactive suggestions** – provides intelligent recommendations based upon your personal information.

- **Reminders** – prompts you according to the time of day, your location, or the person you are in contact with.

- **Search the web, your device, and the Cloud** – find help, apps, files, settings, or anything, anywhere.

- **"Hey Cortana" hands-free activation** – passive voice activation recognizes your voice.

Windows Hello

- **Native fingerprint recognition** – the ability to log in to the operating system using a fingerprint reader.

- **Native facial and iris recognition** – the ability to log in to the operating system using a camera.

- **Enterprise level security** – the ability to log in to the operating system using a 4-digit PIN code or picture.

Windows Hello is new in Windows 10. Facial recognition requires a camera that has RGB, infrared, and 3D lenses.

Multi-doing

- **Virtual desktops** – multiple desktops to separate related tasks into their own workspaces.

- **Snap Assist** – easily position up to four apps on the screen.

- **Snap Across** – easily position apps across different monitors.

Continuum

- **Tablet mode** – an interface appropriate for touch input and navigation using gestures.

- **Desktop mode** – an interface appropriate for mouse and keyboard input, and navigation clicks and shortcuts.

Virtual desktops and **Continuum** are both new features in Windows 10.

Microsoft Edge

- **Web browser** – streamlined for compliance with the latest HTML5 web standards.

- **Reading view** – instantly remove formatting distractions from web pages to make reading easier.

- **Built-in ink support** – add Web Notes to existing web pages then save or share the edited page.

- **Cortana integration** – search the device, web, and Cloud to quickly find what you need.

Microsoft Edge is new in Windows 10. It lets you write **Web Notes** with a digital pen, with your mouse, or with your finger on touchscreen devices.

Editions of Windows 10

There are four main editions of Windows 10 for PCs and tablets:

Windows 10 Home edition
This is the consumer-focused desktop version that includes a broad range of Universal Windows Apps such as Photos, Maps, Mail, Calendar, and Groove Music.

Windows 10 Pro edition
This is the desktop version for small businesses.

Windows 10 Enterprise edition
This is the desktop version for large organizations.

Windows 10 Education edition
This builds on the Enterprise edition to meet the needs of schools.

The following tables list the features in Windows 10 and illustrate that some of the features are specific to certain editions:

Hot tip

There is also a **Windows 10 Pro for Workstations** edition for intensive computing on high-end hardware.

Features	Home	Pro	Enterprise	Education
Customizable Start menu	Y	Y	Y	Y
Defender & Firewall	Y	Y	Y	Y
Fast start & InstantGo	Y	Y	Y	Y
TPM support	Y	Y	Y	Y
Battery Saver	Y	Y	Y	Y
Windows Update	Y	Y	Y	Y
Cortana Digital Assistant	Y	Y	Y	Y
Windows Hello login	Y	Y	Y	Y
Virtual desktops	Y	Y	Y	Y
Snap Assist	Y	Y	Y	Y
Tablet & Desktop modes	Y	Y	Y	Y
Microsoft Edge	Y	Y	Y	Y
Device Encryption	Y	Y	Y	Y
Domain Join	-	Y	Y	Y
Group Policy Manager	-	Y	Y	Y
BitLocker	-	Y	Y	Y
Enterprise Mode IE	-	Y	Y	Y
Assigned Access 8.1	-	Y	Y	Y
Remote Desktop	-	Y	Y	Y

Features	Home	Pro	Enterprise	Education
Client Hyper-V	-	Y	Y	Y
Direct Access	-	Y	Y	Y
Windows To Go Creator	-	-	Y	Y
AppLocker	-	-	Y	Y
Branch Cache	-	-	Y	Y
Start Screen Group Policy	-	-	Y	Y
Side-load Business Apps	Y	Y	Y	Y
Mobile Device Manager	Y	Y	Y	Y
Azure Active Directory	-	Y	Y	Y
Business Store	-	Y	Y	Y
Granular UX Control	-	-	Y	Y
Easy Upgrade (Pro to Enterprise)	-	Y	Y	-
Easy Upgrade (Home to Education)	Y	-	-	Y
Microsoft Passport	Y	Y	Y	Y
Enterprise Data Protection	-	Y	Y	Y
Credential Guard	-	-	Y	Y
Device Guard	-	-	Y	Y
Update for Business	-	Y	Y	Y
Current Branch - Business	-	Y	Y	Y
Long Term Service Branch	-	-	Y	-

There are also three special editions of Windows 10:

Windows 10 S edition
This is a feature-limited version designed primarily for low-end devices in education.

Windows 10 IoT edition
This is an embedded version for use in small low-cost devices intended for data management.

Windows 10 Team
This is a version for the Surface Hub interactive whiteboard.

Windows 10 brings **Xbox gaming** to the PC and is available in 111 languages!

Microsoft OneDrive

A very important function built in to Windows 10 is its ability to utilize what is commonly known as "The Cloud". Essentially, cloud computing is a technology that uses the internet and centralized remote servers to maintain data and applications. It allows consumers and businesses to use applications they don't own, and to access their personal files on any computer that has internet access. The technology enables much more efficient computing by centralizing data storage, processing and bandwidth.

So how do you get into the Cloud? There are actually several ways: One is to open an account with a dedicated service such as Dropbox. You will be given a free amount of storage space; 2GB initially (which can be increased by referring friends), in which you can store virtually anything you choose to. If you need more, you will be charged a fee depending on the amount required.

A second way is to buy a product from a major software manufacturer. A typical example is Acronis True Image – a data backup program that provides huge online storage, which enables you to create Cloud-based backups.

A third way is courtesy of Microsoft OneDrive, which can be accessed online. OneDrive is basically a portal that allows you to access 5GB of free online storage.

Discover more on **Dropbox** Cloud storage at **dropbox.com**

Acronis

Discover more on **True Image** at **acronis.com**

OneDrive

You need a Microsoft account to sign in to **OneDrive**. By default, you get 5GB of free OneDrive storage space with Windows10. Find up-to-date information on plan allowances and pricing at **https:// onedrive.live.com/ about/en-us/plans**

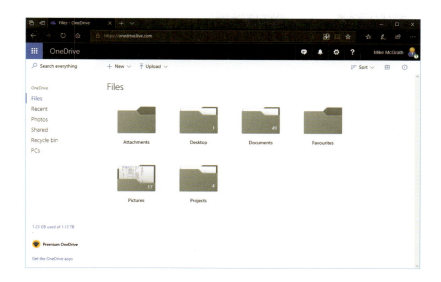

You can log in to access OneDrive with any web browser. Simply visit **onedrive.live.com**

Once logged in, you will see that OneDrive has started you off with a number of pre-configured folders. Windows 10 is supplied configured to automatically synchronize these folders on OneDrive. You can delete these folders, rename them, create more folders, nest folders within folders, and upload/download files.

Once uploaded, your data can be accessed from any smartphone, tablet or PC, from anywhere in the world and at any time. You can also access and upload data from within programs in the Microsoft Office suite of applications.

One of the coolest features of OneDrive is that it enables online sharing and collaboration. For example, you can share your holiday snaps with friends and family regardless of where they are, while business applications provide access to documents while on the move or sharing documents between offices.

If you access OneDrive directly from a browser, you will have a "lite" version of **Microsoft Office** with which to create documents while online.

A key aspect of OneDrive is that it enables data to be synchronized across a range of devices. For example, emails on your PC can be automatically loaded onto your smartphone or tablet, and vice versa. You can also synchronize various settings such as personalization of desktop background, theme, colors, passwords, app settings, and many more. This enables users to maintain the computing environment they are comfortable with across all their computing devices.

Windows 10 connectivity

Windows 10 is terrific at connecting all your devices – whether it's a 3-year-old printer or projecting to your brand new TV with Miracast. Windows 10 is built on a common core and includes Universal Windows Apps, so people using Windows 10 for both their PC and portable devices will get an optimal, seamless experience as they transition between devices throughout the day.

Microsoft recognizes that many people also use iPhone or Android devices but want to ensure their Windows 10 content remains available to them across all the devices they own, regardless of the operating system. So Microsoft has produced a number of apps for Android, iPhone and iPad devices to make them work well with a Windows 10 PC.

So, whatever the operating system, this means that all your files and content can be magically available on your PC and phone:

- With the Cortana app on your phone you can have your Personal Digital Assistant always available.

- With the OneDrive app on your phone, every photo you take can automatically appear on your phone and Windows 10 PC.

- With the Groove Music app you can access and play your music from OneDrive on your phone or Windows 10 PC.

- With the OneNote app on your phone, any note you write on your Windows 10 PC can show up on your phone – and any note you write on your phone can show up on your PC.

- With the Skype app on your phone you can make video calls and messages – free over Wi-Fi.

- With Word, Excel, and PowerPoint apps on your phone you can work on Office documents without moving files around.

- With the Outlook app on your phone you can get your email messages and calendar reminders everywhere.

To help people make everything work together, the Windows 10 Settings screen provides a feature that will help you link your Windows 10 PC to your Android, iPhone or iPad device.

Miracast is a Wireless Display (WiDi) technology your PC can use to project its screen onto any TV that supports Miracast.

Cortana and **Groove Music** are new features in Windows 10.

You must use the same **Microsoft account** on your PC, phone, and tablet to automatically synchronize your content across these devices.

1. Click the **Start** button, then choose the **Settings** item

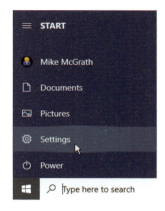

2. Next, click **Phone**, **Add a phone**, **Link phone** to open the "Microsoft account" dialog

3. Enter your phone number in the dialog, then click the button to **Send** button a message to your phone

4. The received message contains a link to install the **Your Phone Companion** app – tap the link and install the app

5. Grant permissions to allow the **Your Phone Companion** app access to your phone's file system

6. Your PC now recognizes your phone as a linked device on the **Settings**, **Phone** screen

You can find the Your Phone Companion app on **Google Play** store.

7. Your phone is now linked to your PC and provides an option to install popular Microsoft apps onto your phone. A **Your Phone** item is added to the Start menu so you can access text messages and photos on your phone from your PC

Microsoft Office Online

Microsoft Office is a very important application for many people, so here we will take a brief look at Microsoft Office Online and see how it fits in with Windows 10.

Office Online includes the core apps: Word, Excel, PowerPoint, Outlook, and OneNote for both PC and touchscreen. Your completed documents, spreadsheets, and presentations can be saved online in your OneDrive for easy access or sharing. Alternatively, they can be downloaded to your computer and saved as a local file – just as you would with an installed app.

You can compare versions of **Microsoft Office** online at products.office.com /en-us/compare-all-microsoft-office-products

1 Open the Microsoft Edge web browser, then navigate to the **office.com** website

2 Click the **Sign in** button then type the email address and credentials for your Microsoft account

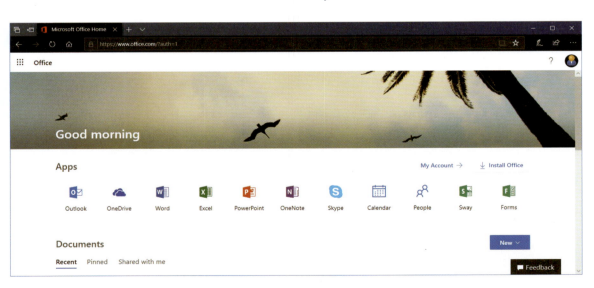

You will need a Microsoft account to sign in to **Office Online** apps.

3 Choose the online app you wish to use. For example, choose the **Word** app to create a cover letter

4 When the Word app opens on a new tab in the browser you are presented with a selection of ready-made templates that you can select. For example, choose the **Business letter** template

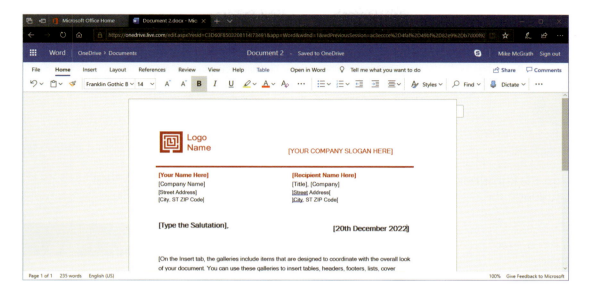

5 Edit the template to suit your requirements by inserting your name and address details, etc.

6 When you are happy with the letter, click the **File** menu item at the top-left of the window

7 Now, choose a save location and document format

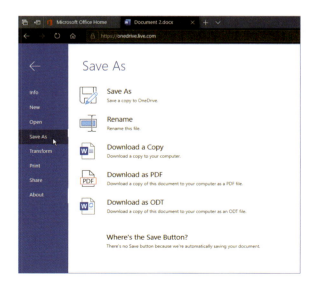

Use the **Rename** option before saving unless you are happy to use the automatically assigned default name.

Windows freebies

Microsoft knows we all like to get something for nothing so they offer free theme downloads with which to personalize your PC at **support.microsoft.com/en-us/help/14165**. The themes are divided into categories of interest, such as "Art (photographic)". To grab a free theme:

1 Click the **See all themes** link then choose a category from the list on the left of the themes page

2 Scroll through the list to choose a theme, then click its **Download** link to get the "themepack" file

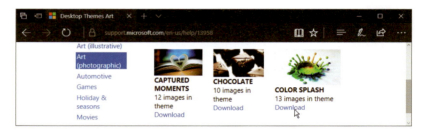

3 When the download completes you will find the themepack file in your **Downloads** folder

4 Right-click on the file icon and choose **Open** to install that theme on your PC

Hot tip

Other free Microsoft downloads are available at this website, such as **Desktop Backgrounds** and **Language Packs**.

Hot tip

You can also download free **Themes** from the Microsoft Store.

Don't forget

You can change or uninstall themes at any time from **Settings**, **Personalization**, **Themes**. See page 99-106 for more information on themes.

2 Choosing your computer

This chapter examines the hardware requirements of both Windows 10 and the computers on which it can be run, describing CPUs, memory, touchscreens, sensors, and much more.

Windows 10 requirements

Traditionally, every edition of Windows has required more in the way of hardware resources than the editions that preceded it. This came to a stop with Windows 7, which ran quite satisfactorily on the same hardware that its predecessor, Windows Vista, did. This has continued with Windows 10, so users upgrading from either Windows 7 or Windows 8.1 do not have to also upgrade their computer hardware.

The official system requirements of Windows 10 are as follows:

- **Processor** – 1GHz or faster, or SoC (System on a Chip).
- **Memory (RAM)** – 1GB (32-bit) or 2GB (64-bit).
- **Disk space** – 16GB (32-bit) or 20GB (64-bit).
- **Graphics** – Microsoft DirectX 9 with WDDM driver.

Please note that the above is the absolute minimum required. While Windows 10 will run on this hardware, it may not do so particularly well. To be more specific, it will probably be on the slow side, and if you run resource-intensive software such as 3D games, Photoshop, etc., it may struggle to cope. If you wish to avoid this, our recommendation is to install twice the recommended amount of memory – i.e. 2GB on a 32-bit system and 4GB on a 64-bit system.

In addition, the following will be required to use some features:

- **Touch gestures** – tablet/monitor that supports multi-touch.
- **Snap apps** – screen resolution of at least 1024 x 600 pixels.
- **Internet access** – wired or wireless.
- **Microsoft account** – required for some features.
- **Cortana support** – speech recognition requires a microphone.
- **Windows Hello** – fingerprint reader or specialized camera.
- **Continuum** – tablet or 2-in-1 PC, or manual mode selection.
- **BitLocker To Go** – a USB drive.
- **Hyper-V** – a 64-bit system with second level address translation (SLAT) plus an additional 2GB of memory.

Processors

The Central Processing Unit (CPU), more than any other part, influences the speed at which the computer runs. It also determines how many things the PC can do concurrently to efficiently multi-task, before it starts to struggle.

With regard to speed, a CPU is rated by its clock speed – for example, 3.4GHz. As described on the previous page, Windows 10 requires a 1GHz or faster CPU. As the slowest CPU currently on the market is 2GHz (twice as fast), the issue of CPU speed is not something the typical home user needs to be too concerned about. It's only important to users who require more power, such as hardcore gamers.

The CPU's, and hence the PC's, multi-tasking capabilities may well be a different story, though. Modern computers are frequently required to do a number of things at the same time. Each task requires a separate process or "thread" from the CPU, so anyone who is going to do a lot of multi-tasking will need a CPU that can handle numerous threads simultaneously.

Don't get fixated with CPU clock speed. You should also consider things like the number of cores and the size of the cache.

This means buying a multi-core CPU. These devices are no faster than traditional single-core CPUs but because they have several cores, their multi-tasking capabilities are increased enormously. Currently, there are two-, four-, six- and even eight-core models on the market and the more your PC is going to have to do, the more cores you will need in your CPU.

There is also the issue of the CPU manufacturer. Currently, the majority of computing devices are laptops and desktop PCs. These both use CPUs from Intel and AMD exclusively. While Intel CPUs are often considered to be better than AMD's offerings, there really isn't much in it – whichever brand of CPU you choose will provide similar performance.

For most users, anything over two cores is overkill. **Don't waste your money** on performance you will never use.

For those of you looking to buy a tablet device, the issue of the CPU is more complicated. This is because the CPU in these devices is usually part of a combination chipset that also houses the system's graphics, memory, interface controllers, voltage regulators and more. This combination chip is referred to as a "System on a Chip" (SoC), and its main benefit is that it reduces the space needed for these components. This, in turn, lowers power requirements and increases battery life.

...cont'd

Things are further complicated by the fact that most SoC manufacturers, including Apple, Samsung, Texas Instruments, and NVIDEA, use a CPU architecture called ARM that is produced and licensed by a company called ARM Holdings. Therefore, this part of a SoC will be identical regardless of the manufacturer – the rest of the SoC, however, will not be. This makes it very difficult to compare SoCs on a like-for-like basis.

Many tablets use SoCs but there are some (usually the more capable ones) that use a specially designed low-power CPU of the same type found in desktop PCs. Intel's Atom CPU is a good example of this.

However, whatever the type of CPU, be it a full-size AMD FX, an Intel Atom, or a SoC, the basic premise of clock speed determining the speed of the CPU and the number of cores determining its multi-tasking capability, or power, is the same.

Hardware capabilities

If you are thinking about upgrading to Windows 10, there's a good chance you may also be considering upgrading your PC. If so, you need to give some thought to the hardware that will be in it. Alternatively, it may simply be time to give it a boost.

Whichever, to ensure your PC is capable of doing what you want it to, there are several components you need to consider. The CPU was discussed on page 27, but there is also the memory, video system, and disk drive to consider.

Random Access Memory (RAM)

As with the CPU, memory is a component that has a major impact on the performance of a computer. You may have the fastest CPU in the galaxy, but without an adequate amount of memory all that processing power will be wasted.

This is a more straightforward issue than CPUs. While there are many different types of memory, as far as desktop PCs and laptops are concerned there is only really one choice – DDR3. This is currently the memory of choice and is installed on all new PCs. DDR2 will be found on many older PCs and is still a perfectly good type of memory.

The only issues for owners of modern PCs are how much memory do they need, and how much can they install? With regard to the former, this is a difficult question to answer – it depends mainly on what type of programs are going to be run on the PC. Applications that move large amounts of data, such as 3D games, video and sound editing, or high-end desktop publishing, will require a much larger amount of memory – typically 6GB or more. Less intensive applications, such as web browsing, word-processing and games like FreeCell, will all run perfectly well on 2GB.

The amount of memory that can be installed is determined by the motherboard. This is not going to be an issue for the average user, as current motherboards can handle anything up to 64GB. However, the computer architecture being used may well be an issue. 32-bit computers running a Windows operating system can utilize a maximum of 4GB of memory regardless of how much is installed. 64-bit PCs, on the other hand, can use an almost limitless amount of memory.

Memory modules are rated in terms of speed, which is another consideration. Currently, speeds range from 1GHz to 2.8GHz. The faster the memory, the more expensive it will be.

Tablet devices require much less memory than desktop PCs. High-end devices of this type currently come with about 1GHz of RAM. They also make more efficient use of the available memory by "suspending" apps that are not being used, thus releasing memory for other apps.

When considering a tablet device, it is also necessary to see what it has to offer in the way of built-in memory for storage purposes, and if it can be expanded by adding larger capacity memory cards.

You might think that tablet devices, which do not generally come with much in the way of internal storage, would almost certainly offer a memory card slot. However, this is not always the case, and is something to look for when choosing a tablet device.

Video system

Video systems produce the pictures you see on the display. Two types are used in computers – integrated video that is built in to the motherboard or CPU, and stand-alone video cards.

If you wish to upgrade the memory on a PC that's more than two or three years old, it will almost certainly be using DDR2. **You will not be able to replace it with the newer DDR3** – this requires a motherboard designed to use DDR3.

Don't worry too much about memory speed. The real-world difference between the slowest and fastest modules is not significant. In any case, to get the best out of the high-speed modules, other parts such as the CPU also need to be top-end. Such a setup will be expensive.

...cont'd

Of the two, video cards produce by far the better quality video – for hardcore gamers, they are essential.

The problem with video cards is that they are expensive to buy, bulky, noisy, and power-hungry. Desktop computers and high-end laptops are large enough and powerful enough to accommodate these demands, but for smaller devices, such as Netbooks and tablet devices, they are impractical.

Therefore, these all use an integrated video system. As described on page 28, in these devices the video will be just one part of a System on a Chip (SoC).

Solid-state drives (SSDs)

Disk drives, or hard drives as they are more commonly known, are the devices used to store a user's data. They are electromechanical devices that provide huge amounts of storage space at a low price.

A relatively recent development in the hard drive market has seen the introduction of solid-state drives (SSDs). These devices employ solid-state memory and contain no moving parts – which makes them extremely reliable.

Other advantages include instant startup, extremely fast data access speeds, completely silent operation, a much smaller footprint, weight (they are much lighter than mechanical drives), and low power requirements.

These qualities all make SSDs ideal for use in low-power devices such as tablets. Apple, for example, uses them in the highly successful iPad, iPhone, and iPod devices.

However, their use in desktop computers is somewhat limited by two factors. The first is the high cost of SSDs compared with mechanical drives. The second is that they provide much smaller storage capacities than mechanical drives. This has lead to low-capacity SSDs, typically around 60GB, being used for the boot drive (where the operating system is installed), with a high-capacity mechanical drive to provide data storage.

The result is a PC that typically boots up twice as quickly, is snappy and responsive to the user's actions, and also has plenty of storage space.

Computer types

When it comes to buying a computer, buyers have quite a few different types to choose from, each having pros and cons that make them suitable for some purposes and less so for others.

Desktop PCs

Traditionally, the desktop PC – comprising a system case that houses the hardware, plus a monitor, keyboard and mouse – has been the most popular type of computer.

Their main advantage is that the addition of peripherals such as printers and scanners turns them into workhorses that enable almost any type of computational work to be done.

A big advantage of **Desktop PCs** is that they are easy to expand and to upgrade.

Other advantages are that they are cheap to buy, easy to upgrade and repair, and easy to expand. Disadvantages are their size, noise, aesthetics, and lack of mobility.

All-in-ones

Increasingly popular due to their small footprint, all-in-one PCs are manufactured by a number of companies, including Apple, Lenovo and Samsung. Pictured below is the Lenovo IdeaCentre.

Other advantages include being lightweight, a minimal amount of messy wiring, many come with touchscreens, and a definite element of style – many of these devices look rather cool and not at all out of place in the living room.

All-in-one PCs are produced by a limited number of manufacturers and tend to be expensive.

The downside is that they are very difficult to repair/upgrade due to lack of accessibility. All-in-ones are also prone to heat issues due to the lack of air space in the case, so this makes them unsuitable for high-end applications. Also, if one part goes wrong the whole unit has to go back – it's all or nothing.

...cont'd

Hybrid computers

Continuing the all-in-one's theme of style and elegance is the hybrid computer. It is comprised of nothing more than a very small and usually stylish case that contains the hardware.

Hybrid PCs are ideal where mobility is an issue. Don't expect to do any serious work or gaming on them though.

The user simply places it where it is to be used and connects a monitor, keyboard and mouse.

These devices have only one real advantage – they are extremely portable. They have the same disadvantages as all-in-one PCs and, as such, are only suitable for lightweight applications.

Laptops

A laptop is basically a desktop PC condensed into a small, flat, portable case. It has the same components as a desktop, albeit on a smaller scale, and is generally as capable as a desktop PC.

Fairly obviously, their main advantage is portability – a laptop can be tucked under the arm and literally taken anywhere.

They also require little space and are easily secured. For example, a laptop can be placed inside a safe.

Laptop PCs may have low-capacity batteries that don't last long before needing to be recharged. Check out the battery capacity if buying with a view to portable computing.

As ever, though, there are downsides. Probably the main one is cost – powerful laptops are considerably more expensive than desktops of equivalent capability.

These devices are also more difficult to use, due to smaller screens and the need for touchpads. There is a high risk of physical damage as they can be dropped, they are easily misplaced or lost, and are prone to theft.

Variations of the laptop theme include Ultrabooks and Netbooks. The former are an Intel invention and manufacturers of these devices must conform to standards set by Intel.

These state that Ultrabooks must use low-power Intel Core CPUs, solid-state drives and unibody chassis. This is to ensure that Ultrabooks are slim, high-end devices able to compete at the top-end of the laptop market against the likes of Apple's MacBook Air.

A Netbook is simply a miniature laptop. They usually have 10-inch screens, scaled-down keyboards and touchpads to match, and are extremely small and lightweight. As a result, they are inexpensive and easily transportable. These have become less popular recently, as their role is being taken over by Tablet PCs and Convertible Computers.

Tablet computers

Tablets are mobile computers that fit in between smartphones and Netbooks. The hardware is built in to a touchscreen, which is operated both by touch and by a keyboard (on screen or attached).

Unlike smartphones, the displays offered by tablets are large enough to enable serious work to be done. For example, with a suitable app you can easily write a properly punctuated letter, an email message, or even a novel.

You'll need to choose a tablet PC that can run Windows 10 with an Intel processor or equivalent, or simply buy a tablet PC with Windows 10 already pre-installed.

Tablet PCs may offer you the best of all worlds. The convenience and ultra-portability of smartphones, a camera, plus the ability to carry out serious computer work. Some even have a phone as well!

Ultrabook PCs are aimed at the top end of the laptop market, while Netbooks are aimed at the bottom end.

Tablet PCs are a good option if you need ultra-portability as well as computational functionality.

33

Convertible PCs present a compromise in that you may consider the tablet too big, or the keyboard too small.

...**cont'd**

Convertible computers

A convertible computer is essentially a tablet computer that can be quickly transformed into a laptop by opening an integrated keyboard. Typically, this is achieved by means of a sliding or hinged mechanism. In all other respects they are just tablets but are popular as they provide a degree of flexibility.

For example, by rotating the hinged keyboard, the Lenovo Yoga convertible computer, shown here, can be used in any one of its Tablet, Laptop, Tent, or Stand modes:

● **Tent mode** – follow a cookery class on your counter.

● **Tablet mode** – touch screen to read, browse, or play games.

● **Stand mode** – ideal hands-free viewing for videos.

● **Laptop mode** – type to be more productive at home, in the office, or on the road.

32-bit versus 64-bit

All modern CPUs support 64-bit architecture. But what is it and how does it benefit the user?

The term "64-bit" when used in reference to a CPU means that in one integer register the CPU can store 64 bits of data. Older CPUs, which could only support 32-bit architecture, could store only 32 bits of data in a register – only half the amount. Therefore, 64-bit architecture provides better overall system performance, as it can handle twice as much data in one clock cycle.

The main advantage provided by 64-bit architecture is the huge amount of memory it can support. CPUs operating on a 32-bit Windows system can utilize a maximum of 4GB, whereas on a 64-bit system they can utilize up to 192GB.

The caveat is that a 64-bit system requires all the software to be 64-bit compatible – it must be 64-bit software. This includes the operating system and device drivers, and is the reason why more recent versions of Windows, including Windows 10, are supplied in both 32-bit (x86) and 64-bit (x64) versions. Note that most 32-bit software will run on a 64-bit system but the advantages provided by 64-bit architecture won't be available.

So who will benefit from a 64-bit system and who won't? The simple answer is that every PC user will benefit, as their system will be more efficient. Don't expect to see major speed gains over a 32-bit system when running day-to-day applications such as web browsers, word processing and 2D games, though, as you probably won't notice any difference.

However, when running CPU-intensive applications that require large amounts of data to be handled – for example, video editing or 3D games – 64-bit systems will be faster. Also, if you need more memory than the current small limit of 4GB possible with a 32-bit system, 64-bit architecture allows you to install as much as you want – up to the limitations of the motherboard.

Users running Windows 10 Pro, Enterprise, or Education editions have access to a virtualization utility called Hyper-V. One of the requirements for building virtual PCs with Hyper-V is that the computer must be running on 64-bit architecture.

To get a 64-bit system, simply buy a modern CPU and install a 64-bit version of Windows.

Modern CPUs automatically detect whether an application or operating system is 32-bit or 64-bit, and operate accordingly.

If you opt for a **64-bit** system, all your software, including device drivers, will have to be 64-bit compatible. Even though 64-bit systems are now common, there is still software on the market that runs only on 32-bit systems.

Multi-touch

An important feature of Windows 10 is its support for touchscreen control. If you are considering buying a touchscreen monitor in order to take advantage of this feature, you should be aware of the following issues:

Bezel design

Some of the touch gestures required to control Windows 10 (opening menus, for example) are done by swiping a finger inwards from one edge of the screen towards the center.

However, it is a fact that many touchscreen monitors currently on the market have a raised bezel, which makes it more difficult than it need be to carry out this particular touch command. Our recommendation is that you choose a monitor in which the bezel is flush to the screen. Alternatively, look for a model that has at least a 20 mm border between the edge of the display and the start of the bezel.

Multi-touch

Multi-touch refers to a touchscreen's ability to recognize the presence of two or more points of contact with the surface. This plural-point awareness is necessary to implement functionality such as pinch to zoom-out, or the activation of predefined programs.

All modern touchscreens have this capability. However, to get the best out of Windows 10's touch feature, you need a touchscreen that supports at least five touch points – this allows you to use five fingers simultaneously.

Screen technology

There are various types of touchscreen technology, but when it comes to computer monitors and mobile devices there are just two: "resistive" and "capacitive". Resistive screens can be operated with any pointed object, such as a stylus or a finger. Capacitive screens rely on the electrical properties of the human body, and thus only react to human touch, or a special capacitive pen.

Of the two, the capacitive type is the one to go for – they are much more sensitive and accurate than resistive screens, which tend to be used more in business environments such as shops and banks. Note that most current touchscreens are of the capacitive type, but do check it out just in case.

You may still find touchscreen devices on the market that only support two touch points – **don't buy one of these**.

36

The downside of capacitive touchscreens is that **they cannot be operated with a gloved finger** (not ideal on a freezing cold day, perhaps!).

Sensors

One of the main differences between static desktop PCs and mobile computing devices is the range of sensors employed by mobile devices. Some of the sensors are important to the operation of these devices, while others add functionality. Sensors that you should look for include:

Ambient Light Sensor (ALS)

This sensor enables screen brightness to be automatically adjusted in accordance with the ambient light level. If it gets darker, then the screen brightness decreases, but if it gets lighter the screen brightness increases. A useful side-effect of this is increased battery life.

Proximity sensor

The purpose of this device is to prevent accidental inputs – something that's easily done on a touchscreen. The most common scenario is the ear touching the screen during a phone call and triggering an event or action.

The proximity sensor is located next to the speaker and thus can detect when the ear, or another object, is close by. Any actions generated are assumed to be accidental and are ignored.

Accelerometer & Gyroscope

These two sensors are used to detect the orientation of a device so that the display can react accordingly. For example, if the device is moved from a vertical orientation to a horizontal one, the display will follow suit. Other uses include the camera – the sensors enable it to know if the picture is being taken in landscape or portrait mode.

Global Positioning System (GPS)

An embedded GPS sensor used in conjunction with a mapping service enables any mobile device to get real-time position tracking, text- and voice-guided directions, and points of interest.

Compass

Sensors that detect direction enable compass apps to be built. Sensors of this type do not sense magnetic fields as do traditional compasses, but rather the frequency and orientation of radio waves. In doing this, compass sensors are assisted by gyroscopes.

Increasingly, **data** from the various sensors in a device is being combined to produce more elaborate applications.

New types of **sensor** are being developed for mobile devices. Examples are altimeters (which will detect which floor of a building you are on, for example), temperature and humidity sensors, and heart rate monitors.

Other hardware features

Windows 10 includes several modern hardware features not seen in early Windows operating systems. Two recent features are briefly described below:

Near Field Communication (NFC)

Near Field Communication (NFC) is a set of standards for mobile devices to establish radio communication with each other by touch or bringing them into close proximity – usually no more than a few centimeters. The technology appears on many devices. Applications include:

- **Purchase payment** – used in conjunction with an electronic wallet, this effectively turns a smartphone into a credit card.

- **Setting up connections** – connections such as Bluetooth can be quickly and easily established.

- **Smart tagging** – touching a smartphone to an NFC tag. For example, "tap-and-go" at the gas pump.

- **Peer-to-peer** – sharing small snippets of information such as contacts, photos, and web pages is a typical use.

NFC is similar in concept to **Bluetooth** but is somewhat slower, yet it consumes less power.

Unified Extensible Firmware Interface (UEFI)

A computer needs an interface between its operating system and hardware to make sure they can work together. Traditionally, this role has been carried out by a chip called the BIOS (this produces the black boot screens you may see when starting your PC).

UEFI is a replacement for the now archaic BIOS. Windows 10 takes advantage of a security feature in UEFI known as Pre-boot Authentication. This prevents any software that doesn't have a recognized and valid security certificate from running and, as a result, rootkits, viruses and malware are unable to load themselves into the system's memory during the boot procedure that runs before the operating system loads. (A virus loaded during the boot procedure could circumvent any antivirus measures on the PC.)

If your PC has UEFI, it can be accessed from Windows 10's **Recovery**, Advanced Options menu.

Another feature of UEFI is its graphical display that allows navigation with a mouse and keyboard. Your computer's motherboard must provide UEFI support, so only modern computers built in the last few years are likely to have UEFI.

3

Installing Windows 10

This chapter describes which editions of Windows can be upgraded to Windows 10 and compares options for upgrading and performing clean installations.

Upgrade paths

There are several upgrade paths to Windows 10 from the previous versions of Windows listed below, but it is not possible to upgrade from all earlier versions of the Windows operating system.

Upgrade to Windows 10 Home

You can upgrade to Windows 10 Home and keep Windows settings, personal files, and applications from the following Windows operating system editions:

- Windows 7 Starter

- Windows 7 Home Basic

- Windows 7 Home Premium

- Windows 8.1

- Windows 8.1 with Bing

Upgrade to Windows 10 Pro

You can upgrade to Windows 10 Pro and keep Windows settings, personal files, and applications from the following Windows operating system editions:

- Windows 7 Professional

- Windows 7 Ultimate

- Windows 8.1 Pro

Upgrades unavailable

You <u>cannot</u> upgrade to Windows 10 from the following operating system editions:

- Windows 7 Enterprise

- Windows 8 (must be upgraded to at least 8.1)

- Windows 8.1 Enterprise

- Windows RT

- Windows RT 8.1

Windows 10 can be bought from the Microsoft Store at **microsoft.com/en-us/store/b/windows** Prices at the time of printing are $139.00/£119.99 for Windows 10 Home, and $199.99/£219.99 for Windows 10 Pro.

Upgrade options

Upgrading an operating system can be done in three ways:

- An inplace upgrade
- A clean installation
- A migration

Perhaps the most common method is an inplace upgrade.

Inplace upgrade

With this method, the operating system is simply installed over the top of the old one. While this is the easiest way to do the job, it may produce the worst results. This is because any problems on the original setup (file corruption, malware, etc.) will be carried over to the new installation. Issues of this type can also cause an upgrade to fail.

The only advantages of upgrading in this way are that the procedure is straightforward, and that the user's data, files and programs are not affected – they will still be there at the end of it.

Clean installation

With a clean installation, all potential problems are eliminated right at the start due to the format procedure, which wipes the drive clean of all data. Therefore, nothing is carried over to the new setup from the old one.

The drawback with this method is that the formatting procedure also removes all the user's data – settings, files and programs. So when the new operating system has been installed, it will then be necessary to redo all the settings, reinstall all the programs and restore the data. Another issue is the time it will take to do all this – allow several hours.

Migration

This is not a true upgrade option but is included here as the procedure does transfer files and settings from one installation to another. It does not transfer programs, though.

To do a migration, you need a suitable application that copies the files and settings from the old setup to a medium such as a USB flash drive, then transfers them to the new setup.

For best results, we suggest you back up your personal data and **perform a clean installation**.

Walkthrough clean install

Unlike an upgrade, which can be initiated from within Windows, a clean install has to be done from an installation disk. If your copy of Windows 10 has been supplied on a DVD disk or USB drive then you're all set. If not, it will be in the form of an ISO image file that will have to be "burned" onto a DVD disk – a procedure that will require a DVD burning program.

If you are upgrading from Windows 7, you have a DVD burner built in. Just pop an empty DVD disk in the DVD drive and follow the prompts from the AutoPlay window that will open shortly afterwards.

If you don't have a built-in burner, you can find a free one on the internet. One that we recommend is ImgBurn from **imgburn.com** that you can use like this:

Microsoft provides a free **Windows 10 Media Creation Tool** that allows you to easily download the Windows 10 ISO image file, which must then be burnt to a DVD. You can also use this tool to download for USB media. Find details at **microsoft.com/ en-us/software- download/windows10**

ImgBurn is just one of many free disk burners available on the internet.

1 At the opening screen, click **Write image file to disc**

2 Under **Source**, click the browse link and select your ISO file

3 Click **Write** and wait while the DVD is burned

Set the boot drive

Having created your installation disk, you now need to configure your computer to boot from it:

1 Start the PC, and at the first boot screen press the key required to open the BIOS. This is usually the **Delete** or **F2** key (it is often specified at the bottom of the screen)

2 On the main BIOS screen, select the **Boot** menu – it's called "Advanced BIOS Features" in the example below

3 Scroll down to **First Boot Device**, then use the Page Up/Page Down keys to cycle through the options and select the CD/DVD drive

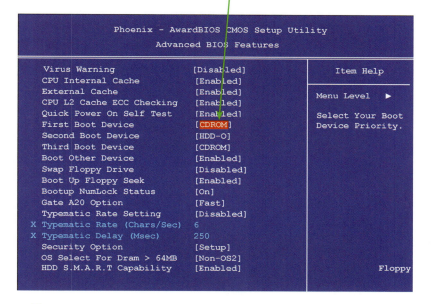

```
            Phoenix - AwardBIOS CMOS Setup Utility
                   Advanced BIOS Features

   Virus Warning                [Disabled]         ┌──────────────────┐
   CPU Internal Cache           [Enabled]          │   Item Help      │
   External Cache               [Enabled]          │                  │
   CPU L2 Cache ECC Checking     [Enabled]         │ Menu Level  ►    │
   Quick Power On Self Test     [Enabled]          │                  │
   First Boot Device            [CDROM]            │ Select Your Boot │
   Second Boot Device           [HDD-O]            │ Device Priority. │
   Third Boot Device            [CDROM]            │                  │
   Boot Other Device            [Enabled]          │                  │
   Swap Floppy Drive            [Disabled]         │                  │
   Boot Up Floppy Seek          [Enabled]          │                  │
   Bootup NumLock Status        [On]               │                  │
   Gate A20 Option              [Fast]             │                  │
   Typematic Rate Setting       [Disabled]         │                  │
 X Typematic Rate (Chars/Sec)   6                  │                  │
 X Typematic Delay (Msec)       250                │                  │
   Security Option              [Setup]            │                  │
   OS Select For Dram > 64MB    [Non-OS2]          │                  │
   HDD S.M.A.R.T Capability     [Enabled]          │           Floppy │
                                                   └──────────────────┘
```

4 Press the **Esc** key to return to the main BIOS screen

Note that you must save the change before exiting the BIOS, otherwise it will revert to the original setting. The BIOS option for this is to **Save & Exit Setup**, typically with the **F10** key.

Hot tip

If you can't find the **key to open the BIOS**, check the motherboard manual. Some devices even have a special button with which to access the BIOS screen.

Don't forget

The **BIOS screen** on your PC may differ from the example on the left – it depends on the age of your PC and the BIOS manufacturer.

Don't forget

All the tools needed to do a clean install of Windows 10 are on its installation disk. So, you must set the CD/DVD drive as the **first** boot device.

Windows Setup

The following pages describe a step-by-step procedure for performing a clean installation of Windows 10.

Before you start this procedure, make sure you have made a **backup** of any data (see Chapter 21) that you want to keep, then configure the PC to boot from the CD/DVD drive.

1 Place the Windows 10 installation disk in the CD/DVD drive and start the PC. When you see a **Press any key to boot from CD...** message, do so. Windows will now begin loading its installation files to the disk drive

2 The first screen you will see is the language, time and currency format, and input method preferences. Make your selections and press the **Next** button

Beware

The steps illustrated in this walk-through **may change** with each release of Windows 10, but the setup procedure will be similar.

44

3 On the second screen, click **Install now** to begin the installation procedure

Hot tip

Notice the option to **Repair your computer**, should you need to use the installer to rectify a serious system problem.

Enter product key

4 Next, enter your product key and click **Next**, or choose the **I don't have a product key** link to continue

You will now be asked to select which version of Windows 10 to install. The installer may offer "N" versions alongside regular versions of the Home and Pro editions. These alternatives exclude some media capabilities to comply with a European ruling on anti-competitive practices – but you're probably going to want to have those media features.

5 Choose the version of Windows 10 you wish to install, then click the **Next** button

Hot tip

The **product key** can be found on the DVD packaging or in a confirmation email if purchased online. If you are replacing Windows 7 or 8.1, the key may be on a sticker on the PC case. You can retrieve an embedded key using the Windows OEM Key Tool. For details, see **neosmart.net/OemKey**

6 Check the box to accept the license terms, then click the **Next** button

Don't forget

You will need a **valid product key** for the version you choose to install in order to complete activation of Windows 10.

Type of installation

The **Upgrade** option is available for an existing version of Windows only – use the **Custom** option for a clean install.

Tools are provided here to modify your system **drive partitions** if required for installation.

7 At the "Which type of installation do you want?" screen, select **Custom: Install Windows only (advanced)**

8 In the "Where do you want to install Windows?" screen, select the required drive or partition, then click **Next**

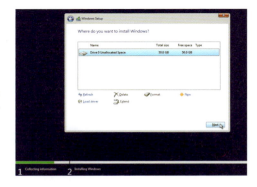

9 Installation will now proceed and your PC will restart – as it does so, remove the installation media so it will not restart from that source

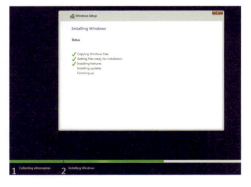

10 The end of the installation routine is signified by screens announcing that Windows 10 is "getting ready" – the PC will then reboot to a setup screen

First start

Setup begins with a Welcome screen where the Cortana personal digital assistant offers to talk you through the setup steps:

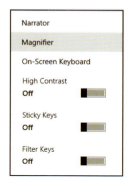

The Windows 10 installer now offers **Cortana voice assistance** for the setup procedure.

Users with physical impairments can click the "Ease of Access" icon to reveal a menu of aids to help with the setup process.

11 Next, you are asked to identify your location. Choose your region, then click the **Yes** button

Drag the slider control on the **setup** screen to see all the options.

12 Now, choose your keyboard, then click the **Yes** button

…cont'd

Hot tip

Dual language keyboards have two characters on each key, so adding a second keyboard layout makes it easy to switch languages.

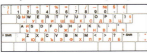

Hot tip

If no internet connection is available you can click this **Skip for now** link to continue with setup.

13 Add a second keyboard layout if required, or simply click the **Skip** button to continue

14 Setup now wants to establish a network internet connection. Connect an Ethernet cable from your network router, or establish a Wi-Fi connection, then click **Next**

15 Unless part of an organization, select **Set up for personal use** if asked, then click the **Next** button to continue

Sign in to your PC

16 Enter your Microsoft account details then click **Next**, or choose the **Offline account** link to continue

Use the **Create account** link if you don't already have a Microsoft account – avoid using an **Offline account** if you want to enjoy all the features and benefits of Windows 10 (see page 52).

17 Unless you chose **Offline account** now, enter the password for your Microsoft account

Use the **Forgot password?** link if you can't remember the password of your Microsoft account.

18 Next, you are given the opportunity to set a PIN – click **Create PIN** if you want to sign in with a 4-digit code

The Windows 10 sign in screen lets you enter either a **password or PIN**, but a PIN is faster and more secure.

19 Enter a memorable PIN code twice, then click **OK**

Finalizing settings

20 If you want to continue what you were doing when you switch to other devices, click **Yes** to activate the timeline feature

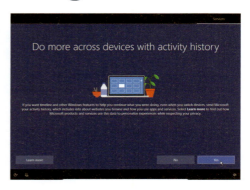

Hot tip

You can **link your phone** and PC later from the Windows 10 Settings – see page 290.

21 If you want to link your phone and PC, enter your phone number and click **Send**. Click **Next** to continue with setup

You are now given the opportunity to use Microsoft's OneDrive facility that provides 5GB of online storage. Windows 10 can make a copy of each file on your PC and store it safely online. This means that you automatically have a backup copy of your files, and they are always accessible to you from any device with internet access – including Android and iPhone devices.

Hot tip

OneDrive is really useful but if you prefer not to use this free facility click the **Only save files to this PC** option.

22 Click **Next** to have Windows automatically save a copy of your files to OneDrive

23 Now, click **Accept** to enable the **Cortana** Personal Digital Assistant

24 Review and adjust **Privacy settings** to your preferred requirements, then click the **Accept** button

If you are concerned with **privacy** you can change Cortana settings later to restrict access.

25 Wait while Windows 10 completes setup before displaying the Desktop on your screen. Windows 10 is now installed on your PC and is configured with the options you selected during the setup process

Heed the **warning** to allow Windows 10 setup to complete before you can turn your PC off.

Restoring your data

You now have a brand new operating system. However, apart from the apps bundled with Windows 10, that's all you have.

The first thing you have to do now is install essential system drivers. The most important of these are the chipset drivers, and they will be found on the motherboard's installation disk. Pop this in the CD/DVD drive and wait for AutoPlay to open the disk's setup utility. Select the option that installs all the chipset drivers.

When the driver installation is complete, the PC will reboot. When back in Windows, the next step is to install the drivers for any hardware connected to the computer. Typically, these include video cards, sound cards, printers, scanners, routers, monitors, mice and keyboards.

Finally, install your programs and any data backed up from your previous installation.

Local Offline accounts

As a final note, on page 49 we mentioned that it is not essential to have a Microsoft account to use Windows 10 and, indeed, it isn't. However, if you choose this option, you will find that some features of Windows 10 are denied to you.

The first is that you won't be able to synchronize your settings, email, passwords, etc. across your various devices. This means that one of the big attractions of Windows 10 – the ability to create and maintain a consistent computing environment regardless of which device you are using – will not be available. While this probably won't be a big deal for many users, for some it most definitely will be.

Also, you won't be able to get apps from the Microsoft Store. It will still be possible to browse the Store, but you won't be allowed to download any apps.

Furthermore, some Windows 10 apps won't work unless the user is signed in to a Microsoft account. Examples include the Mail, Calendar, People, and OneDrive apps.

Don't forget

You may need to install the **drivers** for your chipset and other hardware. If you don't have them, they can be downloaded from the motherboard manufacturer's website.

Hot tip

If you opt for an **Offline account** and don't specify a password, you will be able to automatically log on to Windows 10 without having to enter a password.

The Windows 10 interface

4

This chapter describes the Windows 10 interface and introduces the Cortana Personal Digital Assistant. It also demonstrates how to change user settings for personalization and for access control.

Start Windows 10

When a Windows 10 PC is started, the first thing the user will see (once the boot screens have flashed past) is a black screen with the Windows logo, as shown below:

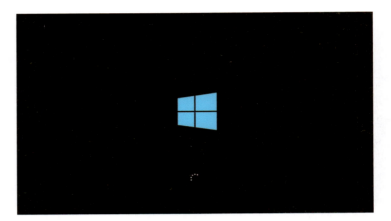

A Lock screen is **not necessary** when Windows 10 is used with a standard monitor. Many users will find it useful though, purely as a means of displaying information.

This is followed by the Lock screen. The basic purpose of this screen is to provide a protective barrier that prevents accidental inputs – this is necessary, as Windows 10 is a touch-supportive operating system.

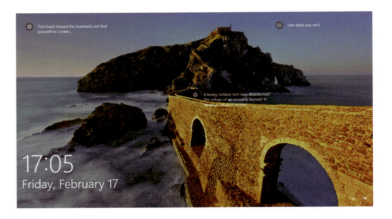

17:05
Friday, February 17

You can **customize** the Lock screen's background (see page 71).

Microsoft has evolved this basic function by enabling users to customize the screen by changing its background, and by specifying various notifications to be displayed.

By default, the Lock screen shows the current date and time, and has power status indicator icons, as in the image above.

Log in

Click or tap anywhere on the Lock screen and the Login screen will open. Above the Login box, you'll see the account picture. (This can be changed, as described on page 74.)

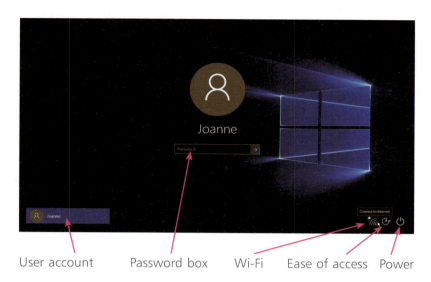

User account   Password box   Wi-Fi   Ease of access   Power

The Login screen will have a User account button for **each account** on the system – so you can choose which account to log in.

- **User account** – a button that selects the user to be logged in to the system.

- **Password box** – an input box to enter the password.

- **Wi-Fi** – an icon button that lets you connect to a network and indicates signal strength if already connected via Wi-Fi.

- **Ease of Access** – an icon button that provides the pop-up menu shown on the right, containing accessibility settings for users with impaired abilities. When this button is clicked, Windows reads and scans the menu as Narrator automatically provides audible guidance. Each item is explained and highlighted in turn. The user can select any item when it's highlighted by pressing the spacebar.

The menus on the Login screen are easy to miss, as they are very **small** and placed right at the bottom of the screen.

- **Power** – an icon button that provides a pop-up menu containing Sleep, Shut down, and Restart options.

55

The **Documents** and **Pictures** buttons are available on the left sidebar of the Start menu so you can quickly open those folders.

In **Desktop mode**, open the Start menu by clicking the ⊞ Start button to see the A-Z list of apps and pinned tiles.

In **Tablet mode**, tap the ▦ button to see the Start menu pinned tiles, then click the ▤ button to see an A-Z list of apps.

Start screen

After logging in to a Windows 10 system you will see the Start screen in Desktop or Tablet mode, appropriate for the device:

Desktop mode

Search box   Start menu   Tiles   Taskbar   Desktop   System Tray

Tablet mode

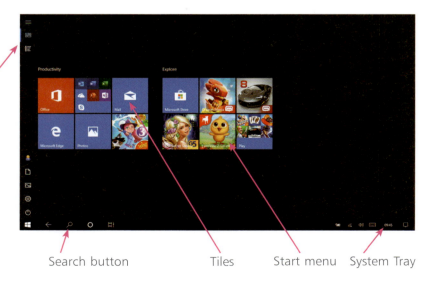

Search button   Tiles   Start menu   System Tray

The Start menu tiles and A-Z list of all apps launch an app within a window in Desktop mode or full-screen in Tablet mode.

Any app can be added to the array of tiles by right-clicking on the listed app and choosing **Pin to Start** from the context menu. This allows you to populate the tiles with your favorite apps, so you can quickly launch them by clicking or tapping on a tile. Apps can also be pinned to the Taskbar in Desktop mode.

Search box

The Search box lets you easily locate anything you need and useful tabs along the top of the box let you easily refine your search:

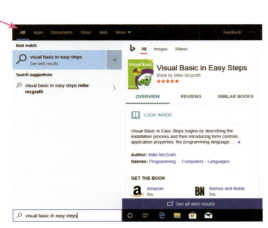

Icons of open or minimized apps appear on the **Taskbar**. Right-click on the Taskbar in a blank space to see its options.

57

System Tray

The System Tray contains icons that typically give access to:

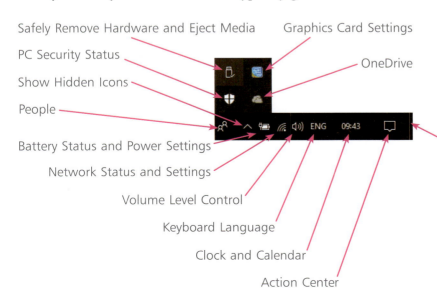

Safely Remove Hardware and Eject Media

Graphics Card Settings

PC Security Status

OneDrive

Show Hidden Icons

People

Battery Status and Power Settings

Network Status and Settings

Volume Level Control

Keyboard Language

Clock and Calendar

Action Center

You can also click the **Show Desktop** button to minimize all open windows, or hover the mouse cursor over here to **Peek at desktop** by minimizing all open windows.

Navigation

In its drive for Windows 10 to be all-encompassing, Microsoft has made it possible to navigate the interface in three different ways: by touch, the mouse, and the keyboard.

Touch

Touch gestures include swiping, sliding, tapping, and pinching. The best way to get to grips with these is to experiment. The following, however, will get you off to a good start:

- **Tap** – opens, selects, or activates whatever you tap (similar to clicking with a mouse).

- **Tap and hold** – shows further info about the item, or opens a context menu (similar to right-clicking with a mouse).

- **Pinch or stretch** – visually zooms in or out, like with a map or picture. Pinch to zoom out and stretch to zoom in.

- **Rotate** – some items can be rotated by placing your fingers on them and turning your hand.

- **Slide to scroll** – dragging your finger across the screen scrolls through screen items (similar to scrolling a mouse wheel).

- **Slide to arrange** – dragging an item around the screen with your finger to position it (similar to dragging with a mouse).

- **Swipe to select** – a short, quick movement will select an item and often bring up app commands.

- **Swipe or slide from right edge** – opens the Action Center.

- **Swipe or slide from left edge** – opens the Task View feature.

- **Swipe or slide from top edge** – enables you to view the title bar in full-screen apps.

- **Swipe or slide from bottom edge** – enables you to view the Taskbar in full-screen apps.

In many cases, the touch commands available are dependent on the application in use. For example, various rotational commands can be used to manipulate objects in drawing and layout applications such as Microsoft PowerPoint.

Mouse

Using the mouse to get around in Windows 10 is no different from any other operating system, although you can spin the mouse wheel while on the Lock screen to open the password box.

Keyboard

Those of you who use the Windows 10 interface without the benefit of a touchscreen are well advised to get acquainted with the various keyboard commands relevant to it. In many cases, just as with keyboard commands and shortcuts in general, they are often quicker than using the mouse.

There is actually a whole bunch of these commands; the following being some of the more useful ones:

The key that will be used most is the Windows key (WinKey). Pressing this key opens and closes the Start menu. It can also be used in conjunction with other keys to perform other actions. For example, pressing **WinKey** + **X** opens the Power User menu while **WinKey** + **C** starts Cortana listening, when enabled in Cortana's Settings.

Press **WinKey**, then **Tab** key three times to "activate" the A-Z list. The Home and End keys now jump from one end of the "All apps" list on the Start menu to the other, while the arrow keys can be used to select a tile. The **Enter** key opens a selected app.

WinKey + **Tab** opens Task View, which allows the user to switch to a different app using the arrow keys to select an app. The Enter key can then be used to exit Task View and activate the app.

Alt + **Tab** opens a Switch list which allows the user to switch to a different app. Note that you must have at least two apps running for **WinKey** + **Tab** and **Alt** + **Tab** to work.

A rarely-used key known as the Context menu key (usually located close to the space bar) brings up a menu of related options when pressed.

The **Windows key** ("WinKey") is usually located at the bottom of the keyboard near to the spacebar, and often has an image of the Windows logo on it.

Two of the most useful keyboard shortcuts are **WinKey** + **C** to start Cortana listening, and **WinKey** + **X** to open the Power User menu.

Action Center

The Action Center provides a notification area for messages and various Quick Action icons that enable you to quickly adjust some settings:

1 Click the Action Center button on the System Tray to open the Action Center

2 Click on **Expand** or **Collapse** to see all Quick Action icons or fewer Quick Action icons

3 Click the Action Center button on the System Tray once more to close the Action Center

When the Action Center is open you can use the slider to adjust brightness or click a Quick Action icon to adjust a current setting:

● **Tablet mode** – switch between Desktop mode and Tablet mode display configuration.

● **Network** – show current connection status and option icons.

1 Click the Wi-Fi icon to turn off the Wi-Fi connection

2 Select how and when you want to turn the Wi-Fi back on

3 Click the Wi-Fi icon to turn on the Wi-Fi connection

- **All settings** – open the Windows Settings screen.

- **Nearby sharing** – toggle Wi-Fi and Bluetooth visibility.

- **Airplane mode** – disable or enable all cellular, Wi-Fi, and Bluetooth wireless transmissions.

- **Location** – reveal or conceal the current global location of the device for GPS tracking.

- **Focus assist** – deny or allow notifications from the system and external sources during specific times.

- **Mobile hotspot** – turn on or off the ability to share the internet connection.

- **Screen snip** – lets you select an area of the screen to save an image of that area to the system clipboard.

- **Bluetooth** – toggle the visibility of Bluetooth devices.

- **VPN** – connect or disconnect to the internet via a Virtual Private Network server for anonymity.

- **Battery saver** – enable or disable Battery Saver mode to control power consumption when running on battery only.

- **Project** – show current screen configuration for "PC screen only" and provide second screen options to Duplicate, Extend, or display on "Second screen only".

- **Connect** – connect wirelessly to another device via WiDi (Wireless Display), such as to a smart TV that supports Miracast technology.

- **Night light** – reduce blue light emissions from the screen to reduce eye strain at night.

The **Action Center** was redesigned completely for Windows 10.

You will need a subscription to a VPN service to connect to the internet via a VPN. Find out more online at **purevpn.com**

You can choose what to include in the Action Center. Go to Start, Settings, System, Notifications & actions, **Edit your quick actions**.

Ask Cortana

One of the great innovations in Windows 10 is the Personal Digital Assistant named "Cortana". This is an enhancement to the Search box feature that allows the user to search, and much more, by verbal communication once it has been enabled:

1 Ensure your microphone is correctly configured, then click the Cortana button  on the Taskbar

2 Click the ⚙ **Settings** button at the left of the Cortana dialog box

3 On the Settings screen, slide the **Hey Cortana** toggle button to the **On** position

4 Now just say "Hey Cortana" at any time to make Cortana listen for your voice

5 Ensure you have an internet connection, then ask Cortana anything you like. For example, try asking about the weather

6 Click the X button at the top right of the Cortana dialog box to close it

Cortana is new in Windows 10 but performance **may vary by region**. If Cortana is not working or enabled in your country, try setting your **Region** to "United States" in Settings, Time & Language, Region. (Note: if you change your region, you might not be able to shop at the Store or use things you've purchased, like memberships and subscriptions, games, movies, TV, and music.)

Note that Cortana may be replaced in the future by an alternative voice assistant, such as Alexa.

...cont'd

The best way to learn Cortana commands is to simply try out different ways to phrase your question. Here are some Cortana commands that worked successfully when we tried them, and demonstrate some of the many things you can have Cortana do:

- **Cortana Search** – "Rhianna discography"
- **Cortana Calendar** – "Create a meeting with David"
- **Cortana Reminder** – "Remind me at 4pm"
- **Cortana Alarm** – "Wake me up in 2 hours"
- **Cortana Maps** – "Map of Washington DC"
- **Cortana Weather** – "What's the forecast this weekend?"
- **Cortana Music** – "Play music", "Pause music", "Resume music"
- **Cortana Pictures** – "Show me a picture of Cortana"
- **Cortana App Launch** – "Notepad"
- **Cortana News** – "Today's news"
- **Cortana Finance** – "Microsoft Stock today"
- **Cortana Sports** – "New York Jets' next game?"
- **Cortana Fun** – "Sing me a song"

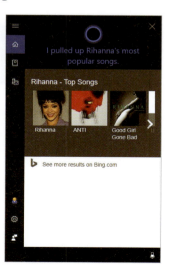

Hot tip

Cortana requires an **internet** connection, so will be unable to answer if you should lose your Wi-Fi connection.

Don't forget

Cortana collects users' personal data to further **personalize** results, and as such is subject to child-protection laws. Therefore, the user must be at least 13 years of age (checked against age data in user profiles) or Cortana will refuse to answer questions.

Cortana remote control

If your PC is idle and the **Hey Cortana** feature is enabled (see page 62), the Cortana interface will appear in full-screen mode. This allows you to read the screen from a distance to control Cortana remotely:

Cortana in **full-screen mode** is a new feature that lets you talk to Cortana anytime.

1 Do not use your PC's mouse, screen, or keyboard for around 10 seconds, then say "Hey Cortana" – to see Cortana appear full screen

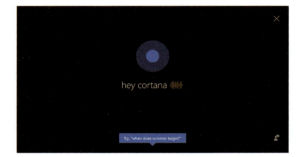

2 Next, issue a command and see Cortana respond

Click the **X button** at the top-right of the screen to exit back to your desktop.

...cont'd

If the **Hey Cortana** feature is enabled you can also enable the ability to use Cortana even when the PC is locked:

1 Click the Cortana button on the Taskbar, then click the ⚙ **Settings** button at the left of the Cortana dialog box

2 On the Settings screen, slide the **Lock Screen** toggle button to the **On** position

3 Next open the Start menu, then right-click your  user icon and select **Lock** from the context menu (or simply press the **Winkey + L** keys) to lock the screen

4 Issue a command to play music and see Cortana respond

If you turn the volume level too high, Cortana **may no longer hear** your voice commands.

Some apps, such as TuneIn Radio (available free from the Microsoft Store) provide voice **playback** controls. You can also ask Cortana "What song is playing?".

Notice that details of the track playing may appear with playback controls on the **Lock screen**.

Cortana reminders

Cortana's Notebook lets you store information about your interests and favorite places. This allows Cortana to provide you with better personalized assistance. Most usefully, the Cortana Notebook also stores reminders you can set to appear only once or at recurring intervals:

1 Click the Cortana button on the Taskbar to open Cortana, then select the **Notebook** icon in the left-hand pane

2 Next, select the **Organizer** tab, then click **Create a reminder** option to add a reminder – or simply say "Hey Cortana, add a reminder"

3 See Cortana now prompt you to add your reminder

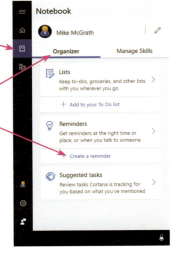

4 You can edit the "Remember to..." text by typing a reminder message in the box – or simply speak a reminder message, such as "Take a coffee break"

5 Select when to be reminded and choose to be reminded just once or at regular intervals by editing the boxes – or simply speak the time, such as "Eleven A.M. every day"

6 Optionally, choose to add a photo to your reminder from a Library or Camera location

7 Click the **Remind** button, or simply say "Yes", to set the Reminder

8 To see the Reminders list, click Cortana's **Notebook** icon, and select **Reminders**

9 Select the reminder you want to edit or delete

10 Next, change any detail in the boxes – for example, change the reminder time to "09:50", then click the **Save** button

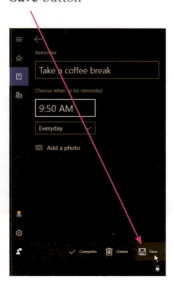

Hot tip

You can click the **+** button at the bottom of the Reminders list to add a **new** Reminder.

11 See the reminder appear at the specified time

Don't forget

Click the **Snooze** button if you want to be reminded again later.

67

Personalization

You can easily customize your Desktop by replacing the default Windows 10 background with a picture of your choice or with a solid color by choosing from a swatch selection:

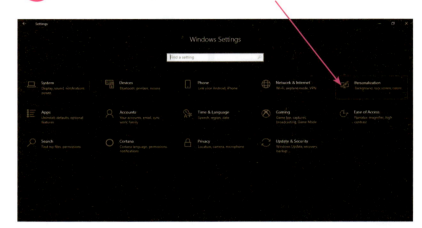

1 Click the Start button, then click the **Settings** icon

2 On the Settings screen, choose **Personalization**

Don't forget

You can click **Browse** to choose an image from your Pictures folder. Search the web for background wallpapers to suit the resolution of your PC screen.

70

3 Click the **Background** drop-down menu and select **Picture**, then choose an image or select **Solid Color**, then choose a color from the swatch that appears

Hot tip

There is also a drop-down option to create a **Slideshow** that changes the background image at a frequency of your choice, and you can choose how to fit images on your screen.

...cont'd

The Lock screen, which appears when you boot your PC or when it's sleeping, can be customized in two ways:

Appearance

1 Go to Settings, Personalization then click the **Lock screen** option on the left-hand pane

2 Click the **Background** drop-down and select a picture

Notifications

If you look below the default Background images you will see options to change the notifications displayed on the Lock screen.

The only app showing a notification on the Lock screen in the picture above is the Calendar app. You can add more simply by clicking one of the **+** add icons.

If you are leaving your PC and want to turn on the Windows 10 Lock screen, simply press **WinKey** + **L**.

You can use the Lock screen to display **useful information** – for example, unread emails.

User settings

The Windows 10 interface provides a range of settings with regard to users. Amongst other things, these include switching accounts and changing account passwords.

Switch accounts

Windows 10 allows two types of account – a Microsoft account, which enables all of Windows 10's features to be used, and a Local account, which has restrictions. To switch from one to the other:

Two types of account can be used with the Windows 10 interface – a **Microsoft** account and a **Local** account.

1 On the Start menu, click **Settings** then choose **Accounts**

2 Click the link to **Sign in with a local account instead**

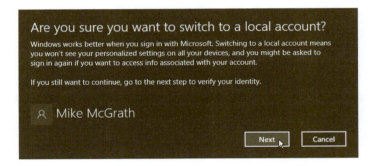

Are you sure you want to switch to a local account?

Windows works better when you sign in with Microsoft. Switching to a local account means you won't see your personalized settings on all your devices, and you might be asked to sign in again if you want to access info associated with your account.

If you still want to continue, go to the next step to verify your identity.

👤 Mike McGrath

[Next] [Cancel]

3 Click **Next**, then enter your current password or PIN

4 In the next screen, enter a username, password and password hint for the new Local account

5 Click **Sign out and finish** to be taken to the Lock screen, where you must log in with the new account's credentials

The **Switch to a local account** option effectively creates a new user account.

← Switch to a local account

👤 Mike
Local account

You're almost done. Make sure you save your work before you sign out, and use your new local account info the next time you sign in.

[Sign out and finish] [Cancel]

Change account password

Should you ever wish to change your account's password, you can do so as described below:

1 On the Start menu, click **Settings** then choose **Accounts**

2 On the left-hand pane, click the **Sign-in options** item then **Change your Microsoft account password**

3 See your browser display instructions. Click the link to **Sign in to your Microsoft account**, then sign in

4 Next, select **Security**, **Change my password**, then confirm your identity and enter your new password

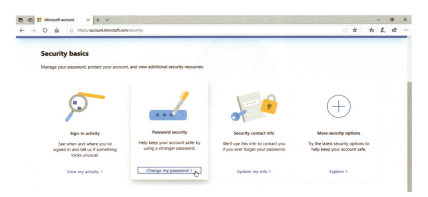

It is recommended that account passwords should have at least **eight** characters and include digits plus mixed-case letters.

PIN code

PIN (Personal Identification Number) codes are another security feature in Windows 10, and enable users to secure their computer with a four-digit code. You may question the need for this as there are already plenty of security options provided, not to mention the fact that a four-digit code isn't particularly secure anyway.

However, the feature is intended for use in tablets and smartphones, where the small keyboards provided make it difficult to enter a complex alpha-numeric password.

Don't forget

The PIN code feature is primarily intended for use on small touchscreen devices, but can make logging on **quicker** and **simpler** on any device.

1 On the Start menu, click **Settings** then choose **Accounts**

2 On the left-hand pane, click the **Sign-in options** item, then choose the **Windows Hello PIN** option

3 Click the **Add** button that appears, then click **Next** and enter your text sign-in password

4 Enter a four-digit PIN twice, then click the **OK** button – the PIN code option is now available at the Login screen

Add a user

An important feature in Windows 10 is the provision for setting up more than one user account. This allows a single PC to be shared by a number of people, each with their own computing environment. The procedure for adding a user is as follows:

1 On the Start menu, click **Settings** then choose **Accounts**

2 On the left-hand pane, click the **Family & other users** item and you will see an **Add someone else to this PC** button for "Other users"

When a user is added to a Windows 10 PC, the account type can be either a **Local** or **Microsoft** account.

3 Click the button, then enter user details of a Microsoft account, or click the link to enter user details without a Microsoft account then enter the user details

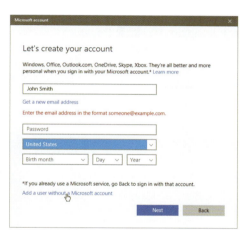

4 The user will be added to the "Other users" list and can log in the next time the PC is started

Close Windows 10

Windows 10 offers several ways of closing the system down:

Desktop mode

Click the ⊞ **Start** button, then click the ⏻ Power button, and choose to "Sleep", "Shut down", or "Restart" from the pop-up menu options.

You can also **Shut down** or **Sign out** from the Power User menu (see page 110).

Tablet mode

Click or tap the ⏻ Power button icon and choose to "Sleep", "Shut down", or "Restart" from the pop-up menu options.

Keyboard

A keyboard command that has been around for a long time is still available in Windows 10. This is **Ctrl + Alt + Del**. Pressing these keys opens the options screen shown on the right – from where you can access the pop-up menu power options.

You may also see a **Change password** option if you have not set up a login PIN code.

Shutdown/Restart shortcuts

1 Right-click on the Desktop, then select **New**, **Shortcut**

2 Enter **shutdown /s /t 0** as the location, then click **Next**

3 Enter "Shutdown" as the name, then click **Finish**

4 Repeat to create a shortcut named "Restart" with the location of **shutdown /r /t 0**

You can also create a "Sign out" tile using the value **shutdown /l**.

You will now see Shutdown and Restart tiles on the Desktop.

5 Windows 10 apps

Apps are an integral part of the Windows 10 interface. This chapter explains how they work, how to access their options, and shows some useful tips. It also describes the apps bundled with Windows 10.

Supplied with Windows 10

Windows 10 comes with lots of pre-installed applications ("apps"). There are familiar traditional programs, such as Notepad, but the A-Z list of apps on the Start menu contains many new "Universal Windows App" programs designed to run on PCs, tablets, and phones. The A-Z list of apps typically looks something like this:

Several of the bundled apps require the user to be logged in with a **Microsoft** account.

Universal Windows Apps are new in Windows 10 and are intended to provide a common experience across many devices.

- 3D Viewer
- Alarms & Clock
- Calculator
- Calendar
- Camera
- Connect
- Feedback Hub
- Game bar
- Get Help
- Groove Music
- Mail
- Maps
- Messaging
- Microsoft Edge
- Microsoft Solitaire Collection
- Microsoft Store
- Mixed Reality Portal
- Mobile Plans
- Movies & TV
- Office

- OneDrive
- OneNote
- Paint 3D
- People
- Photos
- Settings
- Skype
- Snip & Sketch
- Sticky Notes
- Tips
- Video Editor
- Voice Recorder
- Weather
- Windows Accessories *
- Windows Administrative Tools *
- Windows Ease of Access *
- Windows PowerShell *
- Windows System *
- Xbox Console Companion
- Your Phone

If you need apps not supplied with Windows 10, you can find many more apps at the **Microsoft Store**.

Items marked with an * asterisk are folders containing more apps. For example, **Windows Accessories** contains Notepad, Paint, WordPad, Internet Explorer, and many more.

Start apps

Following is a brief look at some of the pre-installed apps – other bundled apps here are reviewed in later chapters.

People

Windows operating systems have always provided a contact manager, which provided a useful means of keeping phone numbers, addresses, etc. in one place. However, the advent of social media websites such as Twitter, Facebook and LinkedIn has seen this type of information stored and used in new ways.

The **People** app is Microsoft's attempt to update its old Contacts manager to make it relevant to today's needs. It stores the data from your contacts in a Cloud-based location, which means they can be accessed from anywhere in the world, via any of your Windows 10 devices.

Furthermore, the app amalgamates data from all supported networks. Thus, people who use more than one social network will be recognized by the app as being the same person, and all their data, whatever the source, is presented as a single contact link.

Skype

This app replaces the Messaging app provided with Windows 8. It allows you to make audio and video calls to other **Skype** users on almost any device, pretty much anywhere in the world, for free.

It is also possible to share files, photos, and web page links with people you're chatting with. When you sign in to the app, all your contacts from the old Messaging app are automatically added to your existing list of contacts.

Calendar

An updated version of a traditional Microsoft application, the **Calendar** app doesn't really offer anything new. It has been designed to be easy to read, and free of unnecessary distractions.

To this end, by default, the content displayed is kept to a minimum. Ease of navigation has been improved, there is a simple interface for adding events, many notification options, and some good advanced scheduling options.

The **People** app also integrates with other Universal Windows Apps. So from the People app you can send emails via the Mail app, map addresses with the Maps app, and you can drag and drop contacts.

The **Skype** app is a new Universal Windows App.

Calendar syncs with Hotmail, Outlook, and Google accounts to bring all your events together for easy viewing.

The **Maps** app allows you to organize your favorites and save places in collections.

The Location service must be enabled in **Settings** > **Privacy** > **Location**, for Directions to work.

The **Get Help** app makes it easy to get help directly from a Microsoft Answer Tech.

...cont'd

Maps

Windows 10's **Maps** app is a particularly useful app. You can enter any address using its Search option and the app will attempt to produce a map showing that location, and a street view photo if available. If the address is found by the app, you can get directions from a starting point of your choice to that address, and discover nearby hotels, coffee shops, restaurants, stores, and museums.

The Directions option lets you seek directions between any two points of your choice, and you can store your maps using the Favorites option.

There is also a 3D Cities option that provides aerial photographic views that you can zoom, tilt, and rotate.

Weather

The **Weather** app provides several menu options. The Home screen displays weather conditions for the current location. This includes an overview, an hourly breakdown, and a range of weather-related details.

The Maps option shows a temperature map of your location and the Historical Weather option displays a graph of past monthly temperature and rainfall at your location.

The Places option allows more locations to be selected to create a Favorite Places list so that multiple locations can be monitored in addition to those displayed on the Home screen.

A News option displays weather-related news items from around the world, describing typhoons, earthquakes, etc.

Get Help

The **Get Help** app aims to provide direct assistance from Microsoft. Its **Accounts & Billing** category provides links to manage your Microsoft account, seek information for Xbox, Skype, or Windows Phone billing queries. It also provides access to get help via online chat or scheduled call to a Microsoft Answer Tech.

The **Technical support** and **Setting up** categories provide links to seek help on Windows installation, settings, activation, errors, performance, and security issues. There are links to seek answers from the Microsoft Community forum, and via online chat or scheduled call to a Microsoft Answer Tech.

These popular apps, which were previously bundled with Windows 10 by default, may now be absent from your A-Z apps list – but they can be easily installed from the Microsoft Store:

Sports

Updated content in real time is provided by the MSN **Sports** app. It is dynamic, and provides an edition related to your location. For example, the US edition is devoted to popular American sports such as football, basketball, baseball, ice hockey, golf, and soccer. The My Favorites option allows you to choose your Favorite Teams and Favorite Sports to follow more closely. Drilling down enables you to access detailed information such as the latest team news, results, fixture lists, and leading players.

News

Most people like to keep abreast of what's happening both in their locality and on the world stage. The MSN **News** app provides the conduit and, like the Sports app, provides an edition related to your location. For example, the US edition is devoted to American news items. The Home screen displays My News items with tabs for categories of news you can customize using the Interests menu option. The Local option allows you to receive items of local news from a location of your choice, and the Videos option shows a selection of recent news videos from the internet.

Money

The MSN **Money** app provides a wealth of finance-related information, with various menu options providing different types of data. You can drill down into items of interest to get detailed information.

The Markets option and World Markets option provide up-to-date stock, commodities, and bond market data. A Watchlist option provides a customizable list of companies you may want to follow closely. Information that can be monitored includes stock market performance (current and historic), revenue, profit, company profile, and more.

The Currencies option provides a handy Currency Converter and up-to-date exchange rates of world currencies. There is also a Mortgage Calculator option to calculate monthly payments.

The new Universal Windows Apps of **Money**, **Weather**, **Sports**, and **News** provide the latest information on any device, wherever you are.

When a news story is clicked in the **Money**, **Weather**, **Sports**, or **News** app it opens up the website that provides it in the app window.

83

App options

In addition to options provided on an app's toolbar, Windows 10 apps offer a range of options on a drop-down menu from a "hamburger button": . Let's start by adding a favorite app to a custom Start group.

1 To add any app to a Start group, first click on the Start button, then find the app in the alphabetical list

2 Next, right-click on the app item to open a context menu, and choose the **Pin to Start** option

3 Click the group title bar above the app icon that has been added to the Start group, and enter a custom group name

Hot tip

A good way to open the Start menu is to simply press the **WinKey**.

Hot tip

To arrange your Start menu groups, use the ▤ icon at the right-hand side of a Start group title bar to **drag** that group.

You can open a context menu of options by right-clicking on any app icon in a Start group. With an open app, clicking the app window's ☰ hamburger button reveals a list of options for that app. The app's ⚙ Settings button can reveal settings options.

4 Launch an app (say, Weather) from the Start menu, then click the app's hamburger button to see the app's options

Windows can display apps in **full screen**, or the window can be resized to display the app in a small floating window.

5 Click the Settings button to reveal the settings options

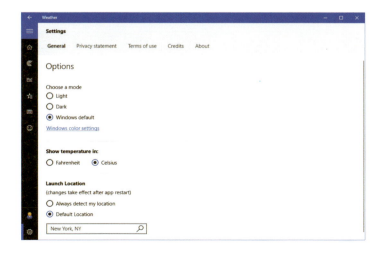

App options offered are related to **each particular app** in use.

App switcher & Task list

The Windows 10 App switcher can be used to quickly switch between running apps. It displays all running apps on the Desktop so you can easily select the one you want to work with. The App switcher is launched using a keyboard shortcut of **WinKey + Tab**.

1 Open the App switcher by pressing **WinKey + Tab**

Don't forget

WinKey refers to the Windows key. This is usually located close to the spacebar (see page 59).

2 Tap or click to select the app you want to work with, or press **WinKey + Tab** again to close the App switcher

Alternatively, you can quickly select a running app to work with from a Task list. This, too, displays all running apps on the Desktop so you can easily select the one you want to work with. The Task list is launched using a keyboard shortcut with **Alt** and **Tab** keys.

3 Open the **Task list** by holding down the **Alt** key and pressing the **Tab** key once

Hot tip

When using the **Task list**, you can also select programs with the arrow keys.

4 Keep the **Alt** key depressed and tap the **Tab** key to move through the list. When the focus is on the app you want to work with, release the **Alt** key to select that app

Snap apps

Windows 10 apps can run full-screen. With the large wide-screen monitors available today, many users will find it irritating to have their entire desktop real-estate taken up by just one program.

To address this issue, Windows 10 offers a feature called Snap, which enables users to run up to four apps side-by-side. The actual number depends on the monitor's resolution. Resolutions of 2,560 x 1,440 pixels can snap four apps. Resolutions of less than this will only be able to snap two or three apps.

Hot tip

For the **Windows Snap** feature to work, the device must have a screen width of at least 1,366 pixels. If you are having problems, check this out by going to Control Panel, Display, Adjust Resolution.

Here, two apps are snapped – the Maps app and the Weather app

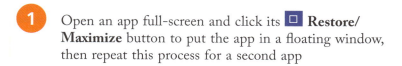

1 Open an app full-screen and click its ▢ **Restore/ Maximize** button to put the app in a floating window, then repeat this process for a second app

NEW

In addition to snapping apps to the left and right, you can snap a **third and fourth** app – but only if the screen resolution allows it.

2 Click on the title bar of the first app and drag it out to the left edge of the screen – then release it to see the window snap to fill the left half of the screen

3 Click on the title bar of the second app and drag it out to the right edge of the screen – then release it to see the window snap to fill the right half of the screen

Don't forget

Most of the time it is **not necessary** to shut an app down. Due to the way that Windows 10 minimizes the system resources required by apps that aren't being used, you can, in fact, have a whole bunch of apps running at the same time without any noticeable degradation of system performance.

Close apps

Closing an app is very simple to do, but it must be pointed out that usually it is not actually necessary to close apps. This is because when a new app is opened, other running apps are switched to a state of suspension in which they use very little in the way of system resources.

However, there may be situations in which it is desirable or even necessary to close down an app. Here are five ways to do this:

- Simply press **Alt** + **F4** – this kills the app instantly.

- Click the Close button on the window bar.

- Right-click the app in **App Switcher** and select **Close**.

- Hover over the app icon on the Taskbar and select **Close** in the pop-up context menu that appears.

- Press **Ctrl** + **Shift** + **Esc** to open the Task Manager, then select the app on the Processes tab and click the **End task** button.

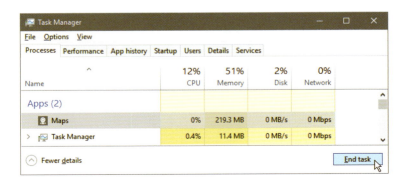

Office app

The Office app lets you easily manage a Microsoft Office subscription. It is also a hub that provides buttons to easily install Microsoft Office apps or to open Microsoft Office apps you have already installed. Additionally, the hub provides a list of Office documents you've recently used, and other useful features:

1 Launch the Office app and click any Microsoft Office app icon to install or open that app

The earlier version of the **Office** app ("Get Office") simply pointed to the Office 365 website, but the app was improved to provide a much more useful hub.

Hot tip

Click the **My Account** option to manage your Microsoft Office subscription.

2 Scroll down to see a list of Microsoft Office documents you have recently used, then right-click one to see options

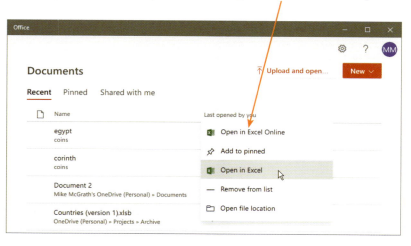

Hot tip

You can also install Microsoft Office **for mobile devices** via the Office app.

Select items from the 3D Objects group, then **decorate** them using Tools, Text, or Stickers that automatically map to the 3D surface.

Don't forget

The **History** feature records every change you make to the object so you can rewind to restart from a previous point.

3D apps

The **Paint 3D** app allows you to create and work with 3D objects and scenes. It also lets you share your 3D art with others via the online Remix 3D community. You can import and edit 3D objects created by fellow community members to build new models and scenes within the Paint 3D app.

The interface of the Paint 3D app comprises a toolbar, workspace, and right-hand pane that displays a collection of items according to the currently selected toolbar button:

An object selected is surrounded by a box with handles on each side that will rotate and zoom the object in space. Multiple objects can be added to the canvas then grouped together to maintain their relative positions when the 3D model is rotated.

The hamburger menu button on the toolbar allows you to publish your 3D art in the Remix 3D community, export it as a 2D image in the popular file formats PNG, JPEG, BMP, GIF, and TIFF, or export it as a 3D image in the 3MF or GLB file formats.

Fans of mixed reality can virtually place objects created in Paint 3D within the real world when viewed through a mixed reality headset, and using the **Mixed Reality Portal** app.

Microsoft HoloLens mixed reality headset.

The **3D Viewer** app is designed to view 3D objects in the 3MF or GLB file formats. It has a Turntable feature that rotates the 3D model through 360 degrees:

3D image files can be huge. **Remix 3D** has a publish limit of 64MB at the time of writing.

The **3D Builder** app is available in the Microsoft Store and can print 3MF or GLB file format objects using a 3D printer:

Dremel 3D printer.

Windows Ink Workspace

Windows 10 has a Windows Ink Workspace that is primarily intended for users of a digital pen on tablet devices. This feature provides Sticky Notes, Sketchpad, and Snip & Sketch pen applications – but these can also be used without a digital pen. Sticky Notes simply allows you to jot down a quick note:

You can use the **OneNote** app for more extensive note-taking.

1 Right-click on the System Tray, then choose **Show Windows Ink Workspace button** to add this button to the tray

2 Click the **Windows Ink Workspace button** to open a sidebar providing quick access to Sticky Notes, Sketchpad and Screen sketch apps, and shortcut tiles to recently used apps

3 Select **Sticky Notes** to open a new blank note on which you can jot down a note with a digital pen or your keyboard

Discover much more on the **Sticky Notes** app on pages 125-127.

4 Click the ... ellipsis button, then click **Delete note** on the menu to remove a note

Sketchpad

Sketchpad is a digital whiteboard that has options for different writing styles with thin pencils, colored pens, and highlighters. There are also nifty ruler and protractor tools to draw straight lines, arcs, and circles – just place the pen on the edge and draw:

Eraser   Clear   Copy

Pens   Tools   Save   Share

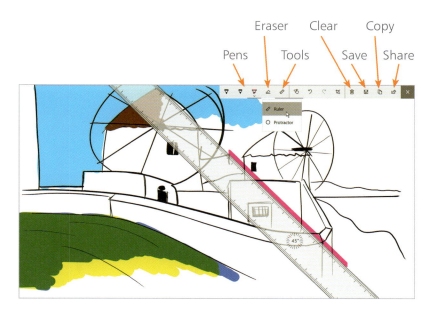

Sketchpad was improved with the introduction of the **protractor** tool.

Snip & Sketch

Snip & Sketch enables you to mark up your current screen, as it displays a screenshot and provides a selection of drawing tools similar to those in Sketchpad:

If you just want to capture your screen, simply use the **PrtScn** (Print Screen) key on your keyboard or use **Alt** + **PrtScn** to capture the current window.

Screenshots marked up in Snip & Sketch and Sketchpad whiteboards can be saved as an image file or sent to others using the Share button on their toolbars.

Another new screenshot feature – press **WinKey** + **Shift** + **S**, then drag the cursor to define a region of the screen to copy onto the clipboard.

OneDrive

OneDrive is a Microsoft facility that allows users to store data in the Cloud via a Microsoft account. To get started, click the OneDrive item on the Start menu and log in with your Microsoft account (if you don't have an account you will need to create one). You will then be asked to choose which folders on your PC you wish to synchronize on OneDrive. Your selection now appears under the OneDrive category on your PC, marked with green check mark icons when they have been synchronized.

The **status icons** denote the sync status of files and folders.

 Online-only

 Available on this device

Always kept on this device

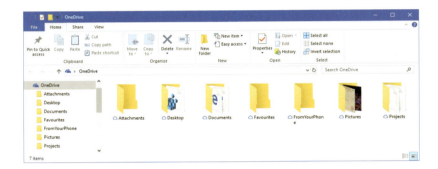

Copies of content added to these local folders are automatically uploaded to your online OneDrive folder to synchronize photos, documents, etc. across devices such as PCs, smartphones, and tablets. Your content can be accessed from anywhere using the OneDrive app on a device or by browsing to **onedrive.live.com** You can create **New** online folders and add files, or **Upload** folders and files to the online OneDrive folder from your device.

A OneDrive account can be accessed in two ways – directly from a web browser, and via the OneDrive app. **More options** are available when it is accessed via a browser.

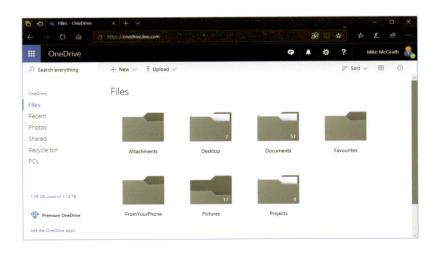

6 Desktop and Taskbar

This chapter describes how Windows 10 displays text and graphics at the right size. It also illustrates how to take advantage of multiple monitors and choose a Desktop theme with the style, appearance and features that most appeal to you.

Switching Desktops

Windows 10 has a virtual Desktop feature called "Task View". This allows you to have multiple Desktops so you can spread out various projects, so that each project is on a separate Desktop. When you need to jump from one project to another you can just switch Desktops and everything is right there waiting for you – no need to minimize and maximize windows to get back to work:

Virtual Desktops have been available in other operating systems for quite some time, but are new in Windows 10.

You can also access Task View by pressing **WinKey** + **Tab**.

1 Click the ⊞ button on the Taskbar to access the Task View feature – thumbnail icons of all running apps and a **+ New desktop** button appear on the screen

2 Next, click the **+ New desktop** button and Desktop thumbnails will appear in a bar at the top of the screen

3 Hover the mouse cursor over either Desktop thumbnail to see thumbnail icons of all apps running on that Desktop

To move a running app to a different Desktop, right-click on the thumbnail icon of the running app, then select **Move to** and choose a Desktop from the context menu.

4 Each Desktop thumbnail icon has a pop-up X button to close that Desktop – apps running on that Desktop will automatically move to an open Desktop

Timeline

Task View also includes a Timeline feature that lets you resume any activity you were working on in the past 30 days. Timeline is essentially a "recent apps" screen that synchronizes activities across all your devices that are logged in to the same Microsoft account. This means that you can quickly resume working on a document at a later date by opening Timeline and selecting that document.

Timeline remembers all kinds of activity including websites visited in Microsoft Edge, articles read in the MSN News app, files created in Microsoft Office apps, Notepad, Paint, and more. Upon its introduction the Timeline feature only detected activity from Microsoft apps, so you may not see activity from apps from other sources until developers add support for this feature.

Timeline appears below Task View, so currently open apps are at the top of the screen (the "now" view) and previous activities appear below in historical order with the most recent highest. There is a side scroll bar that lets you scroll back in time to find a recent activity you may wish to resume:

Timeline is a useful new feature in Windows 10.

1 Open Task View, then scroll down the Timeline thumbnail icons to find a previous activity

You can right-click on any Timeline thumbnail icon and select **Remove** on the context menu to delete that icon.

2 Click the Timeline thumbnail to resume that activity in the appropriate app

You can **launch** any program on the PC from the Search box.

The Taskbar **Search box** is new in Windows 10.

Launching apps

There are various ways of launching an application:

Start menu/Desktop icons

Start menu items and Desktop icons are actually shortcuts that link to a program's executable file. So, to launch an app, just click on the menu item or Desktop icon – this activates the app, which then opens on the screen.

Taskbar icons

Icons on the Taskbar are application shortcuts as well. Click one, and the associated application will open on the Desktop.

Search box

Applications that are located on the Start menu, Desktop, or Taskbar are easy to locate – they are literally right in front of your eyes. How about programs you can't see, though?

Windows 10's Search box is the answer:

1 Enter the name of the app in the Search box

2 Choose the appropriate app from the search results

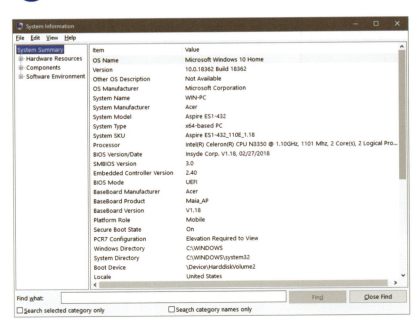

Personalize

You can give your computer a personal touch by changing the computer's window color, sounds, Desktop background, screen saver, and many other aspects. You can change the attributes individually, or select a pre-configured theme:

1 Right-click the Desktop and select **Personalize** to open a Settings screen

2 Choose **Themes** on the left-hand pane to see the currently selected theme

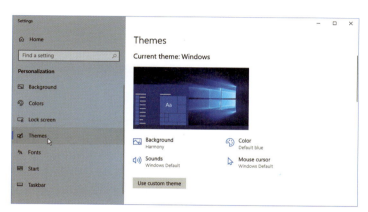

You can click the **Get more themes in Microsoft Store** link on the Personalization, Themes screen to add more great themes to your PC (see page 24).

3 Scroll down to see other available themes and select one to see it get immediately applied to your PC

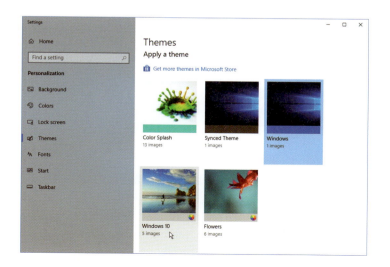

There's no **screen saver** included in most themes since they already include a varying background. However, you can add a screen saver to any theme.

...cont'd

There will be a theme for the **location** appropriate to your installed version – for example, USA or UK.

Don't forget

If your selected theme has a slideshow background, by default the images will advance **every 30 minutes** – but you can adjust the timing and select random images.

One of the standard Windows 10 themes is shown below:

If you don't like the background image of a particular theme, right-click the Desktop, then select **Personalize** and click **Background** to choose another. To retain the previous accent color for icons and tiles, select **Colors** then turn off the option to "Automatically pick an accent color from my background". Below, we see the Windows 10 theme as above, but now with a different background and accent color.

NEW

The Acrylic effect is part of the **Fluent Design System** in Windows 10.

Scroll down the **Colors** screen and set **Transparency effects** to **On** to enable the "Acrylic" feature, which allows the surface behind to shine through the foreground window.

Create a theme

1 Right-click the Desktop and select **Background** on the Personalization screen

2 Next, click **Browse** and select the background image required, then click the **Choose picture** button

3 The selected image now appears in the Preview area

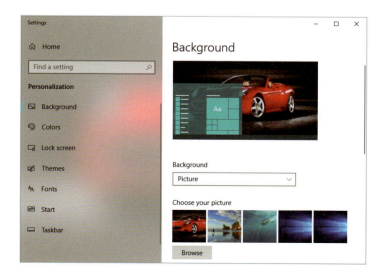

...cont'd

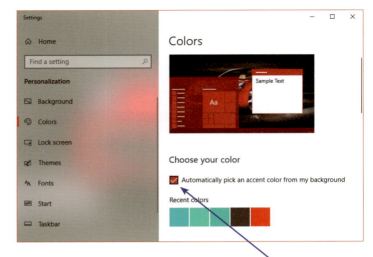

The modified theme is added to the **My Themes** section, as an unsaved theme.

4 Select **Colors** and turn **On** the option to "Automatically pick an accent color from my background" for color tiles

5 Adjust the other toggle buttons for color and transparency on the Start menu, Taskbar, and Action Center. Your changes appear in the Preview area and on your Desktop

You can click the **High contrast settings** link to customize colors for high contrast themes.

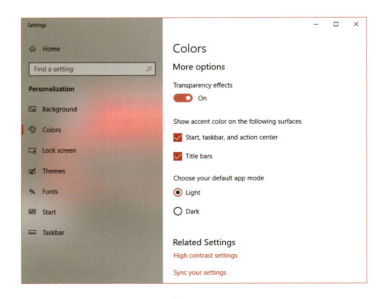

...cont'd

Sound scheme

Next, choose a sound scheme:

1 Right-click the Desktop and select **Themes** on the Personalization screen, then choose the **Sounds** link

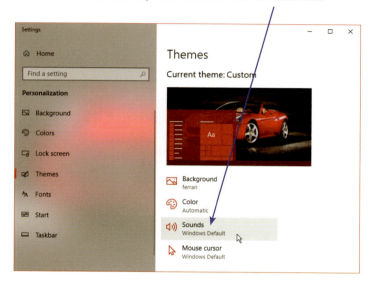

Most of the Windows themes provide their own **sound scheme**, so you can try these out to see which you prefer.

The **default** Windows 10 sound scheme has more mellow sounds than earlier versions.

103

2 Select the **Sound Scheme** drop-down menu, and choose from the predefined sound schemes to find which you prefer

3 Select a Program Event such as "Windows Logon" and click **Test** to listen to the sound

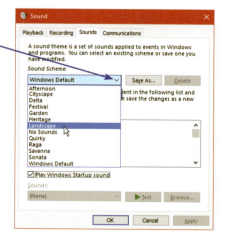

Free additional sound schemes are available online from websites such as **winsounds.com**

Check the **Play Windows Startup sound** box to hear sound when Windows starts up, or uncheck it to avoid the sound.

4 Click **Browse...** to choose a different sound file, then click OK to set it as the new sound

5 Click **Save As...** to save the revised sound scheme

…cont'd

Desktop icons & Mouse pointer settings

Choose which icons to display on the Desktop:

1 Right-click the Desktop and select **Themes** on the Personalization screen, then choose the **Desktop icon settings** link in the "Related Settings" category

2 Check any icon you want on the Desktop, then click **Apply**, **OK**

3 Click the **Mouse cursor** link on the Personalization screen

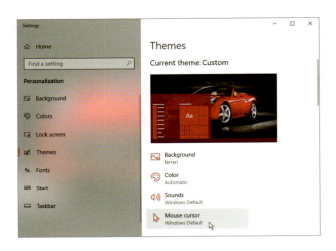

4 Customize the performance of the mouse and the appearance of pointers using the tab options

5 Click **Apply** then **OK** to save the settings

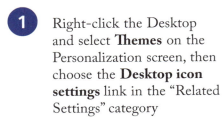

Check the box to **Allow themes to change desktop icons** if you want to use themes with their own custom icons.

Hot tip

The Mouse Properties' **Pointers** tab lets you select from a variety of Windows pointer schemes.

...cont'd

Save the theme

To save your theme:

1 Right-click the Desktop and select **Themes** on the Personalization screen, then click the **Save theme** link

2 Provide a name for your new theme and click **Save**

3 The theme remains in "Themes", under its new name

The theme file is stored in the user's applications data area – e.g. **C:\Users*name*\AppData\Local\Microsoft\Windows\Themes** – along with any Windows themes that have been downloaded.

...cont'd

To make the theme available to other users:

1 Right-click the theme and select **Save theme for sharing**

2 Specify the name and folder for the theme and click **Save**

3 Backgrounds, colors, sounds, and other theme settings are saved in a file of type **.deskthemepack**. Sharing this file will make the theme available to the other users

4 To remove a theme, first ensure it is not currently selected, then right-click and select **Delete**

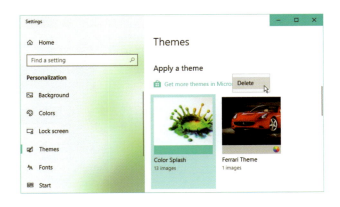

Screen resolution

To adjust the screen resolution:

1 Right-click the Desktop and select **Display settings** from the menu

2 Now, click the **Resolution** box and choose a setting from the drop-down menu

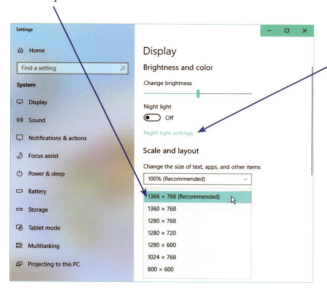

3 See the resolution change for 15 seconds

4 Click **Keep changes** during the change period to retain the new resolution you have selected

5 Drag the slider to adjust the brightness

6 Set the **Night light** to the "On" position to reduce blue light at night

Night light is a new feature in Windows 10. Use the **Night light settings** link to choose your preferred color temperature and schedule.

The **screen resolution** controls the size of the screen contents. Lower resolutions (e.g. 800 x 600) have larger items, so fewer can be displayed. Higher resolutions (e.g. 1920 x 1200) have smaller and sharper items, and more can be viewed on the screen.

You can also change the orientation from **Landscape** to **Portrait** – useful for tablet PCs and for a monitor that can be rotated.

Taskbar

The purpose of the Taskbar is to launch and monitor running applications. The version provided in Windows 10 has two specific regions – a small section at the right called the System Tray notification area, and the main body of the Taskbar on which program buttons and the Start button are displayed. To explore the Taskbar and see what it can do, it is necessary to go into its settings (right-click on the Taskbar and select **Taskbar settings**).

Before you can move or resize the Taskbar, it must be **unlocked**.

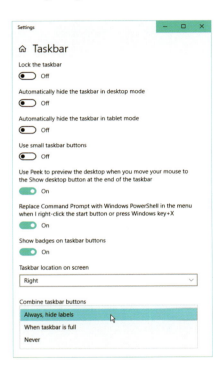

Taskbar settings provides various options including:

- **Lock the taskbar** – when unlocked it can be moved and its depth can be increased.
- **Use small taskbar buttons** – enables the bar to hold more buttons.
- **Combine taskbar buttons**: **Always, hide labels** – each app appears as a single, unlabeled button, even if several windows for that app are currently open.

When the **Use Peek to preview the desktop...** option is enabled, hovering your mouse at the far-right of the Taskbar will temporarily hide all open windows.

- **Combine taskbar buttons**: **When taskbar is full** – each window is shown as an individual button. When the Taskbar becomes crowded, apps with multiple open windows collapse into a single button.

- **Combine taskbar buttons**: **Never** – each window is shown as an individual, labeled button and are never combined, regardless of how many are open. As more apps and windows open, buttons get smaller, and will eventually scroll.

- **Notification area** – customize the area using **Select which icons appear on the taskbar** and **Turn system icons on or off**.

You will also find options for configuring the Taskbar on multiple displays, as shown below – choose to have the Taskbar showing on all your displays, and how program buttons are displayed:

Folders and files cannot be added to the Taskbar. However, they can be dragged to the **File Explorer** icon on the Taskbar and accessed from its jump list. You can pin a folder to the Start menu tiles, then pin that tile to the Taskbar.

Right-click on the Taskbar, then select **Toolbars** to see a list of pre-configured toolbars that can be added to the Taskbar. For example, select **Address** to add an address toolbar to the Taskbar:

By right-clicking on the Taskbar and selecting **Toolbars, New toolbar...**, you can create your own Taskbar toolbars.

Any program can be "pinned" to the Taskbar – simply right-click on its icon in the Start menu, then select **More**, **Pin to taskbar** – or just drag-and-drop the icon onto the Taskbar.

5 Click **Identify** to briefly display the numerals 1 and 2 on the monitor screens for identification

6 By default, the monitors are arranged horizontally, so the mouse moves between them at the screen left and right. To arrange the monitors vertically, so the mouse moves between them at the screen top and bottom, drag one of the monitor blocks above the other, then click **Apply**

Hot tip

When you press **PrtScn** with dual monitors, you will capture an image of both monitors, in the positions as arranged.

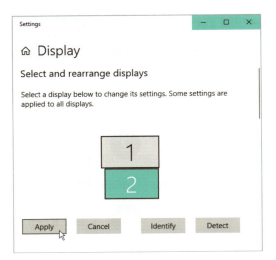

Don't forget

The **Snap Across** feature in Windows 10 allows you to drag an application window from one monitor to the other, or across both monitors.

7 To adjust the resolution of each monitor individually, select a monitor block then change its resolution setting

8 To connect to a wireless display, such as a smart TV with Miracast support, click **Connect to a wireless display**

Application windows

A very useful function in Windows is the ability to move and resize application windows. Apps in the Windows 10 interface can run in full-screen mode and can be resized.

1 To move a window, click the title bar area, hold down the mouse button and drag the window

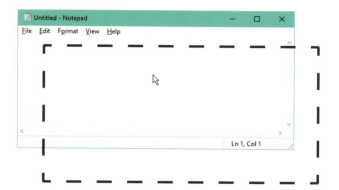

When you drag a **corner** of the window, you can adjust the two adjacent borders simultaneously.

2 To resize a window, move the mouse pointer over any border or any corner until it becomes a double-headed arrow. Then click and drag until the window is the desired size

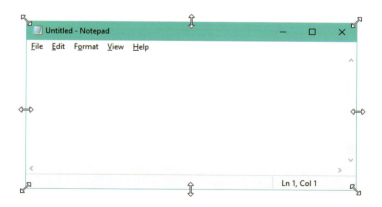

Double-clicking the **title bar** is an alternative to selecting the Maximize and Restore buttons.

3 To make the window full-screen, click the Maximize button. The button will now change into the Restore button – click it again to return to the original size

By default, the window contents show as you drag. To display just the frame, select System Properties, Advanced system settings, and then **Performance Settings**.

Snap and Shake

Windows 10 includes two neat window manipulation features carried over from Windows 7. These are Snap and Shake.

Snap

Snap is a window docking feature that resizes two windows, each to half the size of the screen, and places them side-by-side. It is almost instant, requiring just two clicks to achieve what previously would need much dragging and resizing. Do it as follows:

1 Drag the title bar of a window to the left or right side of the screen until an outline of the expanded window appears

2 Release the window, which then expands to fill one half of the screen

3 Repeat with another window on the other side of the screen. You will now have two windows of equal size, side-by-side and filling the screen, as shown below:

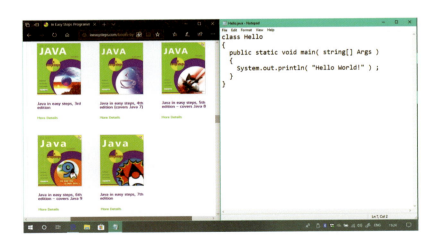

Shake

Ever need to cut through a cluttered Desktop and quickly focus on a single window? Just click the top of a pane and give your mouse a shake. Voilà! Every open window except that one instantly disappears. Shake it again – your windows are restored.

You can also use **Snap** to maximize a window to full-screen by dragging it to the top or bottom edges of the screen.

Snap is improved in Windows 10 with the new **Snap Assist** feature. This provides a thumbnail list of other open apps when you snap one app to a screen edge. Click any thumbnail to snap it to the other edge.

ClearType

ClearType font technology makes the text on your screen appear as sharp and clear as text that's printed on paper. It's on by default in Windows 10, but you can fine-tune the settings.

1 Enter "ClearType" in the **Search box**, then click to **Adjust ClearType text**

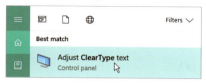

For the full benefit of **ClearType**, you need a high-quality, flat-panel monitor, such as LCD or plasma.

2 Check the **Turn on ClearType** text box (if unchecked)

Windows 10 has improved **Font** management. Go to Start, Settings, Personalization, Fonts.

3 Click **Next** and Windows checks that you are using the native resolution for your monitor

If the monitor is not set to the **recommended** resolution, you are given the opportunity to change it.

115

...cont'd

4 Click **Next** to run the "ClearType Text Tuner"

5 Click the text box that looks best to you, then click **Next**

To review the settings on each of the five pages, click **Next** to accept the default selection.

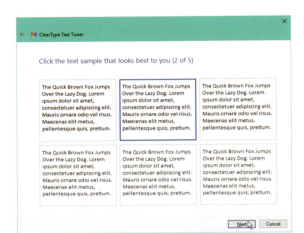

6 Click **Finish** to close the "ClearType Text Tuner"

Any changes apply only to the **current** user. Each user account has its own ClearType settings recorded separately.

7 Built-in programs

This chapter describes programs built into Windows 10 to help you in text processing, scanning, faxing, image management, calculations, and tools to record and process sound and images. It also looks at special tools available, such as Command Prompt and Windows PowerShell.

All apps

Windows 10 comes with a number of applications, services and functions, of which many users may be completely unaware. Usually, these will be features and programs that they will never need to use. There will be times, though, when they miss out on something that would have been useful if only they had known it was there.

To make sure this doesn't happen to you, check to see exactly what is available in Windows 10:

1 Click the Start button

2 Scroll through the alphabetic listing of all available apps

In Windows 10, most items in the A-Z Start list are new **Universal Windows Apps**, whereas traditional programs are found in folders such as "Windows Accessories".

Windows Accessories
Character Map
Internet Explorer
Math Input Panel
Notepad
Paint
Quick Assist
Remote Desktop Connection
Snipping Tool
Steps Recorder
Windows Fax and Scan
Windows Media Player
WordPad

#
3D Viewer
A
Alarms & Clock
C
Calculator
Calendar
Camera
Connect
F
Feedback Hub
G
Game bar
Get Help
Groove Music

M
Mail
Maps
Messaging
Microsoft Edge
Microsoft Solitaire Collection
Microsoft Store
Mixed Reality Portal
Mobile Plans
Movies & TV
O
Office
OneDrive
OneNote
P
Paint 3D
People
Photos

S
Settings
Skype
Snip & Sketch
Sticky Notes
T
Tips
V
Video Editor
Voice Recorder
W
Weather
Windows Accessories
Windows Administrative Tools
Windows Ease of Access
Windows PowerShell
Windows Security
Windows System
X
Xbox Console Companion
Y
Your Phone

Traditional apps

Traditionally, Windows has provided a number of basic, but nevertheless useful, built-in applications such as those below:

- Calculator
- Character Map
- Command Prompt
- Magnifier
- Math Input Panel
- Notepad
- Paint
- Run

- Snipping Tool
- Sticky Notes
- Task Manager
- Voice Recorder
- WordPad
- Windows Fax & Scan
- Windows Media Player
- Windows PowerShell

Microsoft intends the **Windows PowerShell** app to become the preferred default command-line app – rather than the previous Command Prompt app.

Calculator and Voice Recorder have now been reborn as Universal Windows Apps, but other traditional apps are still available in Windows 10 – in the Windows Accessories, Windows Ease of Access, or Windows System folders on the Start menu.

If you intend to use any traditional app often, it will be a good move to pin a shortcut to that app in a handy place. Locate the app in the Start menu, then right-click on the item and choose **Pin to Start** (if you want it on the Start group), or **More, Pin to taskbar**. This is demonstrated in the example below that creates a handy shortcut to the Notepad app on the Start menu:

- Choose **More, Pin to taskbar** and the program will then be instantly accessible from the Taskbar.

- Choose **Pin to Start** and the program will then be accessible from the Start group menu.

If you pin a lot of programs to the Taskbar, you may find yourself running out of room. Create more space by resizing the Taskbar. Right-click the Taskbar and uncheck **Lock the taskbar**, then simply drag its top edge upwards to make it taller.

We'll take a look at the reborn Calculator program and some of the traditional Windows programs in the next few pages.

In Windows 10, **Calculator** is a Universal Windows App with more functionality than the old traditional program. For example, it now has a built-in **Currency converter** facility.

You can also use the numeric keypad to type numbers and operators. Press **Num Lock** if it is not already turned on.

Calculator clears the display when you switch views. You should use the **memory** buttons if you need to retain a number between mode switches.

Calculator

Whilst there's no spreadsheet capability built in to Windows 10, it does offer a handy calculator:

 Open the Start menu, then find **Calculator** under "C"

Click calculator buttons or press equivalent keyboard keys, to enter numbers and operations such as Add, Subtract, Multiply, Divide, Square Root, Percent and Inverse.

 To complete the calculation, select or press the **Enter** key

You can also store and recall numbers from memory, and the History capability keeps track of stages in the calculations.

This is just the Standard calculator. You can also choose to use the Scientific, or Programmer, version of the calculator.

 Click the hamburger button and choose, for example, **Scientific**

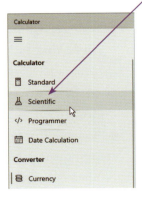

The Scientific calculator includes many functions and inverse functions, including logarithms and factorials. There is also a Programmer calculator view that can perform arithmetic on binary, octal, decimal and hexadecimal values. Converter options usefully convert between many different units of measure.

Notepad

There are several applications that provide various levels of text management capabilities. One of these is Notepad.

The program is a basic text-editing application and it's most commonly used to view or edit text files, usually with the **.txt** file name extension, but any text file can be handled:

1 Open the Start menu, then find **Notepad** under "Windows Accessories". Type some text, pressing **Enter** to start a new line

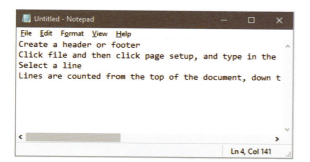

Hot tip

Select **Format**, **Font...** to choose the Font, Font Style and Size. This will apply to all the text in the whole document.

2 Parts of the lines may be hidden, if lines are longer than the width of the window

3 Select **Format**, **Word Wrap** to fit the text within the window width

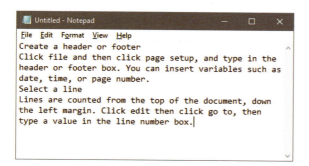

Don't forget

When you print a document the lines are wrapped between the margins, whatever the **Word Wrap** setting.

4 Select **Edit** to cut, copy and paste text, or to insert a Time/Date stamp into the document

5 Select **File** to save or print the document

WordPad

WordPad is a text-editing program you can use to create and edit documents that can include rich formatting and graphics. You can also link to or embed pictures and other documents:

1 Open the Start menu and find **WordPad** under "Windows Accessories". Then, type in some text

The text automatically wraps as you type, and the **Enter** key starts a new paragraph.

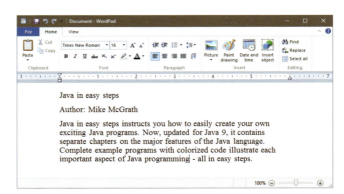

2 Select text and use the formatting bar to change font, etc.

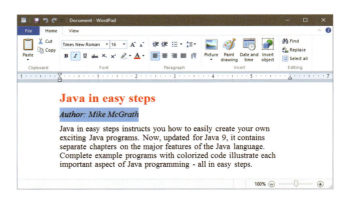

Saving as a **Rich Text Document (.rtf)**, **Open Office XML (.docx)** or **OpenDocument Text (.odt)** will retain the text styling. However, the other formats save as plain text, and remove images or links.

3 Click the **Save** button on the Quick Access Toolbar, type the file name and confirm the file type, then click **Save**

Paint

Paint allows you to create drawings on a blank drawing area or edit existing pictures, photographs, and web graphics. Open the program as described below:

1 Open the Start menu then find **Paint** under "Windows Accessories". The app launches a blank canvas:

File button (for Paint Tooltip)   Quick Access Toolbar   Home tab   Ribbon   Drawing area   Color palette

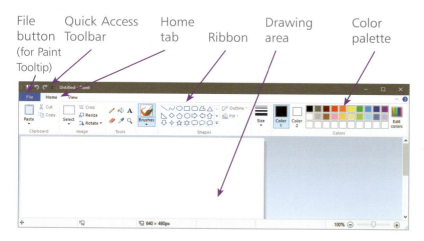

2 Or, right-click an image file and select **Open with**, **Paint**

View tab   Scroll bars

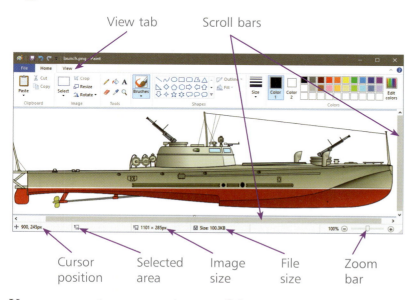

Cursor position   Selected area   Image size   File size   Zoom bar

You can zoom in on a certain part of the picture or zoom out if the picture is too large, and show rulers and gridlines as you work.

There is also a toolbar button giving you the option to open the image in the **Paint 3D** application (see page 90).

Edit with Paint 3D

When you paste an image onto the **Paint** drawing area, it will be automatically resized if necessary to fit the whole image. **Paint** can open and save as a number of image formats, including: **.bmp**, **.jpg**, **.gif**, **.tif** and **.png**.

Snipping tool

This will capture a screenshot, or Snip, of any object on your screen, and you can then annotate, save, or share the image. For example, if there's a window open with information to be copied:

1 Open the Start menu, then find **Snipping Tool** under "Windows Accessories"

2 Select the arrow next to **Mode** to pick the Snip type; e.g. Rectangular

3 Click a corner and drag over the area you wish to capture

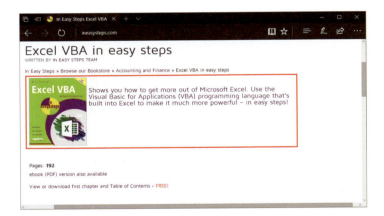

4 Release the mouse, and the Snip is copied to the Clipboard and the mark-up window

5 Use the tools to annotate the Snip if desired then click the **Save Snip** button, adjust the name and click **Save**

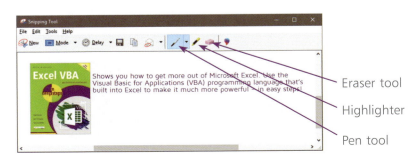

Eraser tool

Highlighter

Pen tool

Hot tip

You can use the **Delay** options to give you time to select, and the **New** button to quickly capture a new Snip.

Don't forget

You can capture a free-form area, a rectangular area, a window or the full screen and save the Snip as file type **.png**, **.gif**, **.jpg** or **.mht** (single file **.html**). You can then include the saved file in documents or email messages.

NEW

There is also a toolbar button giving you the option to open the image in the **Paint 3D** application (see page 90), and you can find an alternative Snipping tool in the **Snip & Sketch** app (see page 93).

Sticky Notes

Sticky Notes

You can keep track of small pieces of information such as phone numbers, addresses or meeting schedules using Sticky Notes. You can use Sticky Notes with a tablet pen or a standard keyboard.

To create a new Sticky Note:

1 Open the Start menu, then find **Sticky Notes** under the "S" category

2 The new note appears on the Desktop with the typing cursor active

3 Type the text of the note or reminder that you want to record

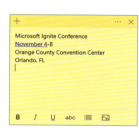

4 Text automatically wraps as you type, or you can press **Enter** to start a new line

5 To change the color of the note, first click the **...** (ellipsis) button then choose a new color from the swatch that appears – see the note change color instantly

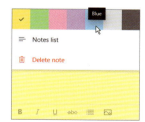

6 To provide simple formatting of the note text, first select the text that you want to change then use one of these keyboard shortcuts to format the text how you like

Ctrl + B	Bold text
Ctrl + I	Italic text
Ctrl + U	Underlined text
Ctrl + T	Strikethrough

Hot tip

Sticky Notes automatically extend in length to accommodate text as you type. You can also drag a corner or edge to resize or reshape the note.

Don't forget

To create another note, click the **+ new note** button. To remove a note, click the trash can icon.

Insights

The Sticky Notes application can be integrated with Cortana Insights to set reminders, send email messages, view web addresses, display stock prices, show flight details, and more:

To enable and use Insights in Sticky Notes:

Beware

Some **Insights** features may only be available to users located within the United States.

1 Click the **...** (ellipsis) button to reveal the drop-down **Menu**, then click the **Notes list** option

2 To reveal the **Settings** options click the gear cog icon

Hot tip

If your Windows device has a **pen** or **stylus**, you can draw or write directly on a Sticky Note.

3 Slide the **Enable Insights** button to the **On** position

4 Click the **X** button to close the **Notes list** – items recognized by Insights will now appear as links

5 Select a date link and click the **Add Reminder** button that appears – Cortana will now ask if you want to set a reminder for this note on that selected date

6 Click **Remind** to set Cortana to display the note as a Reminder on that date

You can now explore some other Insights:

1 Create a new note and add a valid email address

2 Select the email address link to see a **Send Email** button appear that you can use to send a message

3 Create a new note, and add a web address, such as **ineasysteps.com**

4 Select the web address link to see an **Open Link** button appear that you can use to open that address in a browser

The Sticky Note buttons provided for Insights will use the program associated with that link. For example, **Send Email** may open the Mail app, **Open Link** may open the Edge browser, and **Call** may open the Skype app.

5 Create a new note, and add a valid phone number

6 Select the phone number link to see a **Call** button appear that you can use to call that number

7 Create a new note, and add a valid physical address

8 Select the address link to see a **View Address** button appear

9 Click the **View Address** button to open a map window that you can use to locate that physical address

Microsoft will over time **expand** Insights to other languages and regions.

Fax and scan

Windows provides software to support sending and receiving faxes, but you need a fax modem installed or attached to your computer, plus a connection to a telephone line.

There's also support for scanning documents and pictures, but you need a scanner (or all-in-one printer) attached to your computer.

To start Windows Fax and Scan:

 Open the Start menu, then find **Windows Fax and Scan** under "Windows Accessories"

Select **View**, then **Zoom** and you can choose a larger or smaller scale, or fit to page or fit to width, as desired.

An example document is displayed, and this provides guidance for getting started with faxes and scanning

To scan a document or photo, click the **Scan** button, then click **New Scan** on the toolbar, and follow the prompts

When you have scanned a document or picture, you can forward it as an **email** or as a **fax**.

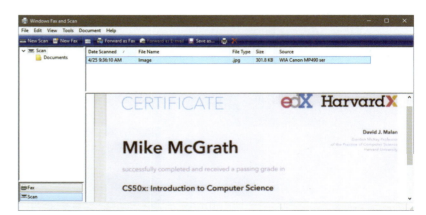

Command Prompt

All versions of Windows have included a command line feature for typing MS-DOS commands and other computer commands.

1 Open the Start menu, then find **Command Prompt** under "Windows System"

Beware

The **Command Prompt** environment is extremely powerful and should be used with great caution.

2 To display a list of commands with a brief description of each, type "Help" and press **Enter**

Don't forget

If the commands you use require authorization, right-click Command Prompt on the Start menu, and select **Run as administrator**.

3 For more details of a specific command, type **Help** *Name* then press **Enter**; e.g. **Help CHKDSK**

4 To adjust Command Prompt options, right-click the title bar and select **Defaults** or **Properties**

Hot tip

Select **Edit** from the right-click menu, and you can mark, copy and paste text onto the command line.

5 To close Command Prompt, type "Exit" then press **Enter**

Windows PowerShell

To support system administrators and advanced users, Windows provides a command-line and scripting environment, far more powerful than the old MS-DOS batch file system.

1 Open the Start menu, then find **Windows PowerShell** under "Windows PowerShell"

2 Type **GET-COMMAND** for a list of PowerShell commands

3 Now you can discover more about any command using the PowerShell help system – for example, to discover more about a particular alias, type **HELP FLUSH-VOLUME**

Windows PowerShell can execute "Cmdlets" (which are .NET programs), PowerShell scripts (file type **.ps1**), PowerShell functions, and executable programs.

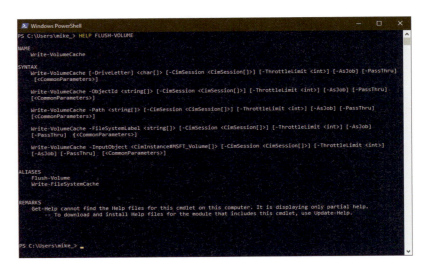

4 The PowerShell help system can be updated online using the command **UPDATE-HELP**

Administrative tools

Administrative tools are intended for system administrators and advanced users. To see the list available on your system:

1 Open the Start menu then find all the tools under "Windows Administrative Tools"

2 Here you will see a range of tools that enable you to manage the way the PC is used

3 Click **Services** and you will see a list of all services available and running on the PC

4 Double-clicking a service reveals options for starting and stopping the service. This enables you to disable the ones that aren't necessary. A typical example is network-related services – if you don't use networking, you can safely disable these and gain a small performance boost

Hot tip

You can use the **System Information** tool to discover details of the hardware, components, and the software environment of your entire system.

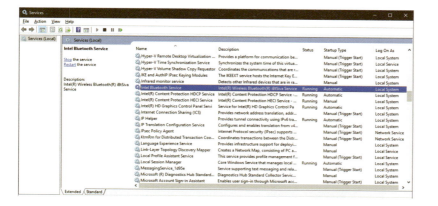

Hot tip

Explore each item in **Windows Administrative Tools** to see how they might be useful to control your PC.

131

Unknown file types

A problem you may come across occasionally is trying to start a program, only to be greeted by a message like this one:

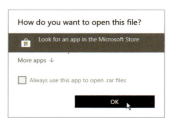

The reason for the message is that Windows cannot recognize what program is associated with the type of file you are trying to open – so has no idea how to open that file.

Initially, you are offered an option to look for an app in the Store. Clicking this will take you to the Microsoft Store where, if you aren't already, you will have to log in with a Microsoft account. Once done, a search is made automatically for apps capable of opening the file in question. If one is found, you are offered the option of downloading it – remember, you may have to pay for it.

If the results inform you that a suitable app hasn't been found for this type of file, you can return to the message box to retry.

Clicking the "More apps" link will reveal a list of suggested programs. However, if none of these work either, your last recourse is the internet. There are quite a few sites that provide lists of file types and the programs associated with them. For example, you could try looking online at **filext.com**

Beware

If you try any of the suggested programs, make sure the "Always use this app to open XXX files" option is not selected – **unless you are sure** the program is the one you want.

Change default program

All files are designed to be opened with a specific type of program. For example, graphics files such as JPG and GIF can only be opened by a graphics editing program such as Paint, or with a web browser such as Microsoft Edge.

A common problem that many users experience is when they install a program on their PC that automatically makes itself the default program for opening related files. If the user prefers the original program, he or she will have to reassociate the file type in question. Alternatively, the user might want to set a different program as the default:

1 Go to **Start, Settings, Apps, Default apps** then click the link to **Choose default apps by file type**

2 Select the file type you want to reassociate. For example, to open **JPEG** files with a different app

3 You will now see a list of programs on the PC capable of opening that file type. Select the one you want to use; e.g. **Paint**

4 See the selected app is now associated with that file type

Search the web for software

There was a time when if you wanted a specific program, you either had to visit a store to buy it, or order it online – the instant downloads of today were very rare due to painfully slow internet connections. Because of this it was almost impossible to "trial" a program – you had to pay for it and hope it did the job.

Nowadays, thanks to broadband, the situation is completely different, and there are several very useful sources of software:

Manufacturer websites
Without doubt, the best source of software is the manufacturers' websites. The vast majority of them allow users to download time-limited or feature-limited versions of their products to try out before parting with the cash.

The big advantage here is that the software is guaranteed to be the real deal, and with no unwelcome attachments in the form of viruses and malware. The downside, of course, is that once the trial period is up, you have to pay for the program if you want to keep using it.

Download websites
Software download sites are set up specifically to provide an outlet for the legions of small software developers. Many of these programs are free (freeware), others are time- or feature-limited, (shareware), while others require up-front payment.

Popular download sites include **download.cnet.com**, **tucows.com/downloads**, **downloads.zdnet.com**, and **soft32.com**. These sites offer a vast number of programs of all types. However, you do have a risk of picking up viruses and malware hidden in the programs, and many free programs also come with irritating nag screens or ads.

File sharing
File sharing is a common internet activity that makes use of peer-to-peer networks. Users install a program that connects to these networks and lets them share designated files on their PC with other users.

This enables all types of data (software, video, images, etc.) to be downloaded at no cost. The practice is quite legal. However, actually using the data is often illegal. There is also a high risk of virus and malware infection.

When you need a certain program only temporarily, download a time-limited **trial** version for free.

Watch out for **phishing** sites that imitate those of major manufacturers and rip you off.

Software acquired from download sites can be poorly coded and thus contain **bugs**. These can cause problems on your computer.

8 Windows downloads

This chapter explores some of the most popular Windows downloads to complement the great apps that come bundled with Windows 10.

CCleaner

ccleaner.com/ccleaner

CCleaner is a utility that cleans out the junk that accumulates over time – temporary files, broken shortcuts, and other problems. The program also protects the user's privacy by clearing the contents of the history and temporary internet files folders.

1 At the website, **Download CCleaner** on the drop-down Download menu

2 Next, click the **Download from:** URL link to download the free version of CCleaner

3 Click **Install** to run the Setup Wizard

4 Click the **Analyze** button to see a summary of "Trackers" and "Junk" that can be safely deleted, by clicking the **Clean All** button

Hot tip

Uncheck the box on the Setup dialog to install **Google Chrome** unless that is what you want.

Hot tip

CCleaner also provides a **Registry Cleanup** tool that keeps the system's registry in good shape, and a **Drive Wiper** tool that lets you safely remove data from a drive.

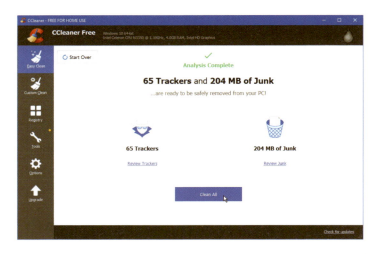

CDBurnerXP

cdburnerxp.se/en/home

CDBurnerXP is a burning utility that enables a wide variety of disks such as CDs, DVDs, Blu-ray and HD-DVDs to be created. Other useful options include the ability to create ISO image files and bootable disks.

1 At the website, click the **Free Download** button

2 Install the program by running the **Setup Wizard**

3 When the program is run, you are offered disk burner options to create a Data disk, Video DVD, Audio disk, Burn an ISO image, Copy a disk, or Erase a disk

Hot tip

Another free disk authoring utility with a good reputation is **ImgBurn**, which you can download free from imgburn.com

IrfanView

irfanview.com

IrfanView is a very fast and compact graphic viewer for Windows that is freeware (for non-commercial use). It supports many graphics file formats, including multiple (animated) GIF, multi-page TIF and videos.

1 Visit the website and select any of the IrfanView **download** options. For example, choose the link to get the 64-bit Windows 10 App from the Microsoft Store

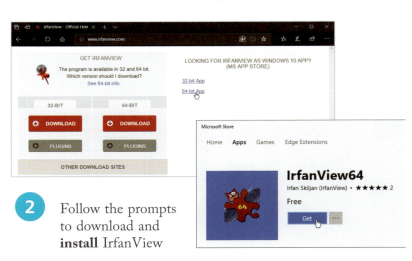

Hot tip

Select the download for **Plug-ins** shown in the image in Step 1 to get support for the full set of file formats.

2 Follow the prompts to download and **install** IrfanView

3 Launch IrfanView, then use its **Open** button to view any image

4 Click the forward or back buttons to scroll through all the images within the current folder

Don't forget

IrfanView is designed to be simple for **beginners**, and powerful for **professionals**. It also provides an extremely quick way to scroll through picture folders.

5 In this example, image 3 of 3 is showing

140

Notepad++

notepad-plus-plus.org

Notepad++ is a free text editor and Notepad replacement that is particularly designed for source code editing. It supports over 50 programming languages, including C, C++, C#, HTML, CSS, JavaScript, Java, and Python.

1 On the website, make sure the current version is selected on the left of the screen then click **Download**

In addition to language support, the main advantage over the built-in Notepad is **tabbed** editing, which allows you to work with multiple open files.

2 Follow the prompts to run the **Setup Wizard** and install Notepad++

3 Launch the app, then open any text file

4 Choose **Settings**, **Style Configurator** options for color syntax highlighting

If you are interested in **programming**, you can download the source code for this application.

Apache OpenOffice

openoffice.org

Apache OpenOffice is an open-source suite with a powerful set of applications that are very similar to those in Microsoft Office, and include techniques such as macros and templates, but have the advantage of being free to use.

1 Visit the website and select **I want to download...**

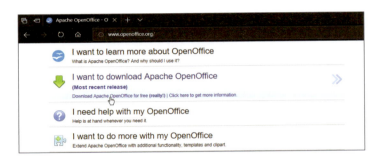

Don't forget

This website is the entry point for all aspects of **Apache OpenOffice**, with help, documentation, templates and clipart, as well as installation.

2 Select **Download full installation** for your system

Hot tip

You'll be invited to contribute, but it's your **time and effort** they want, not your money, since the product is built on user participation.

3 Follow the prompts to unpack and save the installation files ready for the actual installation

4 Provide your **name** and, optionally, your organization, as they are to be used in OpenOffice documents

5 Select the **Typical** setup, and click Next to install all OpenOffice apps, or choose **Custom** and click Next if you prefer to install only specific apps

6 Upon completion, click **Finish** to end the Wizard

7 Click the shortcut placed on the **Desktop** to start Apache OpenOffice

143

Apache OpenOffice has these six components: **Writer** (word processor) **Calc** (spreadsheet) **Impress** (presentations) **Draw** (vector graphics) **Base** (database) and **Math** (formula editor)

Paint.NET

getpaint.net

Where the Windows Paint app doesn't have the power you need, Paint.NET gives you more powerful editing facilities.

1 Click **Download** or click the **paint.net** link

Paint.NET is not equivalent to the **Adobe Photoshop** app, but it is just what's needed for casual graphic design tasks.

2 Click the **Download Now** button for free Paint.NET

3 Click **Free Download Now** link to download a compressed installer **.zip** file

Paint.NET is a **free** app, but you are encouraged to contribute to its future development. You can also buy it from the Microsoft Store for a small fee.

4 Extract the executable installer **.exe** file from the compressed download file, then run the installer to launch the installation wizard

5 Choose **Express** for the install method, then click **Next**

6 Agree terms and conditions, then continue

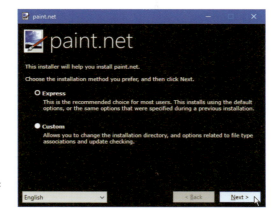

During the installation, Paint.NET will be **optimized** for best performance on your particular system.

7 Follow the prompts to complete the installation

8 Click **Finish** to start Paint.NET

Select **Effects** to see the range offered: Photo, for example, with Glow, Sharpen and Soften, as well as Red Eye Removal. Adjustments also applies various changes to the appearance.

7-Zip

7-zip.org

7-Zip is a free file compression utility that can handle more compressed file formats than the built-in Windows 10 file compression tool. Additionally, it can compress large files into its own **.7z** file format, which produces smaller compressed archive files than the ubiquitous **.zip** file format:

1 Click **Download** and run the installer

To use the Windows 10 file compression tool, right-click and choose Send to, Compressed (zipped) folder to create an archive file, or choose **Extract All...** to decompress an archive.

2 Right-click on a compressed archive file and see a **7-Zip** item has been added to the context menu

3 To decompress the archive, choose **Extract Here** from the 7-Zip menu options

7-Zip can create archives in several formats including **.zip**, **.7z**, and **.bzip2**, and extract many archive formats including **.cab**, **.chm**, **.iso**, **.lzh**, and **.rar**.

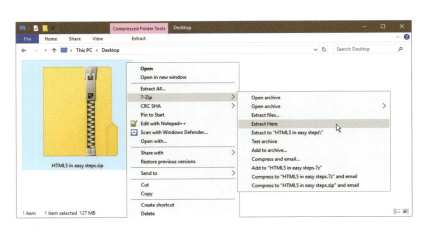

4 See 7-Zip decompress the archive and extract all of its contents alongside the compressed archive file

5 In this example, notice that the compressed **.zip** archive of 127MB is expanded to 229MB when decompressed

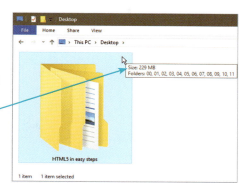

6 To compress the folder into a compact archive, right-click on the folder, then choose **Add to** *filename*.**7z**

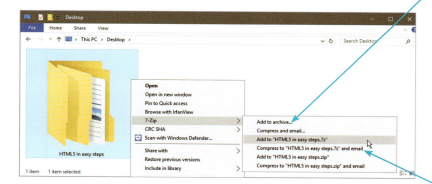

7 See 7-Zip create a new archive alongside the folder

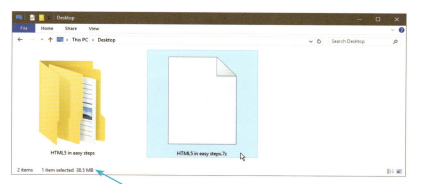

8 In this example, notice that the compressed **.7z** archive is just 38.5MB – considerably smaller than the **.zip** version!

μTorrent

utorrent.com

μTorrent (also referred to as uTorrent) is a freeware but closed-source BitTorrent client. The μ in its name implies the prefix micro, in deference to the program's small size, but it can handle very large downloads very rapidly.

1 At the μTorrent website, click the **Download μTorrent Web** button

2 Right-click on the downloaded **.exe** file, then choose **Run as administrator** to install

3 Uncheck the options to install optional additional software, then click **Finish** to complete the installation

4 Open μTorrent to launch the app in your web browser, then **Search** for an item of interest to find a torrent

Make sure that files you select for downloading via μTorrent are in the public domain and **not subject to copyright**.

9 Microsoft Store

You can choose apps to run on your Windows 10 devices from the Microsoft Store. This chapter describes how to access, search and navigate the Store, how to install apps, keep them updated, and how to manage them.

Accessing the Store

When you need apps, the Microsoft Store is the place to go. It is, in fact, the only place to go – official Windows 10 apps are not available from any other source. To access the Store:

1 Click any **Microsoft Store** launcher

The Microsoft Store has been redesigned to be a **one-stop-shop** for all Windows 10 devices.

Select an item from the menu, then scroll down the page to find the list of **Categories** for that item located at the bottom of the page.

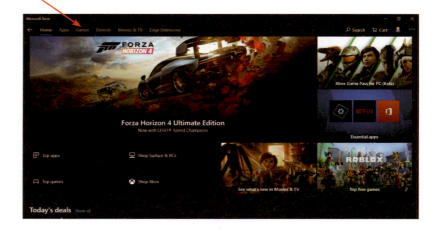

Store categories

The Microsoft Store organizes its products into specific categories to make it easier to find what you are looking for. These frequently change, but look like this at the time of writing:

Apps:				
Books & reference	Food & dining	Medical	Personal finance	Shopping
Business	Government & politics	Multimedia design	Personalization	Social
Developer tools	Health & fitness	Music	Photo & video	Sports
Education	Kids & family	Navigation & maps	Productivity	Travel
Entertainment	Lifestyle	News & weather	Security	Utilities & tools

Games:				
Action & adventure	Educational	Other	Shooter	Tools
Card & board	Family & kids	Platformer	Simulation	Video
Casino	Fighting	Puzzle & trivia	Social	Word
Classics	Multi-player battle	Racing & flying	Sports	
Companion	Music	Role playing	Strategy	

Devices:				
Microsoft Surface	Laptops & 2-in-1s	Xbox consoles	Gaming PCs & desktops	Xbox accessories
Windows Mixed Reality headsets	Audio and entertainment			

Movies & TV:				
Action/Adventure	Documentary	Horror	Sci-Fi/Fantasy	
Animation	Drama	Other	Sports	
Anime	Family	Romance	Thriller/Mystery	
Comedy	Foreign/Independent	Romantic Comedy	TV Movies	

Edge Extensions:				
Newest	Ad Blockers & Password Managers	Productivity	Shopping	Social & entertainment
For developers				

There you will also find related items grouped into collections as you scroll down the page, such as the **Best-rated games** collection on the Games page.

Navigating the Store

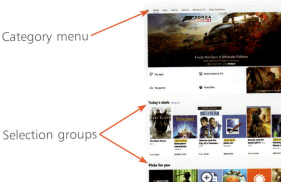

Category menu

Selection groups

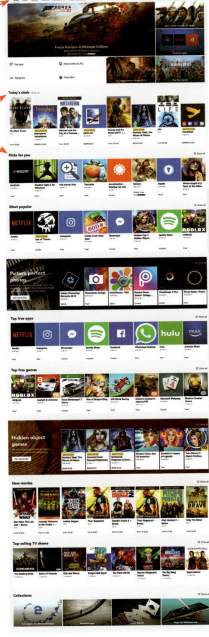

Don't forget

You can select the **Home** menu item at any time to return to the Store's Home page.

Scroll down the **Home** page of the Store to see these selection groups:

- **Today's deals**
- **Picks for you**
- **Most popular**
- **Top free apps**
- **Top free games**
- **New movies**
- **Top-selling TV shows**
- **Collections**

Use the Store's category menu bar at the top-left of the Store window, to review categories of:

- **Apps**
- **Games**
- **Devices**
- **Movies & TV**
- **Edge Extensions**

Exploring categories

On the Home page, a small selection of featured apps are presented in selection groups, which can be accessed directly from the Home page.

If you can't see what you want here, then you need to dig deeper. Select a Store category, then refine your requirements.

1 To open a Store category, click its name on the category menu – for example, select the **Games** category

2 The category page will open and is laid out like the Home page, but features only items relevant to that category

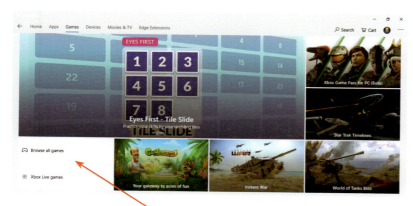

3 The category page also provides a menu with which to explore that category further – for example, on the Games category page, select the **Browse all games** menu item

4 Sub-categories are provided to refine your requirements

Hot tip

Use the **Back** button at the top-left of any Store window to return to previous pages.

Search the Store

Search is an extremely important component of modern user interfaces, and currently is one of the most common ways for customers to find things when browsing online stores.

In Windows 8, the Microsoft Store didn't have a Search box – you had to search using the Search charm, which many users found confusing. The revamped store in Windows 10 does provide a Search box, though, and this can be found at the top-right of any Store page, as shown below:

Search begins looking for results as soon as you type **two** characters into the Search box.

If you know the name of the app you want or are looking for apps by a specific publisher, enter the name into the Search box. In the page that opens, you'll see the results of your search, as in our "video" search below:

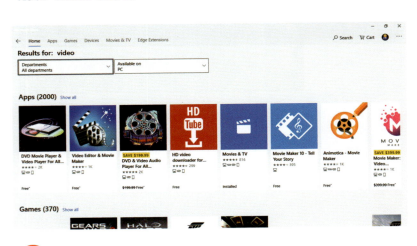

1 If any of the apps shown appear to be of interest, just click one to open it and get further details

An important aspect of the Windows 10 search is that it is universally accessible, meaning you can search for an app no matter where you are in the Windows 10 interface – you don't need to be in the Store. We see how this works on the next page.

...cont'd

In the example shown below, you're using the Microsoft Edge app to browse a site about Mahjong. This triggers in you a sudden curiosity to see if there are any Mahjong apps available.

1 Type the word "mahjong" into the Taskbar Search box

2 Next, click the "Apps" item on the results list

3 Click the link to **Search for apps in the Microsoft Store**

4 A Store window opens, revealing items related to Mahjong

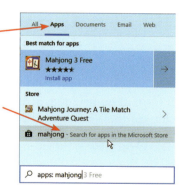

Hot tip

As you type in the Taskbar Search box, **suggestions** immediately appear in the results list.

Select an app

To select an app, simply click on its tile. As an example, we have searched for the Netflix app as shown below:

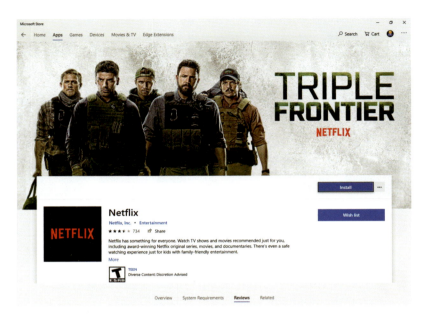

The page begins with a brief description of the app and age rating information, together with **Install** and **Wish list** buttons. Below this are four link items you can select:

- **Overview** – providing a more detailed description of the app.

- **System Requirements** – operating system version needed.

- **Reviews** – gives you the average rating figure, the total number of ratings, and the total number of reviews.

- **Related** – similar apps for your consideration.

Before paying for an app it's worth checking out the **reviews**.

Download and install

Microsoft has made it simple to download and install apps from the Store in Windows 10:

1 Click the **Install** button above the app description

2 Wait until you see the **This product is installed** confirmation

3 The app will now appear on the Start menu, under its alphabetic A-Z heading, and will also appear under the **Recently added** heading

4 Click the menu item to launch the app as usual

You must be logged in with a **Microsoft account** before you can download an app.

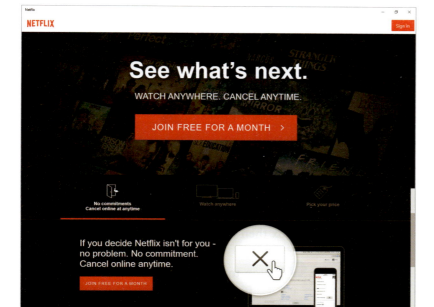

The customizable Start menu is a great new feature in Windows 10. Right-click on an app tile then choose **More** to see the options. Select **App settings** to open the settings page for that particular app.

You can reduce the size of the large tiles to create more space on the Start menu, which reduces the amount of scrolling necessary. Just right-click on a tile, select **Resize** and choose from the available options.

Manage apps

App tiles on the right of the Start menu are much larger than the Start menu list items. The more congested the Start menu becomes, the more scrolling will be necessary to find an app, so it's a great idea to arrange the Start menu tiles conveniently. It's best to place your most frequently-accessed apps at the top of the Start menu tile area where they will be on view by default. To do this, just left-click on the tile, then drag it to where you want it.

Create and organize groups

App tiles are automatically placed in groups, which can be moved around the Start menu in blocks. This makes it easier to arrange your Start menu, and having your apps in specific and related groups makes it much easier to locate them as and when required. At the top of each group is a bar bearing the name of that group. Drag this bar across the Start menu to move the group.

Tiles can be easily switched from one group to another group. Drag a tile from any group to see the other tiles move to accommodate that tile within a different group, as shown below. If you take any heading group bar and drag it across the Start menu you'll see other groups move to accommodate that group.

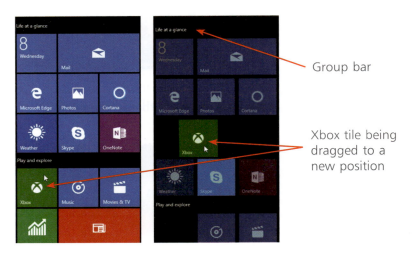

Group bar

Xbox tile being dragged to a new position

If you want to start a new group, drag an app item from the Start menu's A-Z list onto the right-hand part of the Start menu, and release it above an existing group bar – the new group is created. Add more tiles to it as already described.

...cont'd

The group bar of a new group may not be visible until you **place the mouse over** its position.

Name a group

You can assign a name to a group by editing its group bar. Simply click on a group bar then type a name of your choice into the box.

You can **edit** the name of any existing group using its Name box.

163

Create Start menu folders

You can group the tiles on your Start menu into folders, too. Just drag a tile onto another, then drop it to create a folder that can contain multiple tiles. Click on the folder to see it expand to reveal the tiles it contains, then click again to collapse the folder:

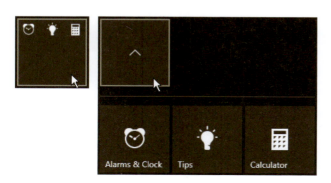

Desktop apps

Although the Microsoft Store provides a huge range of apps, some traditional Desktop programs are not included and must be downloaded directly from the publisher's own website. For example, the popular Photoshop image editing program must be acquired directly from Adobe:

1 Enter "adobe photoshop" in the Taskbar Search box, then select a link from the results to visit the Adobe website

When you buy a Desktop program outside the Microsoft Store, don't forget that updates to the app must be downloaded from the publisher's website – they **won't** be provided through the Store.

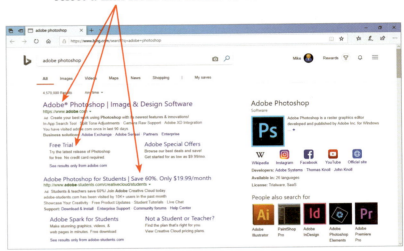

2 Click the **Buy now** button to download and install the program directly from Adobe

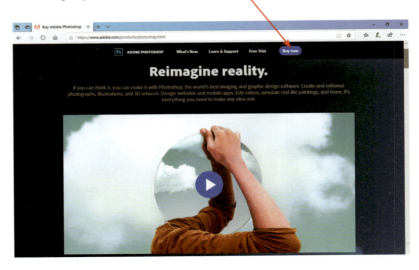

10 Search techniques

This chapter describes many ways to help you find the programs, utilities and information that you need. There's a Search box in every File Explorer folder, and the Taskbar Search box is always readily available.

Start screen search

When you need to search for something it's remarkably simple in Windows 10 – all you have to do is type what you want to find into the Search box located on the Desktop Taskbar.

Search box

As you begin to type, the search results will instantly update, displaying the search results in a list above the Search box:

The Taskbar **Search box** is another great new feature in Windows 10.

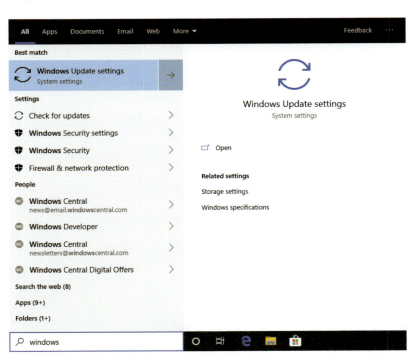

Illustrated above are results when searched for "windows". Due to its tight integration with Microsoft's Bing search engine, the results of the search allow you to search further on the internet and in the Store.

Search filters

The default action of Windows 10's search function is to search the apps and folders on your PC. This can bring too many results, unrelated results, or not the desired results. There are four things you can do to refine the results:

Apps filter

The first is to use the apps filter built in to the Search box to return only results related to applications:

1 In the results, choose the **Apps** button to limit results to apps on your PC and apps available in the Store

Documents filter

The second is to use the documents filter built in to the Search box to return only results related to documents:

2 In the results, choose the **Documents** button to limit results to document files

There is also a useful **More** button that provides six secondary filters to further refine your search.

Email filter

The third is to use the email filter built in to the Search box to return only results related to emails:

3 In the results, choose the **Email** button to limit results to email messages

Web filter

The fourth is to use the web filter built in to the Search box to return only internet-related results:

4 In the results, choose the **Web** button to limit results to a list of online suggestions

File Explorer search

The Search utility is considered by some to be one of the best features in Windows 10, and provides quick and very comprehensive search results – sometimes too many, in fact. While secondary local filters help to narrow searches down, general and system-wide searches can produce too many results.

The Search facility provided by File Explorer is extremely useful in situations such as these, as it enables searches to be restricted to specific parts of Windows, thus producing fewer but more relevant results.

Don't forget

Results from a folder search will include any **subfolders** the folder may contain.

1 Open a **File Explorer** window (it doesn't matter which)

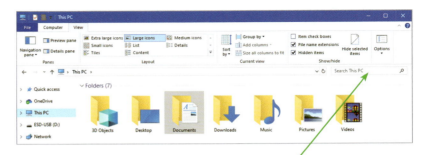

2 At the right, you will see a **Search box**. By default, searches made from this will be restricted to the contents of the current folder, plus any subfolders

3 Clicking in the Search box also reveals a **Search Tools**, **Search** tab on the ribbon toolbar that provides a **Recent Searches** feature where you can repeat a search or clear the search history

Hot tip

You can change the location from any folder to search anywhere in the computer by selecting where you want to search in the **Navigation** pane.

Navigation pane

To the left of the File Explorer window, you'll see the Navigation pane. By default, this shows links for favorite folders such as Desktop, Documents, and Downloads. There are also links for OneDrive, This PC, and Network. These links enable any folder or drive on the computer to be accessed and thus searched. You can do this as follows:

1 Hover over the left-hand pane to see arrows beside the links

2 Click a right-arrow **>** to expand a list, or click a down-arrow **V** to collapse a list

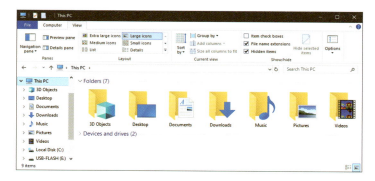

3 Select a folder name to display its contents and find files. For example, double-click the **Pictures** folder to explore the folders and files it contains

4 At any point you can use the folder Search box to search within a particular folder

Hot tip

If you prefer a single-click action, select **View**, **Options**, **Change folder and search options**, then choose the single-click option on the **General** tab.

Hot tip

Double-click any folder name to **expand** that folder and display its contents with one action.

169

Don't forget

Click the arrows or double-click the names to **expand** or **collapse** the entries.

Search tools

Windows provides a number of filters with which folder searches can be made even more relevant. These can be accessed from the ribbon toolbar found at the top of File Explorer folders.

This is a toolbar that provides options related to the task at hand – it is "contextual". We'll take a closer look at this later on, but for now we'll see what it has to offer in the way of search options.

Open a folder you want to search, and click in the Search box. The Search tab on the ribbon toolbar will immediately reveal the search tools. These are listed below as they appear on the toolbar:

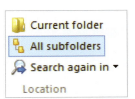

- **Current folder** – restricts the search to the current folder.
- **All subfolders** – includes subfolders in the search.
- **Search again in** – list of locations in which to repeat the search.

- **Date modified** – allows you to search specific dates or ranges of dates. Options provided are: Today, Yesterday, This week, Last week, This month, Last month, This year, and Last year.

- **Kind** – choose the kind of file from a list of types, such as Movie or Program.
- **Size** – choose from a list of sizes ranging from Tiny to Gigantic.
- **Other properties** – choose from a list of properties for Date taken, Tags, Type, Name, Folder path or Rating.

Recent searches and **Save search** are not filters.

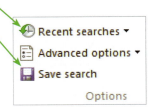

- **Advanced options** – lets you change the indexed locations to search, and allows searches to be limited to File contents, System files, or Zipped (compressed) folders in non-indexed locations.

Favorites

The Navigation pane includes a "Quick access" section where you can keep shortcuts to the locations on your system that you may often view. To view your File Explorer **Quick access** favorites:

1 Open File Explorer then click View, Navigation pane and ensure that **Navigation pane** is checked – to be visible

2 Now, click on the **Quick access** item at the top of the Navigation pane to reveal your current favorites

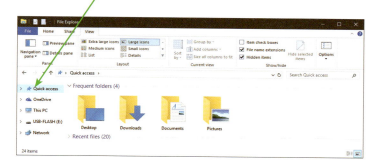

To add a folder location to your **Quick access** favorites:

3 Click on a folder in the Navigation pane – to select it ready to be added. For example, select the **Music** folder

4 Next, click the **Home** tab on the File Explorer ribbon

5 Now, click on the **Pin to Quick access** link on the ribbon to add the selected (Music) folder to your favorites

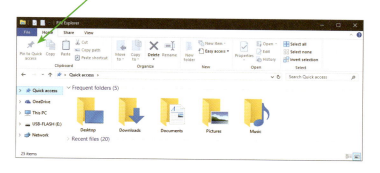

171

Hot tip

To remove a favorite location from the **Quick access** section, right-click on its folder icon and choose "Unpin from Quick access".

Don't forget

The **Quick access** favorites can also be returned to an earlier state by choosing "Restore previous versions" from the right-click context menu.

Folder and search options

You can change the way files and folders function and how items are displayed on your computer using **Folder Options**.

You will also find **Folder Options** under Appearance and Personalization, File Explorer Options in the Control Panel.

1 Open a folder, click the **View** tab, click **Options** then click **Change folder and search options**

2 When **Folder Options** displays, select the **General** tab

From this panel you can:

● Choose to open each folder in the same window, or in its own window.

● Use double-click to open an item, or use the browser-style single-click to point and select items.

● Control **Quick access** privacy.

● Restore Defaults after changes.

3 Select the **View** tab

From here you can:

● Apply the view for the current folder to all folders of the same type.

● Reset folders.

● Apply Advanced settings to files and folders.

● Restore Defaults after changes.

● Hide empty drives in the **This PC** folder.

Hot tip

You can choose to **hide** or **show** hidden files, folders and drives. You can also hide or reveal file extensions.

160

4 Scroll down to reveal the remaining settings

Among these settings are options to:

- Automatically open the folders that you were using when you last shut down Windows whenever you start your computer, thus restoring your work session.

- Hide or show file tips that display when you point to files or folders.

- Use check boxes to select items.

Make a **note** of the options that you would normally prefer, since the Restore Defaults will undo all changes, not just recent changes.

5 Select the **Search** tab

The Search settings let you manage what to search and how to search.

- Don't use the index when searching file folders for system files.

- Include system directories.

- Include compressed files.

- Search file names and contents.

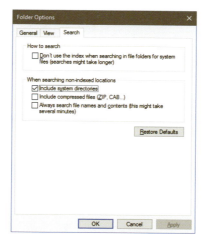

You can click the **Restore Defaults** button to undo any changes that might previously have been applied.

Indexing options

When you add a folder to one of the libraries, that folder will automatically be indexed. You can also add locations to the index without using libraries.

 1 Go to Settings and search for **Indexing Options**

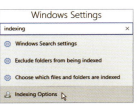

Windows uses the **index** for fast searches of the most common files on your computer. By default, folders in libraries, email and offline files are indexed, but program and system files are not.

2 Click **Modify** then expand the folder lists and select new locations to index – for example a USB drive – and click **OK**

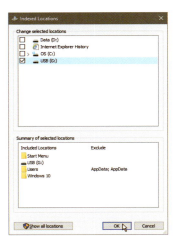

Indexing proceeds in the **background**, and may slow down during periods of user activity.

3 The contents of the new locations are added to the index

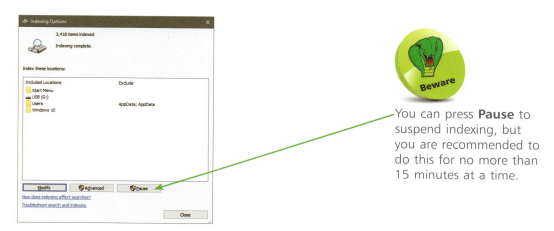

You can press **Pause** to suspend indexing, but you are recommended to do this for no more than 15 minutes at a time.

4 To make changes to the settings for indexing, click the **Advanced** button and select the **Index Settings** or **File Types** tab

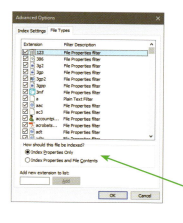

You can choose to index encrypted files, ignore accents on characters for matching, change the index location, or delete and rebuild the index. You can also specify file types that are indexed by **Properties** only or **File Contents** and Properties.

Address bar

The address bar at the top of the folder contains the location path of the folder or library, and you can use this to check the actual folder path and to switch to other libraries and folders.

If a library rather than a folder is being displayed, you'll see a library **path** rather than a drive.

1 Click the space in the address bar to the right of the location names (and left of the down-arrow)

2 The current location is shown in the standard drive and folder path format

3 Click anywhere in the folder to revert to the location path

Click the arrow to the **right** of the location name to show all the folders that are stored within that location.

4 Click a location name – for example, the user name – to switch to that location

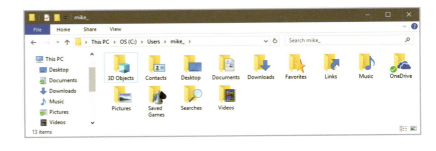

5 Click the arrow to the right of a location name – for example, **Users** – to display all the user folders

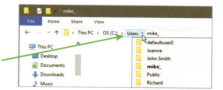

6 When the folders are displayed, you can select any folder to switch to that location

7 Click the back arrow to redisplay the previous folder visited

8 Click the arrow at the left to see a drop-down menu listing all the top-level system locations

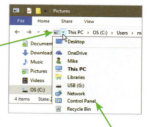

The libraries, user folders, network folders, etc. are included as special folders in Desktop, along with **This PC** and any Desktop icons. Note that File Explorer can also be used to display the Control Panel.

9 Select **Desktop** on the drop-down menu to see the complete structure of your system components

Save searches

If you regularly search for a certain group of files, it might be useful to save your search. You can save a search like this:

1 Carry out a search as previously described

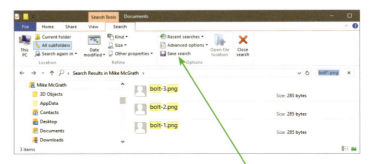

2 When the search is complete, click **Save search**

3 Type a name for the search, and then click **Save**

4 The search itself will be saved in your Searches folder

Move and copy

You can use the search results and the Navigation pane to help move or copy files and folders from their original locations.

1 Use Search to display the items you wish to copy or move (in this case all Word files named "Minutes" within Users)

179

Hot tip

Select the first item, then hold down **Shift** and select the last item to select a sequential range. Press **Ctrl** on individual items to select a non-sequential range.

2 Select the items to copy, using **Shift** or **Ctrl** as necessary

3 Expand the Navigation pane (clicking the arrows, not the folder names) to show the target folder

Don't forget

If the destination is on the same drive as the selected items, the default is **Move**, otherwise the default becomes **Copy**. However, you can still make your preferred selection.

4 Right-click part of the selection and drag the items onto the Navigation pane, over the name of the target folder

5 Release the mouse and click **Move here** or **Copy here** as appropriate, and the files are added to the destination

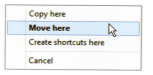

...cont'd

6 As soon as the move takes place, Windows Search adjusts the search results, in this case showing Users documents

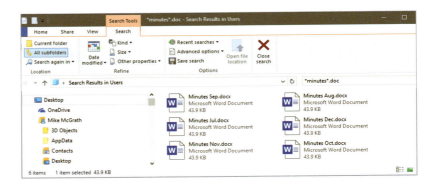

7 Select the target folder, and you'll see all the items added

You can simply click and drag any selected items to your preferred destination then release the mouse button to have Windows move or copy them there immediately, with no menu.

Force move or copy

With either a left-click or right-click, you can force the action you want, whether the same or different drives are involved:

1 Press **Shift** as you drag, and Move becomes the default action

2 Press **Ctrl** as you drag, and Copy becomes the default action

11

Manage files and folders

This chapter describes how to use File Explorer to manage your files, folders and libraries, sorting and organizing the contents. Windows 10 provides libraries for documents, music, pictures and videos but you can define your own libraries for your projects or to manage information.

Files, folders and libraries

Data storage devices are defined as blocks of fixed-size sectors. These are managed by the file system, which defines a root drive directory containing folders and files. Each folder can contain further folders and files. This gives a hierarchical structure.

Files of the same or related types will usually be stored in the same folder. For example, the **Users** folder within the root drive directory will be organized along the following lines:

Windows uses the **NTFS (New Technology File System)** file system for disks and large storage devices. One of the older **FAT (File Allocation Table)** file systems is normally used for smaller storage devices such as memory cards and flash drives.

Each file has a starting block and links to the subsequent **blocks**, with the last link being the end of file marker. The blocks are not necessarily allocated in sequence, hence the potential for fragmentation.

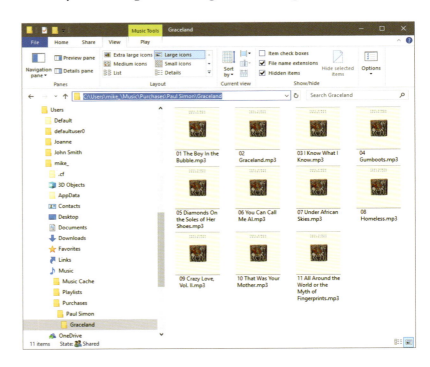

The root drive directory includes the **Program Files** folder which contains applications installed on your system, and the **Users** folder which contains the folders and files associated with each user account. In your user account folder, you will see a number of folders, including your **Music** folder. The example above shows the MP3 music files within a purchased album of a particular artist.

Windows 10 goes a stage further and associates folders with similar content into libraries. The folders included in the library may be stored separately on the disk, or may be on a different disk on the computer or elsewhere on the network. To manage the files, folders and libraries, Windows uses the File Explorer application.

File Explorer

There are several different ways to start File Explorer or change the particular files and folders being displayed.

1 Click the **File Explorer** icon on the Taskbar or open the Power User menu and select **File Explorer**

Quick access is new in Windows 10, replacing the classic Favorites of previous versions. You can also press **WinKey + E** to open File Explorer to see **Quick access**.

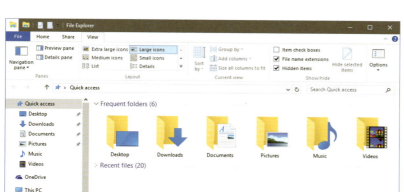

2 The **Quick access** feature displays your **Frequent folders**

3 Click an entry on the Navigation pane to display those contents instead – for example, select the **Music** folder

Don't forget

If you don't want to have File Explorer start in **Quick access**, click View, Options, **Change folder and search options**, then on the General tab choose **Open File Explorer to: This PC**.

4 To retain the current entry and open another, right-click the newly-required entry and choose **Open in new window**

...cont'd

The Taskbar button for the program initially shows a single icon. When you open another window, or more, a second icon gets stacked alongside the first icon – to indicate that multiple File Explorer windows are currently open. You can use the Taskbar like this:

1 Move the mouse pointer over the **Taskbar button**, and thumbnails for the open windows are displayed, as shown below:

2 Click on a **thumbnail** to open that window in File Explorer

You can also open the ribbon toolbar by clicking a File Explorer tab – **Home**, **Share**, or **View**.

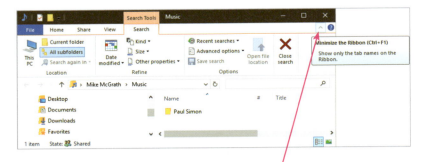

3 Click the down-arrow to open (or up-arrow to close) the File Explorer **ribbon toolbar**

File Explorer layout

This shows all the elements for File Explorer, apart from the ribbon toolbar, which is described on page 186.

Back & Forward Quick Access Toolbar Up Level Menu Bar Address Bar Search Box Resize and Close

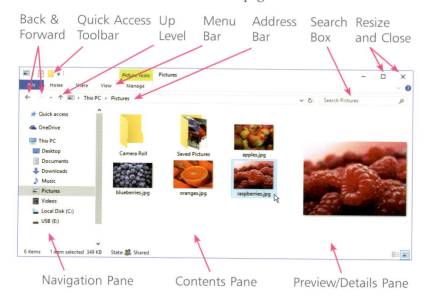

Navigation Pane   Contents Pane   Preview/Details Pane

File Explorer preview

The type of preview displayed depends on the file type. For recognized document types, you will see part of the first page.

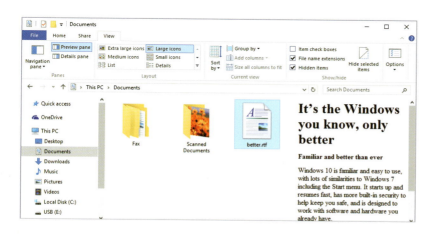

For file types Windows does not recognize, or when a folder is selected, you will see a message saying: **No preview available**.

File Explorer ribbon

A feature in Windows 10 is the File Explorer ribbon toolbar, which is situated at the top of every File Explorer folder. By default, it is hidden – to reveal it just click the down-arrow located under the **X** close button at the top-right.

In essence, the ribbon consists of a File menu plus three core tabs (Home, Share, and View) that are always visible. Other tabs include Manage, Computer, and Network. The ribbon also shows colored contextual tabs, the display of which depends on the type of object selected by the user. For example, when a video folder is opened or a video file is selected, the Video Tools tab appears and provides related options such as Play, Stop, and Pause.

This system of core and contextual tabs enables the ribbon toolbar to offer some 200 different management commands. The user gets the required options as and when required without having to wade through unrelated toolbar menus, right-click menus, etc.

Hot tip

The **File** tab offers a variety of options:

Home tab

View tab

Share tab

Computer tab

Manage tab

Folder contents

You'll also find that the way in which the contents of folders are displayed varies depending on the type of file involved.

In these example views, the Navigation, Details, and Library panes have been hidden, to put the emphasis on the Contents pane.

Documents
Details view:
>Name
>Date modified
>Type
>Size

Music
Details view:
>Name
>Contributing artists
>Album
>Track number
>Title

Pictures
Large Icons view

Program Files
Medium Icons view

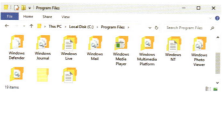

Libraries
Tiles view

Documents and Music both use the **Details** view, but the fields displayed are appropriate to the particular file type.

The Videos library also uses the **Large Icons** view, while Network and Computers use the **Tiles** view, the same as Libraries.

Since views can easily be varied, you might find the setup for some of the folders on your system may be different.

Change view

1 Open the folder whose view you want to change, then right-click in an empty part of the folder

The View menu option, available by right-clicking in an open folder, provides a quick way to change a folder's view, but the **View** menu on the ribbon toolbar offers more, and more easily accessible, options.

2 Hover the mouse on the **View** menu option, then select the required view. Using our example above, we are changing the view from **Large icons** to **Medium icons**. You can see how the view has changed below

The information provided in the **Content** view depends on the file type – for example, Pictures has **Date taken**, and Music has **Track length**.

3 The same commands, and more, are also available from the **View** tab on the File Explorer ribbon toolbar

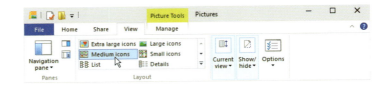

Sort contents

You can sort the contents of any folder by name, date, size or other attributes, using the **Details** view. You can also group or filter the contents.

1 Open the folder and select the **Details** view

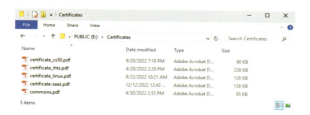

On the first selection, alphabetic fields such as **Name** or **File Type** are sorted in ascending order. Number fields such as **Date** or **Size** are sorted in descending order.

2 Click on a header such as **Size**, and the entries are sorted

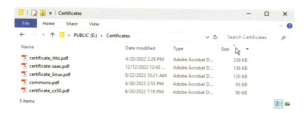

3 Click the header again, and the sequence is reversed

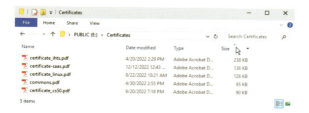

4 Change the view, and the sequencing that you have set up will be retained for the new view

Click the arrow that appears when you hover over any header, to group the entries in **ranges**. By excluding some of the ranges, you can filter the contents displayed.

...cont'd

You can reorganize the contents from views other than Details.

1 Open the folder, and right-click an empty part of the contents, being sure to avoid the icon borders

The space between icons can be very **narrow**, so you must take care to choose an empty area.

2 Select **Sort by**, to change the sort field or sequence

3 Select **Group by**, and select the field (**Size,** for example) by which you want to arrange the entries in ranges

4 To remove the grouping, select **Group by**, then **(None)**

Click **More** to add other attributes that can be used for grouping or sorting. The selected fields would also appear on the Details view.

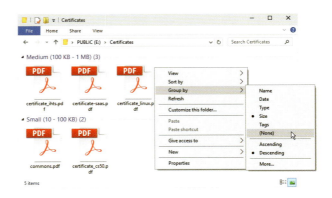

Windows 10 libraries

Windows 10 comes with default libraries such as Camera Roll, Documents, Music, Pictures, Saved Pictures, and Videos. You can add them to the Navigation pane by clicking the View tab in any folder, clicking Navigation pane and then clicking Show libraries.

1 Click **Libraries** on the Navigation pane

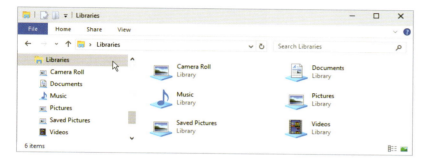

You can include other **locations** in the existing libraries, and you can also create your own libraries.

191

2 Double-click a library (**Pictures**, for example) to open it

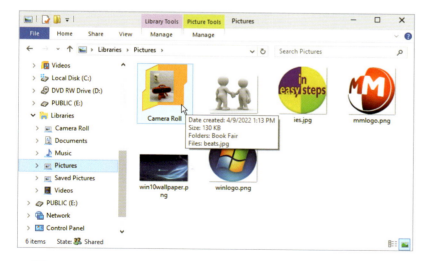

3 Here we can see the library includes the **Camera Roll** location. The files and folders at that location are listed when you hover over the Camera Roll icon

Manage library

1 Open the Libraries folder and click the down-arrow under the **X** close button to reveal the File Explorer ribbon toolbar

2 In the folder contents section, select one of the default libraries such as Camera Roll, Documents, Music, Pictures, Saved Pictures, or Video

3 Click the **Library Tools** tab on the quick launch section of the ribbon to reveal the link options offered

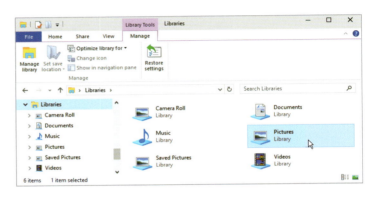

● **Manage library** – this link enables you to add new locations to an existing library – see pages 193-194.

● **Set save location** – this link allows you to specify a default save location within a library. For example, if a library has two or more locations, you can set one of them as the default.

● **Optimize library for** – the default libraries all have different arrangement options appropriate for their respective contents. If you create a new library, this link enables you to quickly set suitable arrangement options for the content of that library.

● **Show in navigation pane** – this link lets you hide or show the Libraries link in the Navigation pane.

● **Restore settings** – Click this link to undo all configuration changes made to the Libraries feature.

Add a location

1 Open the Libraries folder and access Library Tools as described on page 192, then click **Manage library**

Don't forget

This lists the **currently-defined** locations and indicates the **default** save location, where new files would be added.

2 Click the **Add...** button next to Library locations

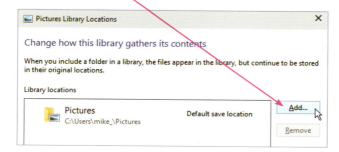

3 Open the drive the required folder is located on

4 Select the folder and then click **Include Folder**

Hot tip

You could **select** folders from your hard drive, as in this example, or from a second internal hard drive, or from an external hard drive.

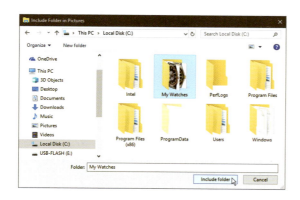

...cont'd

Beware

You **cannot** use folders from devices with removable storage. You can add folders from removable drives, but only if they appear in the hard disk drive section.

5 The selected folder becomes a new location in the library

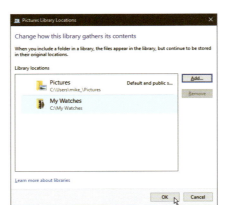

6 Click **OK** to see the added folder content

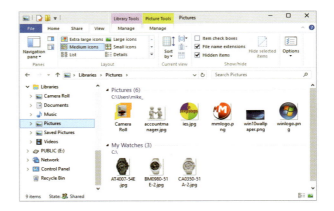

7 Right-click on the library's icon and choose **Give access to** then select an option if you want to share this library

Arrange library contents

Library contents are usually organized by
location and folder, but you can change this.

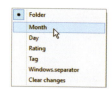

1 Right-click in the library files
window, then choose **Arrange by** and
select an alternative to Folder, such as
the **Month** option

2 The contents of all the folders are gathered together in
groups by month and displayed as stacks

3 Right-click in the library files window
and choose **Arrange by** again, then
select another alternative; e.g. **Rating**

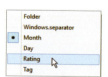

4 The contents of all the folders are gathered together in
groups by their star rating, or as "unspecified" if unrated

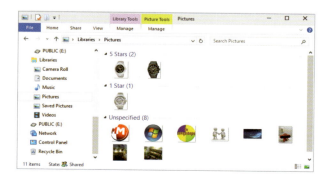

Hot tip

Files can be given star
Rating and **Tag names**
using the Details tab
on their Properties
dialog. Right-click on
a file icon and choose
the Properties item on
the context menu, then
select the Details tab and
edit its star Rating or Tag
name values there.

Create a library

1 Open the Libraries folder, right-click in the folder and select **New**, **Library**

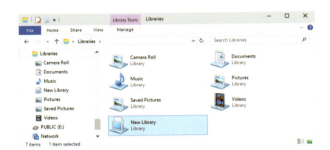

Don't forget

You can create a library of your own to manage other **collections** – for example, project plans or family history.

2 Edit the library name, for example type "Projects", then press **Enter**

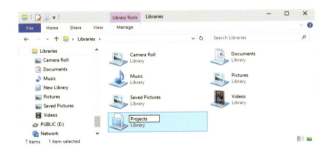

3 Double-click the new library to open it, and you'll be invited to add folders

Hot tip

The first folder that you add will be assigned as the **save** location, but you can change this later if you wish.

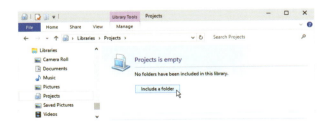

Adjust properties

When you've added folders, the library appears on the Navigation pane and shows locations and folders, just like default libraries.

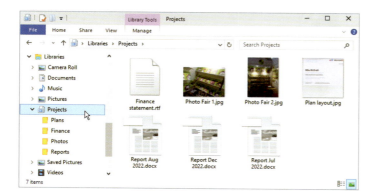

From the right-click menu you can open the library in a **new window**, **share** it with other users, and **hide or show** it in the Navigation pane, as well as displaying properties.

1 Right-click the library name in the Navigation pane or in the Libraries folder and select **Properties**

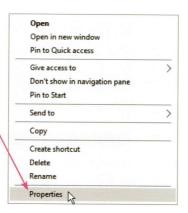

From here you can:

- Select a location and click **Set save location**

- **Add** a new folder or location

- **Remove** an existing location

- Hide or show in **Navigation pane**

- Check **Shared** status

- **Restore Defaults** after making changes

- **Apply** the changes you make

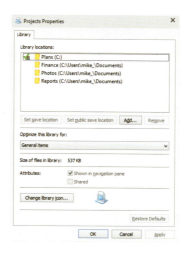

2 Click **OK** to save your changes, or click **Cancel** to abandon your changes

By default, the library will be optimized for the type of file it contains, or for general items if the file types are mixed. However, you can choose a **particular file type** if you prefer.

Customize folders

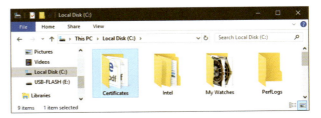

1 Right-click the folder and select **Properties**

To customize a folder in a library, access it from your hard disk, or right-click its folder and select **Open file location**.

2 Click the **Customize** tab on the Properties panel

3 To specify a folder picture, click the **Choose File...** button

4 Find and select the picture image and click **Open**

By default, the folder will be optimized for general items, but you can choose a **specific** file type if you wish.

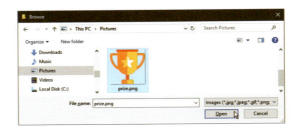

5 Click **Apply, OK** on the Properties panel to add the image as the custom folder image

You can only add images on drives defined with the **NTFS** file system with its extended attributes. They cannot be added to drives defined with a **FAT** file system.

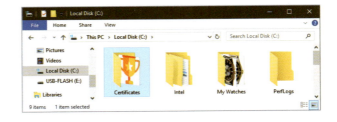

12 Email messaging

This chapter describes the communication tools built into Windows 10 that let you communicate with others, send messages and attachments to individuals or groups of contacts, and the Calendar facility that helps you manage your schedule.

Mail app

Windows 10 provides an app named simply "Mail" for all your email requirements. This has plenty of great features and can be easily configured for multiple email accounts:

1 Go to Start, **Mail** to launch the email app for the first time, and you will be asked to add an email account. Click the **Add account** link

2 Next, you are offered a variety of email services on a "Choose an account" list. Select the type of email account you wish to add – for example, choose **Outlook.com**

You can choose the **Other account** option if you don't see the email service you want to add.

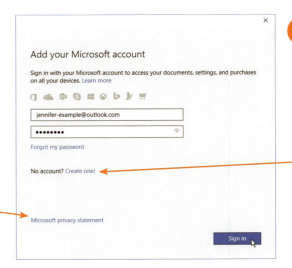

3 Now, enter details of your Microsoft account and click **Sign in**, or click the **Create one** link then follow the Wizard to get an account

Consult the **Microsoft privacy statement** to discover how your personal data may be collected and used.

4 The Outlook account is now added to the **Mail** app and is ready to use. Click the **Add account** link once more if you want to add further accounts – for example, a **Yahoo!** email account

If you don't want to add further accounts simply click the **Go to inbox** link to open the Mail app immediately.

5 Select **Yahoo!** from the "Choose an account" list, then **Sign in** to the Yahoo! email account

6 The Yahoo! account is now added, and the **Mail** app opens, listing the added accounts in the left-hand pane

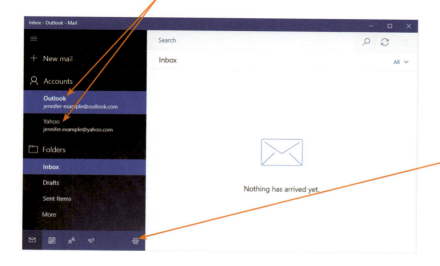

You can add or remove accounts at any time – click the **Settings** button, then choose **Manage Accounts**.

Reading messages

Messages that the Mail app considers suspicious are automatically placed in a **Junk Email** folder.

Messages received by any accounts added to the Mail app accumulate in the account's "Inbox" folder, waiting to be read. The left-hand pane of the Mail app screen contains navigation buttons to select an account and folder. Selecting the **Inbox** folder in the left-hand pane displays a list of received messages in the center pane, for the currently selected account. Selecting any message from the list in the center pane displays its contents in the right-hand pane.

Left-hand pane (navigation)　　Center pane (message list)　　Right-hand pane (message content)

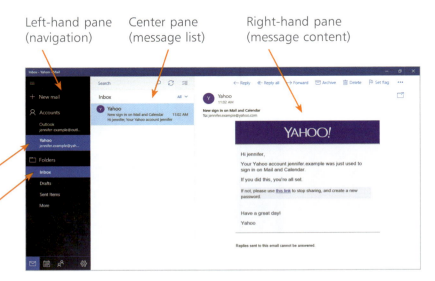

The currently selected items in the left-hand pane remain **highlighted** to identify the account and the folder that is open.

With the Inbox folder selected, you can click on a different account to see received messages for that account:

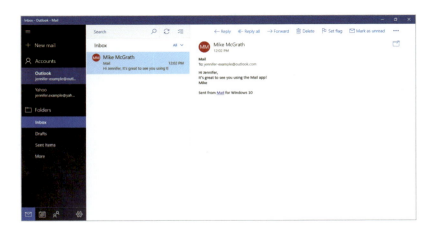

Notice that the messages are automatically given **colored icons** displaying initials – for easy identification of the message sender.

The Mail app learns from your email habits and begins to separate received messages in the Inbox message list. Important messages are placed under a **Focused** tab, and lower priority messages are placed under an **Other** tab. This lets you focus on important messages and helps you keep an uncluttered Inbox.

You can turn off the **Focused Inbox** feature if you don't like it – see page 215.

While you are reading a message you will see a number of links appear above the contents in the right-hand pane:

Actions

Open message in a new window

The links are mostly self-explanatory and let you perform various tasks with the message – for example, click the **Delete** link to remove a message after you have read it and need not save it. More options are available if you click the **...** (ellipsis) button to reveal the **Actions** menu. The **Find** action is particularly useful to search a lengthy message. It opens a Search box above the message content where you can type a word to seek. Results are highlighted in the message, and a count of matches is provided:

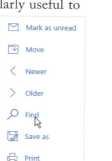

Some messages may arrive with small print – use the **Zoom** option to read those clearly.

Saving messages

When you want to retain email messages, the Mail app provides a number of solutions. Most simply, the app provides an "Archive" folder in which to save your received messages:

1 With a message open for reading, click the **Archive** link to instantly move that message to the Archive folder

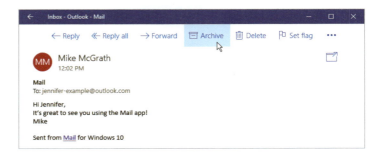

You can click the
⬚ button to open
a message in a **new**
window, without the
navigation pane and
folder pane.

2 Alternatively, select the message in the Inbox list then click the **Archive** button to move the message instantly

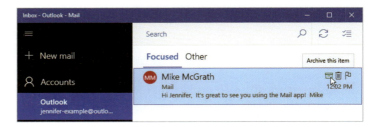

You can also right-click
on a selected message in
the Inbox list to see this
context menu appear,
which provides options
including Archive, Move,
or Delete the message.

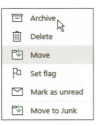

3 Now, in the left-hand pane, click **More**, then choose **Archive** in the pop-up **All folders** list to see your saved messages

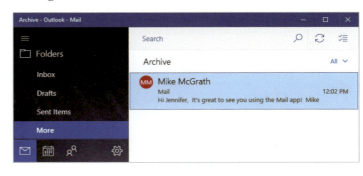

As the **Archive** folder fills up pretty quickly, you may prefer to create your own individual folders in which to save messages:

1 In the Inbox list, click the **Enter selection mode** button

2 Next, click the **Move** button, to open the "Move to..." list

3 Click the **+** button and type a folder name

4 Now, hit enter to see your new folder appear in the list

5 Click on the new folder in the list to move the message

Hot tip

If you save lots of email messages you can create a hierarchy of folders. Right-click on a folder, then choose **Create new subfolder** to add a nested folder inside the selected folder.

Don't forget

Click **More** in the left-hand pane at any time to see the **All folders** list.

Writing messages

The Mail app allows you to easily format the messages you write and check their spelling before you send them, then automatically stores a copy in its **Sent Items** folder for reference later:

1 Click on **New Mail** in the left-hand pane to start a new message

2 In the right-hand pane, type the recipient's email address in the "To:" box – you may select a recipient from a list of contacts that appears as you begin to type

3 Add a subject then type your message. Much like the tags in social media, you can use **@mentions** to tag a contact within the message – type "@" and a list of contacts will appear. Select a contact to tag them in the message body so they will get a copy of your message

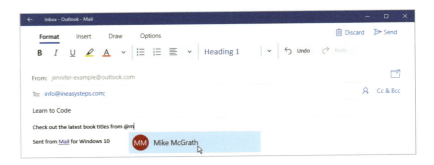

4 Complete the message, then add style with **Format** tools

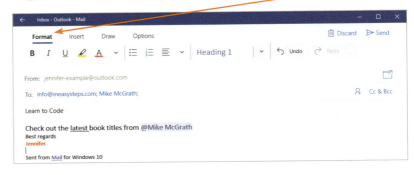

5 Next, select the **Options** item on the toolbar

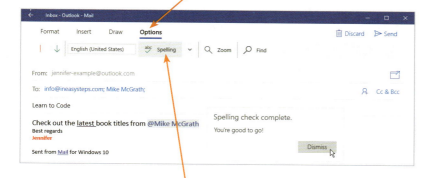

Adjust the language for appropriate **spellings** in the recipient's location.

6 Now, click the **Spelling** tool to check your message for spelling errors. Click **Dismiss** if none are found

7 When you are entirely happy with your message, click the **Send** button to deliver it to your chosen recipients

If you decide not to send the message, simply click the **Discard** button to remove it from the app. If you don't send or discard the message, it will automatically be saved as a draft.

8 To review your message later, click on the **Sent Items** folder in the left-hand pane, then open a copy from the list there

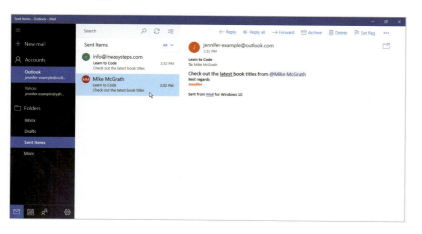

You can also use the keyboard shortcuts **Alt** + **S** or **Ctrl** + **Enter** to send a message from the Mail app.

Adding attachments

They say a picture paints a thousand words, so attaching images to your email messages can mean a lot. The **Mail** app in Windows 10 makes it easy to include any type of file with your messages. You can insert images within your email to enhance the message, and clip attachments alongside the message for further reading:

You can also include links to online images and files in your email messages using the Mail app's **Link** menu item.

1 Type your message, then click the **Insert** menu item

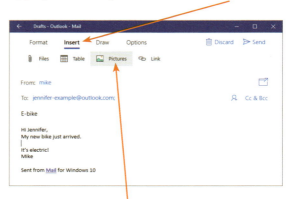

Use an image editor to **reduce** the file size of images you include in your emails to minimize the download for the recipients – they may receive your message on a metered connection where charges could apply.

2 Next, choose the **Pictures** option, then browse to a picture you would like to include in your message

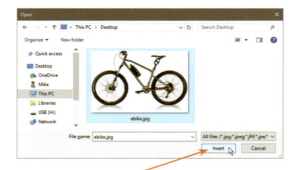

3 Click the **Insert** button to include the picture in your message, then click the **Insert**, **Files** menu item

4 Now, browse to a file you would like to attach to your email message

You can **drag** a file onto the Mail app and **drop** it onto a message you have written to attach that file to the message.

5 Click the **Open** button to attach the file to your message, then click the **Send** button

You can also select the **Draw** menu item to insert a canvas area upon which you can draw using pen tools.

6 Your message is received with the selected picture inserted and the selected file attached

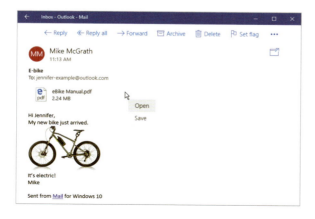

The recipient's email app must **allow** automatic inclusion of images to see them in your message. Some people prefer to deny this due to security concerns.

7 The recipient can right-click the attachment and choose to **Open** or **Save** the file you sent

Syncing options

If you often use a metered internet connection, you might like to configure the frequency at which the Mail app checks for the arrival of new email messages:

1 Launch the Mail app, then click its ⚙ **Settings** button and choose the **Manage accounts** option

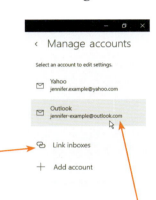

You can unify multiple email accounts into a single Inbox by clicking the **Link inboxes** option.

2 Next, select the account you want to configure and see its **Account settings** dialog open

Select the **Default Font** settings option to choose a preferred font, size, and color for an account.

3 Now, click the **Change mailbox sync settings** option to see the account's current synchronization settings

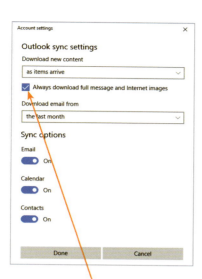

Different mail accounts may provide differing **syncing** options.

4 Uncheck the checkbox if you prefer to receive only previews of your messages

5 Open the top drop-down menu and select an option to check for messages less frequently

If you choose the option to download messages **manually**, the Mail app will never check for messages automatically. Choose an interval such as **every 30 minutes**, to avoid manual syncing.

6 Click the **Done** button to close sync settings, then click **Save** on the Account settings dialog to apply the changes

Automating responses

The Mail app can be configured to automatically send replies to email it receives. This is useful when you cannot respond in person but want to ensure the message sender does not feel ignored:

1 Launch the Mail app, then click its ⚙ **Settings** button and choose the **Automatic replies** option

2 If you have more than one email account, choose the one you want to automate in the drop-down box

3 Slide the **Send automatic replies** toggle button to the **On** position

4 Next, check the box to **Send replies outside of my organization**

5 Type your automated message in the text box below the checkbox

6 Senders of email to your account will now receive automatic replies

< Automatic replies

Select an account

Outlook ⌄

Send automatic replies

⬛ On

Inside my organization

Enter your message here

☑ Send replies outside of my organization

Thank you for your email.
I'm out of the office and will be back next Monday. During this period I will have limited access to my email.

For immediate assistance please contact me on my cell phone at 555-1234.
Best Regards,
Jennifer

☐ Send replies only to my contacts

Hot tip

Automatic replies should advise the length of your **absence** and provide an alternative method of contacting yourself or a colleague.

Don't forget

The automatic reply does **not** maintain formatting of line breaks or paragraphs.

← Inbox - Outlook - Mail — ☐ ✕

← Reply ⇇ Reply all → Forward ▭ Archive 🗑 Delete •••

J jennifer-example@outlook.com
11:56

Automatic reply: Contract Meeting
To: Mike McGrath

Thank you for your email. I'm out of the office and will be back next Monday. During this period I will have limited access to my email. For immediate assistance please contact me on my cell phone at 555-1234. Best Regards, Jennifer

You can also automate your signature at the end of every email so you need not type it manually. This is also useful if you would like to append a disclaimer at the end of each message:

1 Launch the Mail app, then click its **Settings** button and choose the **Signature** option

2 If you have more than one email account choose the one you want to append a signature to in the drop-down box, or check the box to **Apply to all accounts**

3 Slide the **Use an email signature** toggle button to the **On** position

4 Type your signature or disclaimer message in the text box below the toggle button

5 Click the **Save** button to store your signature message

Your **signature** may not be appended to automatic replies.

6 Your signature or disclaimer will now be automatically appended to each new email message you write

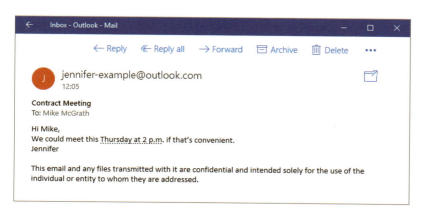

Disclaimers in email messages may not be legally **enforceable**, but they are in common use to underline confidentiality.

Choosing preferences

The Mail app settings provide various options to customize appearance and performance to suit your personal preference:

Personalization

- **Colors** – choose from a selection of 10 colors, or choose to use your Windows accent color, to customize both the Mail and Calendar apps instantly.

- **Modes** – choose Light mode for a white background in the folder and message list panes, or choose Dark mode for a black background in those panes.

- **Backgrounds** – choose from a selection of several default background images, or browse to find a suitable background image on your computer. The background image will appear in the content pane when you are not viewing a message. A portion of the background image can also appear in the left-hand pane but is faded so you can see the items.

Message list

- **Swipe actions** – choose what will appear when you hover the mouse over a message in the message list. When swipe actions are turned on, a Set/Clear flag button and a Delete button will appear by default when you hover over a message in the list.

Turn off the option to **Fill entire window** if you prefer to only see a background image in the content pane – when you are not viewing a message.

Swipe actions determine what will appear when **touchscreen** users swipe left or swipe right.

Reading pane

- **Mark item as read** – choose when to internally denote that you have read a message.

- **Caret browsing** – choose to turn On the option to navigate through messages using the keyboard arrow keys if you're a fan of Caret Browsing.

- **External content** – choose to turn Off the option to automatically download external images if you want to limit data costs over a metered connection.

‹ Reading pane

Auto-open next item
● On

Mark item as read
● When selection changes

Caret browsing
Use the caret to navigate the reading pane.
● On

External content
Select an account
Outlook

☐ Apply to all accounts

Automatically download external images and style formats.
● On

Hot tip

You can discover more about **Caret Browsing** on page 242.

Focused inbox

- **Focused Inbox** – choose to turn Off the option to sort messages into Focused and Other if you don't want to see these separate tabs in the message list.

‹ Focused inbox

Select an account
Outlook

Sort messages into Focused and Other
● On

Notifications

- **Show notifications in the action center** – choose if you want to see a banner and hear a sound when a message arrives.

Show notifications in the action center
● On

☑ Show a notification banner

☑ Play a sound

Hot tip

The Mail settings also provide a **What's new** option that opens a web page in your browser detailing the latest developments in the Mail and Calendar apps.

215

People app

Windows 10 provides a contacts manager called the **People** app that is closely integrated with the Mail app and the Maps app. The People app is useful for storing information such as email addresses, phone numbers, and physical addresses.

The People app has the ability to amalgamate all of your contacts across a range of different email services and social media websites. It allows you to easily call a contact from a phone, send an email to a contact, or retrieve a map of the contact's location:

The **People** app lets you add up to five contacts to the Taskbar for quick access.

1 Go to Start, People, or click the button in the Mail app, to launch the **People** app

2 If you are signed in to the computer with a Microsoft account, the **Contacts** page will open, otherwise you are asked to connect accounts from which to gather contacts

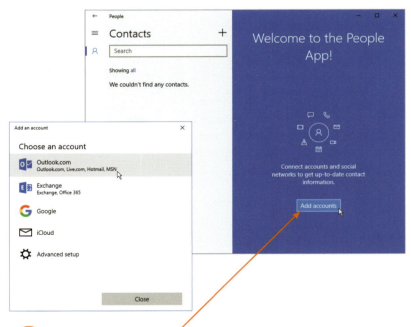

People can link the same contacts from different networks under one profile. There is also an option that allows you to link contacts manually.

3 Click the **Add accounts** button, then choose an account – for example, choose **Outlook.com** to add that account

4 Sign in to the account to add contacts to the People app

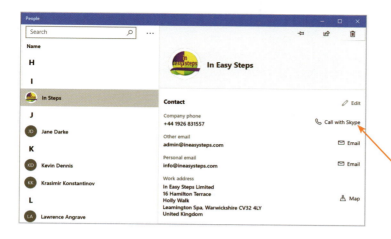

You can tap the **Call with Skype** button beside a telephone number in the contact's profile to call that contact.

5 Scroll down the contacts list and select any one to see their profile details

6 Click the **Email** button beside an email address in a profile to launch the **Mail** app, ready to send that contact a message

7 Click the **Map** button beside a physical address in a profile to launch the Maps app, to see that contact's location

The People app can be used with the **Maps** app to plan a route to a contact's address.

Calendar app

Windows 10 provides a useful Calendar app in which to keep track of forthcoming events. The app is powered by Exchange ActiveSync (EAS) technology that is the backbone of Microsoft services such as Hotmail, Exchange, and Office 365. It can also connect to other EAS-based calendars, such as Google Calendar. As with many Windows 10 apps, Calendar uses a browser-like form of navigation. When using a mouse, you'll see small navigational arrows appear near the top-left of the calendar. Or you can use the keyboard – **Ctrl + Up arrow**, **Ctrl + Down arrow**, **Ctrl + Left arrow**, and **Ctrl + Right arrow** for calendar navigation. A cool feature is that moving backwards or forwards in time is done within the context of the current view – for example, going back while in Week view takes you back a week; going forward while in Day view takes you forward to tomorrow:

The **Calendar** app is a new Universal Windows App in Windows 10.

1 Go to Start, Calendar, or click the 📅 button in the Mail app, to launch the **Calendar** app

You move around the Calendar app using the **arrow** buttons.

2 If you are not signed in to the computer with a Microsoft account you will be asked to sign in, otherwise the Calendar will open in Month view

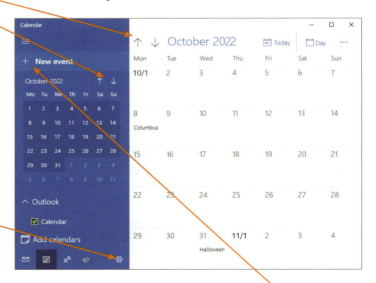

You can import calendars into the Calendar app from Hotmail, Outlook and Google by clicking the Calendar app's Settings button then Manage Accounts, **Add an account**.

3 Add an entry to the calendar by clicking the **New event** link, or by clicking on a date in the calendar to open the event **Home** page

4 On the event Home page, enter details of the event name, location, and duration

5 If you would like a reminder of the event in advance, specify a notice period on the toolbar

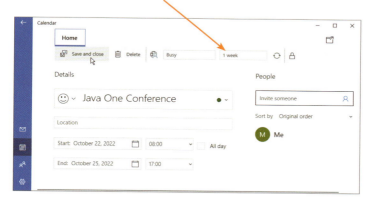

6 Click the **Save and close** button to return to the calendar view and see the event has now been added

Some of the options may be hidden if the Calendar is viewed in a small window. The options to select Day, Week, Month, or Year view are located to the right of the **Today** option, but not all options are visible in these screenshots.

7 You will receive a Cortana notification reminding you of the forthcoming event at the time specified by the notice period

...cont'd

The **Work week** view shows a five day week.

The Calendar app toolbar options let you choose to view **Today, Day, Week, Month,** or **Year,** to change the calendar view as required. Other options, such as **Work week,** are available from the Day and Week drop-downs. Changing from Month view to Week view provides rows for each hour under each day's column. This is useful for noting daily agenda schedules of events for each day. The hamburger button collapses the left-hand pane for extra space.

Calendar can show detailed information regarding your next event on the **Lock** screen.

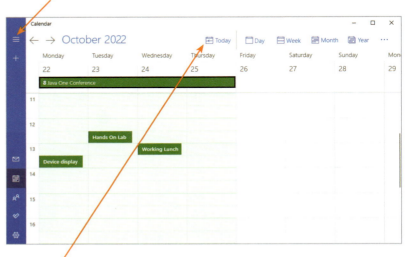

The **Today** button returns the Calendar view to the current date and retains the left-hand pane position – full or collapsed.

The Calendar app has buttons for the **Mail** app, **People** app, and **Calendar** settings, plus a button to open a **To-Do List** app – but you may need to install this from the Microsoft Store if it is not present.

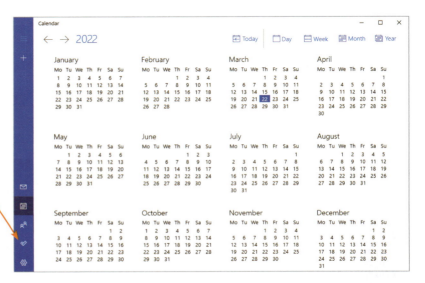

13 Microsoft Edge

Windows 10 includes
Microsoft Edge as the
default web browser. This
chapter describes its features
and demonstrates the
innovations it brings to web
browsing.

Better browsing

Windows 10 introduces the next-generation web browser named Microsoft Edge. This replaces the Internet Explorer web browser that has been around for many years. Microsoft Edge is a brand new, faster, more streamlined web browser.

Microsoft Edge has a new rendering engine that replaces the Trident rendering engine used in Internet Explorer. The new browser doesn't support old "legacy" technologies, such as ActiveX, but instead uses an extension system similar to those in the Chrome and Firefox web browsers. There is, however, a version of Internet Explorer included with Windows 10 for backward compatibility. Not supporting legacy technologies in Microsoft Edge has a number of benefits:

- Better interoperability with other modern browsers.

- Enhanced performance.

- Improved security and reliability.

- Reduced code complexity.

In addition to these benefits, there are several great innovations in the Microsoft Edge web browser:

- Integration with the Cortana Personal Digital Assistant for voice control, search, and personalized information.

- Annotation of web pages that can then be easily stored on OneDrive for sharing with other users.

- Compilation of web pages into a Reading list that synchronizes content between devices.

- Elimination of formatting distractions in Reading view mode that allows web pages to be read more easily.

The Microsoft Edge web browser is uncluttered in appearance, as its design intends to emphasize web page content. Browsing the web simply requires use of the familiar "navigation buttons":

The **Microsoft Edge web browser** app is a new Universal Windows App in Windows 10.

If you need to view a web page that uses legacy technology, you can find **Internet Explorer** under Windows Accessories on the A-Z Start menu.

Back Forward Reload

Interface layout

When the Microsoft Edge web browser is launched it shows just the Start page and provides the interface features shown below:

Set Aside   Close Tab   New Tab   Tab Preview   Favorites   Web Note   Share

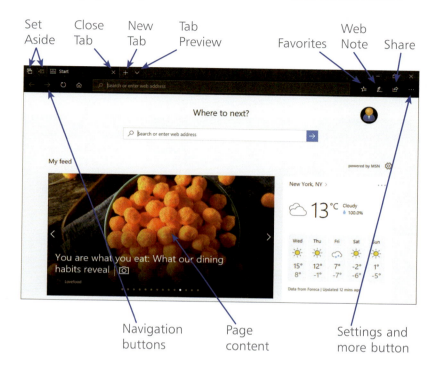

Navigation buttons   Page content   Settings and more button

Beware

Optional interface features of the toolbar, such as the Favorites button, are initially hidden. Click **Settings and more**, **Show in toolbar**, **Favorites** to make it visible.

Clicking the **+ New Tab** button opens a new tab containing a Search box and, by default, an intelligent selection of **Top sites** tiles that may be of interest to you.

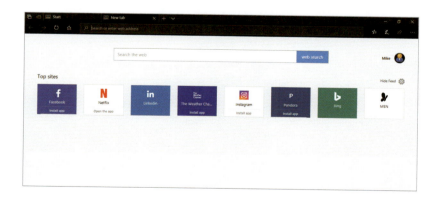

Hot tip

Use the **Customize** option on the new tab page if you wish to include your news feed or wish to exclude the Top sites list.

Tabbing pages

The ability to open multiple pages on separate "tabs" is available in other modern browsers, but Microsoft Edge provides great additional features to better control your open tabs.

Tab Preview

To quickly view the pages you have opened on multiple tabs:

1   Click the **Show tab previews** button after the final tab

Simply select any **tab** to view the page that is open on that tab.

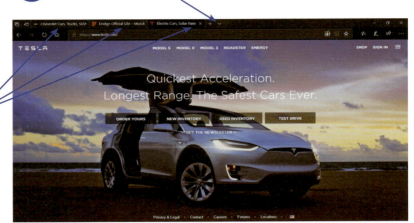

2   See the Tab Preview panel open at the top of the window

You can also right-click on any Tab Preview to choose an **option** from this context menu. There is also an option to **mute** audio playing on an open web page.

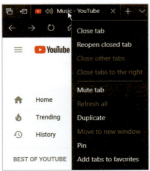

3   Click any preview to switch to that page, or click the **Hide tab previews** button to close the preview panel

...cont'd

Set Aside

If you add many tabs, the Tab Preview panel provides Forward/Back scroll buttons for navigation, but you can clear the panel by "setting aside" all open tabs for later:

1 Click the **Set Aside** button on the Edge toolbar

You can right-click any tab from the **Tabs you've set aside** preview and choose **Remove** to delete that individual tab.

2 See only a New Tab now appear in the Tab Preview panel

3 Click the **Tabs** button to reveal the tabs you've set aside

4 Click the **Restore tabs** link to see the tabs you've set aside reappear in the Tabs Preview panel

Opening options

Typing a URL address or search phrase into Microsoft Edge's Address Bar will, by default, display the search results or specified website in the current window area. It is, however, often preferable to retain the current window and open search results or specified websites in other tabs or windows:

1 Click on the Address Bar to make it active, then type in a search phrase and hit **Enter** to see the search results

If the Address Bar is **hidden**, you can click to the right of the navigation buttons to make it appear.

2 Now, place the mouse cursor over one of the result links and right-click to see a context menu appear

3 Select the menu option to **Open in new tab**

The **Copy link** menu option copies the URL address of the selected link onto the clipboard.

4 Now, click the new tab that appears, to see the page contents of the link displayed in that tab

...cont'd

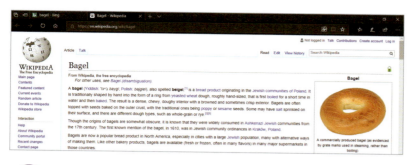

You can also use the keyboard shortcut **Ctrl + Tab** to move forwards and backwards between tabs.

5 Click the original tab to see the search results once more

6 Place the mouse cursor over a different result link, and right-click to see the context menu appear

7 Select the menu option to **Open in new window**

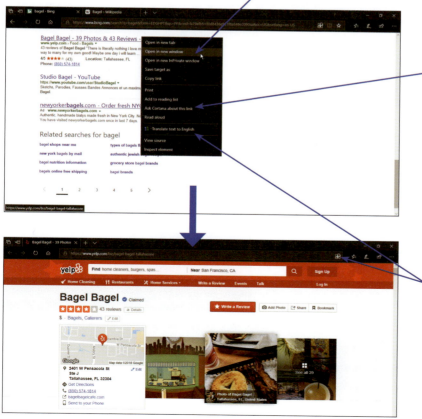

Select the **Ask Cortana...** option to see further links related to a particular search result.

Text translation of non-English web pages can be made available by installing the **Translator for Microsoft Edge** extension, which provides this menu option. Click **...** (**Settings and more**), **Extensions** to see available extensions.

Saving favorites

If you've found a website that you are likely to visit frequently, it can be made quickly accessible as a saved Favorite:

1 Open the website then navigate to a page of interest

2 On the toolbar, click the **Favorites** star icon

3 Edit the favorite **Name**, if desired, then choose **Favorites** from the **Save in** drop-down menu, and click the **Add** button

4 To open a saved Favorite, if the Favorites Bar is not enabled, first launch Microsoft Edge then click the **Favorites** button

5 On the left pane, click the **Favorites** star icon to see saved Favorites

6 Click the saved Favorite from the displayed list, to open that website once more

Hot tip

If the Favorites button is hidden, click **Settings and more**, **Show in toolbar**, **Favorites** to make it visible.

Hot tip

The Favorites Bar is hidden unless enabled in **Settings and more** (**...**), Settings (see page 241).

Don't forget

Remove a saved Favorite from the list by right-clicking on it and choosing **Delete** from the context menu.

Pinning websites

A website that you are likely to visit frequently can alternatively be made quickly accessible as a link pinned to the Start menu:

1 Open the website in the Microsoft Edge browser

2 Click the ellipsis (**...**) **Settings and more** button

3 Select **More tools** menu, then choose the **Pin this page to Start** option to create a link to the current website

See pages 240-241 for further on functions of the **Settings and more** button.

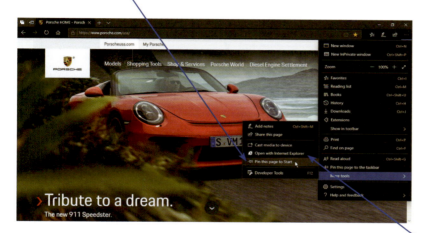

4 Confirm you want to pin this tile to the Start menu by clicking the **Yes** button

Do you want to pin this tile to Start?

Yes   No

You can choose the option to **Open with Internet Explorer** for legacy websites that do not perform well in the Microsoft Edge browser.

5 Open the Start menu, then click on the link tile to launch Microsoft Edge and open that website once more

To remove any tile or pinned link from the Start menu just right-click on it then choose **Unpin from Start** on the context menu.

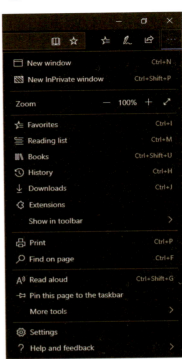

Customizing Edge

The drop-down menu from the (...) **Settings and more** button in Microsoft Edge provides typical options to **Zoom** the page view, **Print** the page or **Find** text within the page. It lets you open a **New window** or, if you prefer, a **New InPrivate window** that does not store cookies, history, or temporary files on your PC. The **More tools** option provides **F12 Developer Tools** to build or debug web pages, and the **Settings** option provides several customization possibilities:

1 Click the (...) **Settings and more** button, then select the **Settings** option

2 In Settings, General under the **Choose a theme** section, click the down arrow and select the **Dark** option from the drop-down menu

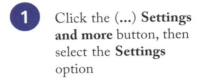

3 Next, click the **Import or export** button and select a browser from the list that appears

4 Now, slide the **Show the favorites bar** toggle button into the **On** position

5 For **Open Microsoft Edge with**, select **A specific page or pages**

6 Next, enter the URL of a preferred start page

7 In Settings, slide the **Show the favorites bar** toggle button to the **On** position

Hot tip

8 Slide the **Show the home button** toggle button into the **On** position – to add a **Home** button on the toolbar

You can add the URL of a Start page to open when you click the **Home** button, or leave this blank to use the default Start page.

9 Click the **Privacy & security** button, then slide the **Block pop-ups** button to the **On** position – to block annoying pop-up dialogs

10 Click the **Passwords & autofill** button, then adjust the **Save passwords** and **Save form data** toggle buttons to suit your preferences

11 Click on the **Advanced** button, then be sure to slide the **Use Adobe Flash Player** button to the **Off** position – to avoid malicious content

Beware

The Adobe **Flash Player** plugin is a known security risk. It is strongly recommended you do not enable this feature.

Selecting text

When selecting text in a web page it can be difficult to select precisely what you want without also selecting adjacent text and images, as shown below:

With Microsoft Edge, the Caret Browsing feature helps solve this problem. This lets you use the keyboard instead of the mouse to make selections, and it offers much more precise control.

You can activate Caret Browsing like this:

Hot tip

If you find Caret Browsing useful you may want to enable it permanently by checking this box. It can be temporarily disabled by pressing **F7** at any time.

1 Press the **F7** key to see a dialog box appear

2 Click the **Turn on** button

3 Place the cursor beside the text block you want to select

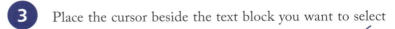

Beware

You will not be able to select text that appears within an image – you can only select **actual text content** in a document.

4 Hold down the **Shift** key and use the arrow keys (the < left arrow key in this example) to highlight the text you want

14 Digital images

This chapter describes how Windows 10 helps you easily manage and organize digital images that you can display on your TV and share with your family, friends, and colleagues.

Movies & TV app

Windows 10 provides two video players – the Windows Media Player app and the **Movies & TV** (Films & TV) app. The new **Movies & TV** video app is the one described below and assumes that you're signed in to the PC with a Microsoft account.

The **Movies & TV** app is a new Universal Windows App in Windows 10. It may be called **Films & TV** in your region.

1 Open the app by clicking the **Movies & TV** item on the Start menu, then select the **Personal** menu option – the screen prompts you to add folders containing videos

Don't forget

Only videos placed in your Videos folder will be accessible from the **Movies & TV** app initially.

2 Click **Add folders**, then click the + button to specify folders to include

3 Click **Done** to see icons appear for each video – click any icon to start playing that video

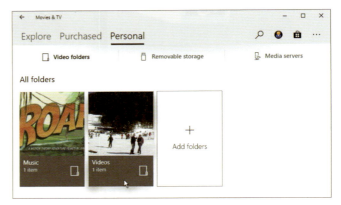

The **controls** disappear as the video begins to play. Hover the mouse over the Video app window to see the controls reappear.

4 Controls to Play/Pause, back 10 seconds, and forward 30 seconds appear at the bottom of the app window

5 Click the back arrow at the top of the app window, then select the **Explore** menu option – to discover movies and TV shows you can rent or buy

You will need to be **signed in** with a Microsoft account to rent or buy videos.

6 Select the **Purchased** menu option to see movies and TV shows you have already bought

Free **trailers** are available for most movies.

Photo apps in the Store

If the Photos app described on pages 246-251 does not meet your requirements, a large selection of other photo apps are available in the Microsoft Store.

1 Open the **Microsoft Store** from the Start menu

2 Type "photos" into the Search box to see a suggestion list

3 Select an app from the list, or select **Top Photo Apps** to see the most popular apps for this search term

Adobe Photoshop Express is a popular **free** photo-editing app.

Many of these apps provide image-related options other than just organizing and sharing. For example, you will find apps that:

● Map pictures to specific locations with "geotagging".

● Create photo albums.

● Provide editing tools.

● Provide camera functions.

● Import pictures from other devices.

● Create slideshows.

15 Windows games

Traditional Windows games such as FreeCell Solitaire are included with Windows 10, and there are a huge number of games available in the Microsoft Store.

This chapter describes some of the most popular games.

Solitaire Collection

Gaming has always been a very popular use of computers and, in recognition of this, Windows operating systems have traditionally provided a selection of games with which users can amuse themselves. No games were included with the Windows 8 operating system by default, but a selection of games is bundled with the Windows 10 operating system. The Microsoft Solitaire Collection is available on the Start menu, and contains a selection of popular traditional Windows card games remade as modern apps.

If you want more games in Windows 10, you can **download** them from the Microsoft Store.

The Microsoft Solitaire Collection in the Windows 10 typically includes guaranteed **solvable** decks for the Klondike, Spider, and FreeCell Solitaire games.

Surprisingly, the standard edition of the Microsoft Solitaire Collection supplied with Windows 10 now contains advertisements. You can, however, upgrade to the Premium edition (at a cost) to remove the adverts and receive other game benefits. The Menu button produces a menu that includes an **Upgrade to Premium** option.

Not all the traditional Windows games are available in **Universal Windows App** versions.

FreeCell is, perhaps, the most popular Solitaire card game in the Microsoft Solitaire Collection.

1 Open the Microsoft Solitaire Collection app, then click on the **FreeCell** tile to begin the game

As shown here, you are notified if you attempt to make an **invalid** move.

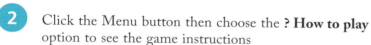

Windows 10 provides a Games Bar to record game play – that you open by pressing the **Winkey** + **G** keys.

2 Click the Menu button then choose the **? How to play** option to see the game instructions

3 Arrange the cards to create four stacks of card suits to complete, then you can review your gameplay statistics

If you quit a game before completion it is counted as a **loss** in your game statistics.

Candy Crush Soda Saga

The highly addictive and popular Candy Crush Soda Saga match-3 game is available as a Universal Windows App on Windows 10.

Candy Crush Soda Saga has **many levels**, and game instructions are provided on screen during the early levels.

Click the **Settings** icon in the bottom-left corner of the app for options to control the music and sound effects.

1 Launch the Candy Crush Soda Saga app from the Start menu, then click on the **Play** button to begin the game

2 Match three or more candies to meet the target score within the limited number of available moves

3 On success you will see and hear the phrase "Soda Crush", then follow the options and the game will proceed to the next level

Xbox Console Companion

The new Xbox Console Companion app on Windows 10 now makes Xbox features available on PCs and tablets. It allows you to keep track of friends on Xbox Live, record game play clips using its Game DVR, join in an Xbox One multi-player game without leaving your desk, and easily acquire Windows 10 games.

1 Launch the Xbox Console Companion app from the Start menu, then click on the 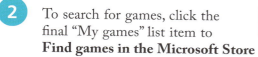 **My games** button

2 To search for games, click the final "My games" list item to **Find games in the Microsoft Store**

3 Choose a game such as "FarmVille 2: Country Escape"

4 When the game is installed it appears in your "My games" list, with a **Play** button you can click to launch that game

The **Xbox Console Companion app** is a new Universal Windows App in Windows 10.

Xbox One consoles can **stream** games and media to your Windows 10 PC using the Xbox app. See pages 262-263 for details.

Streaming Xbox games

The Xbox Console Companion app is a great new **Universal Windows App** in Windows 10 that brings Xbox gaming to your PC.

You must **sign in** to both the Xbox console and Xbox app using the same Microsoft account.

If you have an Xbox console on the same network you can stream games, video, and music to your PC:

1 Turn on your Xbox console and controller, then sign in using your Microsoft account

2 On your PC, launch the Xbox app from the Start menu, then sign in using the same Microsoft account

3 To have the Xbox app search for your Xbox device, click the **Connection** button in the left-hand toolbar

4 Connect an Xbox controller to your PC using a USB to micro-USB cable, so you can interact with your Xbox app

5 Select the Xbox console with which to connect, then click the **Stream** link

6 Your Xbox console screen now loads in the Xbox app

Hot tip

You can search the Store for Xbox game demos to play on a **trial** basis.

7 Use the Xbox controller to select a game to stream to your PC, then play – just like on your Xbox

Beware

To use a wireless Xbox controller after using it on your PC you will have to **re-sync** the controller, using the console's Sync button or a USB cable.

Microsoft
Mahjong

Mahjong

Microsoft Mahjong is a tile-based game that can be played on the PC, a tablet, or online. The purpose of the game is to remove all the tiles from the board by matching them with identical tiles.

1 Download the app from the Microsoft Store, as described in Step 1 on page 265

2 The Home page shows a number of sections – select from **Choose Puzzle**, **Daily Challenges**, **Themes**, **How to Play**, **Awards and Achievements**, and **Statistics**

3 If you are new to Mahjong, click **How to Play** to discover how to play the game, then click **Choose Puzzle**

4 Next, select your skill level. Initially, you are restricted to the first game in each level – when you have completed this, you can move up to the next one

5 Click pairs of matching tiles to remove them from the board. Clear the board completely to win

Hot tip

If you play a lot, the **Statistics** section on the Home page will be interesting.

Hot tip

If you get stuck or just want to take a break, click the **Menu** button – the **Hint** option will reveal a matching pair and **Pause** will stop play until you choose to resume.

Minesweeper

Microsoft Minesweeper is another fun and tactical game. The aim is to uncover all empty squares in a grid while avoiding the mines.

Microsoft Minesweeper

1 On the Home page, select your skill level – **Easy**, **Medium**, or **Expert**. There is also a **Custom** option, which allows you to set your own degree of difficulty

2 At the top of the screen there is a timer and the number of mines on the board

3 As you reveal empty squares, numbers appear on them. These indicate how many mines are touching that square, and thus help you determine which squares are mines

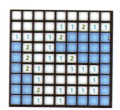

4 If you hit a mine, that's it – the game is over

5 When all the empty squares are uncovered, you win

209

Hot tip

The more difficult the **skill level** you choose, the more squares and mines there are on the game board.

Hot tip

Right-clicking on a square that you suspect contains a mine will put a **warning flag** on the square.

Sudoku

Microsoft Sudoku

If you're a fan of logic puzzles you can play the popular game of Sudoku – to fill a 9x9 grid so that each column and row, and each of the nine 3x3 sub-grids, contain all of the digits from 1 to 9.

1 Download the app from the Microsoft Store, as described in Step 1 on page 265

2 On the Home page, select your skill level – **Very Easy, Easy, Medium, Hard,** or **Expert**

3 The grid is partly filled with digits. Click an empty square, or use the arrow keys to select an empty square

The quantity of each **remaining** digit is shown on these tiles, in the top right-hand corner of each number.

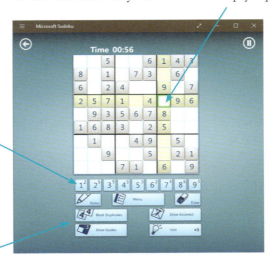

Use the **Block Duplicates**, **Show Guides**, and **Show Incorrect** buttons for assistance if you are new to the Sudoku game.

4 Type a digit that is not already present in the selected row, column, or grid

5 Complete the grid with the missing digits to win

16 Music and sound

This chapter describes how to play music, listen to internet radio, and play videos with audio tracks. It also illustrates how to share your media files with others on your network and how to use a microphone to dictate to your computer.

Audio connections

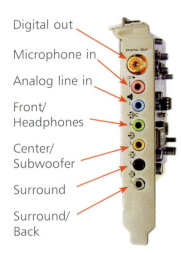

Digital out

Microphone in

Analog line in

Front/
Headphones

Center/
Subwoofer

Surround

Surround/
Back

Desktop and laptop computers are equipped with audio facilities that can produce high-fidelity audio playback. On desktop machines, the sound card can provide the connections for various types of speakers, ranging from simple stereo speakers to multiple speaker sets with surround sound.

For a laptop or notebook the options are often limited to microphone and headset sockets, though some laptops include more sophisticated connections, such as the SPDIF (Sony Philips Digital InterFace) used for home theater connections.

You may have speakers attached to your PC, or built into your laptop. You can check their configuration, like this:

1 Go to **Settings**, **System**, **Sound**, then click the **Sound Control Panel** option under the Related Settings heading

2 On the Playback tab, select **Speakers** and click **Configure**, then select your configuration and click **Test** to check

Hot tip

On a desktop computer, the sound card may be incorporated into the **motherboard** or provided as a separate **adapter card**, as shown here.

Don't forget

The configurations listed depend on the features of your sound card. To check operation of the speakers, click the **Test** button. Note that some software only uses the main speakers, especially for tracks that are two-channel stereo only.

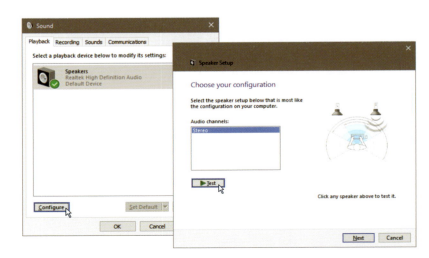

Groove Music app

The Groove Music app in Windows 10 allows you to play your owned music and arrange it into playlists:

1. The first thing to do is place all your music in the Groove app's "My music" folder – to make it accessible in the app

2. Open the Groove app and click the buttons to see your music listed as **Songs**, **Artists**, or **Albums**

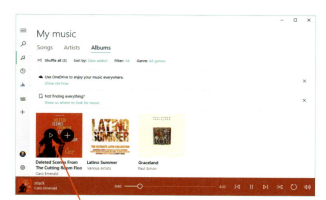

3. Click the **Play** button to begin playing the tracks, or click the tile to open an Album and see its tracks listed

4. To play a listed track, double-click it, or select it then click the ▷ **Play** button at the bottom of the screen

5. Explore the playback controls at the bottom of the screen

The **+ Add to** option allows you to create playlists by adding tracks.

Streaming music

The Spotify Music app is available from the Store for Windows 10 and lets you freely stream music and podcasts while online:

Spotify replaced the availability of **music** in the Microsoft Store.

1 Install and open Spotify and search for an album, artist, or song – for example, search for the artist "Caro Emerald"

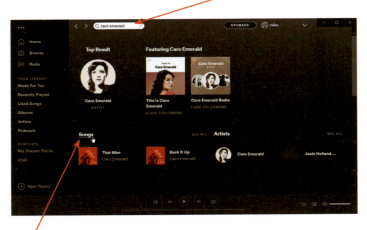

2 Click the **Songs** link – to see available songs by this artist

Hot tip

These **Go back** and **Go forward** buttons let you navigate between screens in the Spotify app.

3 Click the **Play** button beside any song – to play that song

4 Click the **< Go back** button to return to the first screen, then click the **Albums** link – to see albums by this artist

Select any album to reveal all its songs, then click the Play button to begin playing **all** songs, or click the Play button beside any song to play an **individual** song.

5 Click the < **Go back** button to return to the first screen, then click the **Playlists** link – to see albums by this artist

An artist playlist typically combines songs from several albums. You can create your own playlists by clicking the **New Playlist** button.

6 Select any playlist, then click the Play button to begin playing all songs, or select individual songs to play

If you want to own the songs you need to subscribe to the Spotify Premium service. Click this **Upgrade** button to become a subscriber.

273

Windows Media Player

Windows Media Player (WMP) has long been one of the best applications in Windows, and the version supplied in Windows 10 is no exception. Windows Media Player can handle just about any media-related task.

Windows Media Player supports an extensive list of media **codec** (coder/decoder) formats to ensure it can play most types of audio, video, and image media.

These capabilities of Windows Media Player include:

- Playing music

- Viewing your pictures in a slideshow

- Playing video

- Streaming media on home networks

- Ripping music

- Burning media to disks

- Downloading media files

- Listening to music on the internet

- Creating playlists

- Synchronizing media on your devices

- Accessing online media sources to rent or buy music

Hot tip

Windows Media Player features **brightness**, **contrast**, **saturation** and **hue** adjustment controls. It also provides a 10-band **graphic equalizer** with presets, and an SRS (Sound Retrieval System) Wow audio post-processing system to personalize audio to your preferences for rich listening experience.

Play CDs

Providing you have a CD/DVD drive on your computer, you can use your sound card and speakers to play an audio CD.

1 Insert the disk in the drive, and AutoPlay asks what you want to do

2 Select **Play audio CD** Windows Media Player

The CD begins to play, as an unknown album and showing no details other than the track numbers and their durations.

Hot tip

Click the box **Always do this for audio CDs**, and the selected option is carried out automatically in future, whenever an audio CD is identified.

If you are connected to the internet, Windows Media Player will locate and download information about the CD, and display the album and track titles. You can also change the Visualization to display the album cover image.

Hot tip

Right-click the window and select **Visualization** to choose the effects to display – for example, Album art (cover image).

Local media streaming

Anything that you can play in Windows Media Player can be shared with other computers and devices on your local network.

Hot tip

Optionally, you can select other items on the drop-down **Stream** menu to grant further access.

Hot tip

You can also use right-click on media files and choose the **Cast to Device** menu option to select any Miracast compatible local device to cast the media to.

1 Open Windows Media Player, select the Library view and click **Stream**, **Turn on media streaming...** – to launch the "Media streaming options" dialog

2 Next, enter a name for this media library – for example, type "Remote Music Library" into this box

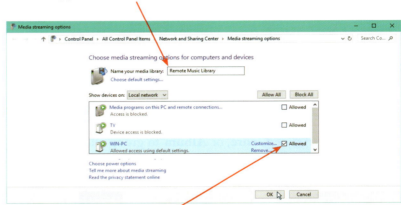

3 Choose a device on your local network that you wish to allow streaming – in this case, a device named "WIN-PC"

4 Now, click the **Choose default settings** link below the library name to open a settings dialog

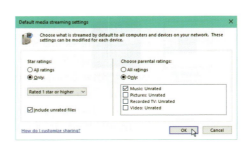

5 Select which categories you wish to allow streaming access – for example, only allow access to all music content

6 Click **OK** to close the settings dialog, then click **OK** to close the "Media streaming options" dialog

7 Open Windows Media Player on the device that has been granted streaming access – "WIN-PC" in this case

8 See that the "Remote Music Library" on the other device is now added on the navigation pane on this device

You may have to **wait** a few moments as the list of contents is transferred from the other computer.

9 Expand the "Remote Music Library" and select any item in its Music category

10 Click the **Play** button to hear the music on this device – streaming across your local network from the other device

Other categories of the remote library, to which access has **not** been granted, simply display a "No files have been found" message if you try to open them.

Streaming Xbox Music

If you have an Xbox console on the same network you can stream games, video, and music to your PC:

You must **sign in** to both the Xbox console and Xbox app using the same Microsoft account.

1 Turn on your Xbox console and controller, then sign in using your Microsoft account

2 On your PC, launch the Xbox Console Companion app, then sign in using the same Microsoft account

The Xbox Console Companion app is a great new **Universal Windows App** on Windows 10 that brings Xbox gaming to your PC.

3 To have the Xbox app search for your Xbox device, click the **Connection** button in the left toolbar

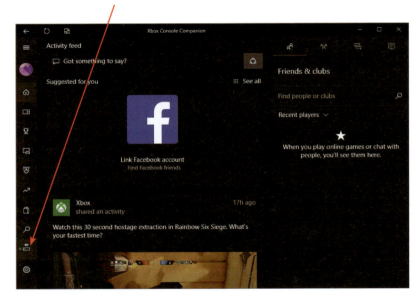

4 Connect an Xbox controller to your PC using a USB to micro-USB cable, so you can interact with your Xbox app

5 Select the Xbox console with which to connect, then click the **Stream** link

6 Your Xbox console screen now loads in the Xbox app

Hot tip

Spotify provides free **music** streaming (see pages 274-275).

7 Use the Xbox controller to select the **Spotify** app tile from the "Apps" screen on your Xbox

8 Browse through the various current offerings, or use the Search box to find a song, then select the item to hear it play on both your PC and the TV connected to the Xbox

9 Click the + button to add any favorite songs to the "Your Music" screen on your Xbox so you can easily replay them

Don't forget

You can still use the mouse to **continue** working on your PC while streaming music from your Xbox.

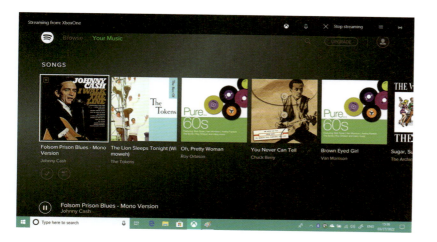

Beware

To use a wireless Xbox controller after using it on your PC you will have to **re-sync** the controller, using the console's sync button or a USB cable.

285

Internet radio

The ability to listen to internet radio stations is no longer available in Windows Media Player. The solution, therefore, is to download a third-party program. One we have tried and can recommend is the TuneIn Radio app that is available from the Microsoft Store:

Hot tip

Around **60,000** stations worldwide are available via the TuneIn Radio app.

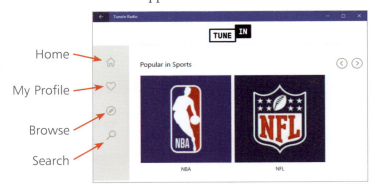

Home

My Profile

Browse

Search

The **Home** screen will show recommended stations listed by various categories. Scroll through the list and click on any station to listen, or click the **Browse** button to further filter categories. You can also search for songs, artists, and stations:

1 Click the **Search** button, then enter the name of a station – for example, the music station "Gold Radio"

Beware

Searching by song may return mere **mentions** of the song – rather than the song itself.

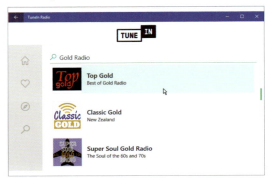

Hot tip

You can also browse for **podcasts** of pre-recorded audio programs that are available on the internet.

2 When the station is found, simply click on the **Play** button to begin listening to the live broadcast

Text to speech

You can let the computer talk to you, using the text to speech facilities of the Narrator app.

1 Go to the Start menu, then in the "Windows Ease of Access" folder choose **Narrator**

2 Narrator starts up, and you can configure how it performs by choosing the **Settings** option

Hot tip

You can open Settings, Ease of Access, Narrator, then check the **Start Narrator after sign-in** option to have the app start automatically.

3 Scroll down and choose your preferences for the Narrator's **Voice**, **Speed**, **Pitch**, and **Volume**

4 Scroll down again, then choose your preferences for the level of detail you would like to hear from the Narrator when **reading** items

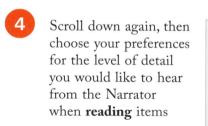

5 Scroll down once more, then choose your preferences for what you would like to hear from the Narrator when **typing** items

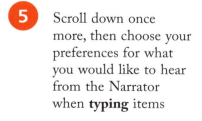

Beware

Narrator does not read the text content of all programs, so its value is somewhat **limited** in comparison with Speech Recognition.

Dictate to your computer

One way to interact with your computer is to simply tell it what you want to do, with Windows Speech Recognition.

1 Go to Start, "Windows Ease of Access" and choose **Windows Speech Recognition** to launch the "Set up Speech Recognition" wizard

2 Read the "Welcome" screen, then click **Next**

3 Select the type of your microphone – a headset mic is best for speech recognition – then click **Next**

4 Follow the advice to position the microphone effectively, then click **Next**

5 Read the specified text sentence aloud so the microphone volume can be set, then click **Next**

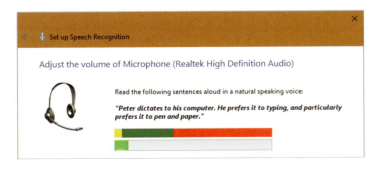

6 Click **Next** again to continue setting up

7 Select **Enable document review** to improve accuracy, then click **Next**

Speech Recognition is supported in **all** editions of Windows 10 and is available in the English, German, French, Spanish, Japanese and Chinese languages.

All the users on the computer should carry out their own **training sessions**, so that each has a separate profile.

8 Unless you are planning to always control your PC by voice, select **Use manual activation mode**, then click **Next**

9 Click the **View Reference Sheet** button and read the online list of commands to which your PC can respond, then click **Next**

You can print the **Speech Reference Card** so that you have it to hand when you are practicing with the system.

10 Uncheck the option to **Run Speech Recognition at startup** unless you plan to use this often, then click **Next**

11 Click **Start Tutorial** to launch Speech Recognition and watch an online video describing how it can be used

12 See that when you start Windows Speech Recognition, having chosen manual activation mode, the app launches in its "Off" state (not listening)

13 Right-click the Speech Recognition bar and select the status option to **On: Listen to everything I say**, or click the mic button, to change the app to its "Listening" mode

Speak **slowly and clearly** into the microphone, or the Speech Recognition app may not instantly recognize the command.

14 Speak any recognizable command to perform an action on your PC – for example, say "What can I say?" to view the Speech Reference Card

Recording

To record stuff on your computer, you need a working microphone and the Voice Recorder app that is included with the Windows 10 operating system:

The Voice Recorder app is a new **Universal Windows App** in Windows 10.

1 Open the **Voice Recorder** app from the Start menu, then click its microphone icon to begin recording – this starts the timer

2 Click the icon again to stop recording – the recording is saved as a file in your **Documents**, **Sound recordings** folder and gets added to the Recording list in the app screen

3 Click an item in the **Recording** list to select it – the app screen changes to display the playback controls

On the playback screen use the ⬆ **Share** button to email your recording, or the ✛ **Trim** button to edit the recording length. You can use the 🗑 **Delete** button to remove recordings, and the ✎ **Rename** button to give your recording a descriptive title.

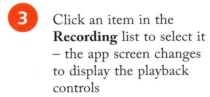

4 Click the || **Pause** button to halt the voice recording – the button changes to a > **Play** button so you can resume playback

17 Devices and printers

This chapter describes how to manage your devices in Windows 10. You can add various types of printers and scanners to your PC, and Windows usually provides the drivers needed to manage the devices.

Virtual printers

You may have some items in **Devices and Printers** that are not physical devices but are software programs that act as virtual printers. You can use these like this:

Fax   Microsoft Print to PDF   Microsoft XPS Document Writer

WordPad is chosen here as it supports **text and graphics**, but you could use almost any Windows program that prints.

1 Open a document with text and graphics in WordPad

2 Open the File menu and click **Print**

3 Choose one of the virtual printers – for example, "Microsoft Print to PDF"

4 Click the **Print** button

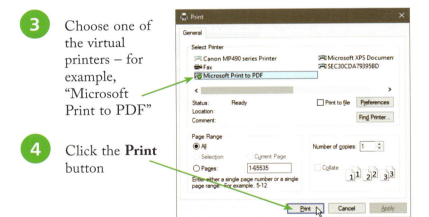

5 You'll be asked to confirm the location and file name, then click Save, and a PDF version of the document is saved

...cont'd

Alternatively, you can use a different virtual printer, like this:

1 Select **Microsoft XPS Document Writer** as the printer

2 Provide a name, and save in Open XPS document format

Some printer drivers pass control on to other programs:

1 Select **Fax** as the printer and Fax Setup is started

2 Choose your setup, then complete the cover page, and send your document as a **.tif** image file

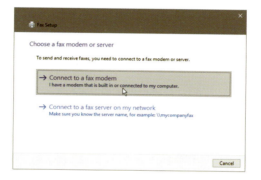

Brother fax machine

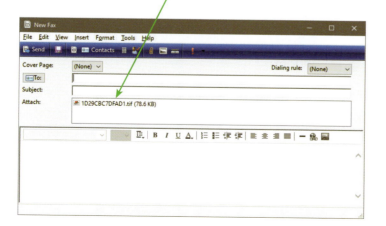

If you are not ready for Fax Setup, click **Cancel** and you can create a fax and save it as a draft to send later.

Generic/text only printer

You can create a useful generic/text only printer, like this:

1 Open **Devices and Printers**, click **Add a printer** and then click **The printer that I want isn't listed**

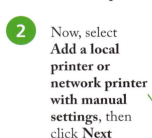

2 Now, select **Add a local printer or network printer with manual settings**, then click **Next**

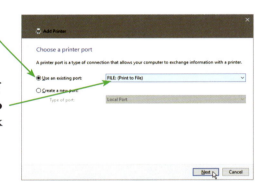

3 Select **Use an existing port** and choose the drop-down menu option of **FILE: (Print to File)**, then click **Next**

You can install a generic/text only printer driver in Windows 10 as a way to capture **text information** in a file, or for use with an application that requires this type of printer driver.

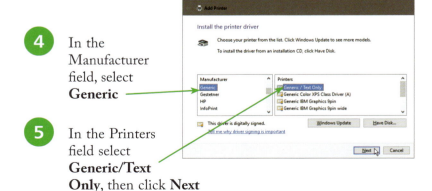

4 In the Manufacturer field, select **Generic**

5 In the Printers field select **Generic/Text Only**, then click **Next**

If you are creating support for an old printer, you'd choose the port it uses – **COM1**, for example.

...cont'd

6 Accept or amend the suggested name, then click **Next**

7 Select **Do not share this printer**, then click **Next**

Since this printer creates files on your system, it is best to **avoid** making it shareable.

8 Finally, click **Finish** to see the printer is added to the list of Printers in **Devices and Printers**

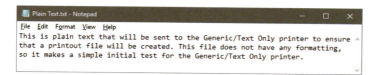

You can check out the operation of this printer, like this:

1 Create a simple plain text document using Notepad

2 Select **File, Print** and choose the **Generic/Text Only** printer

3 Provide the file name (type **.prn**) and click **OK**

When you print from a formatted source, the graphics and formatting will be **stripped out**. You may find the resulting text disorganized, as a default line of 80 characters is assumed.

Add a scanner

You can install a scanner to the **Devices and Printers** folder.

1 To install a USB-connected scanner, such as the Canon CanoScan, insert the USB cable and switch on

2 If the driver is available, the scanner will be installed. If the driver is missing, an **Action Center** error message may be displayed, helping you to download the driver

Canon scanner

Don't forget

Windows 10 will have the drivers for **many** scanners, but may not include older devices.

You can test the operation of the scanner, like this:

1 Right-click on the scanner in **Devices and Printers**, then choose **Scan Properties** to open the Properties dialog

2 Select the **General** tab, then click the **Test Scanner** button

Hot tip

Windows checks its **compatibility** database and identifies where to find the missing driver.

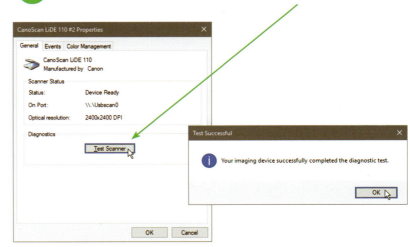

Using the scanner

There are several ways to access images from your scanner, such as with the traditional **Windows Fax and Scan** program. The Microsoft Store also provides a new easy-to-use free app called "Windows Scan".

1 Connect your scanner and insert an item to be scanned

2 Go to the Store and install the free Windows **Scan** app

3 Launch the **Scan** app, then click the **Show more** link to see scanning options

4 Choose your preferences for file type, etc. then click the **Preview** button to see how your item looks in the scanner

5 Drag the handles in the **Scan** window to fit your item

6 Click the **Scan** button to save the image as a file of your specified type, color mode, resolution, and location

The **Scan** app is a new Universal Windows App, listed in the Store as "Windows Scan".

The Scan app saves the **image** files, with the name set to the date they were scanned.

...cont'd

Image editing programs such as Paint provide the ability to import an image directly into the program for manipulation.

1 Connect your scanner and insert an item to be scanned

2 Go to the Start menu and launch the **Paint** program

3 Click **File**, **From scanner or camera**, to open the scanner dialog box

4 Choose your option preferences

5 Click the **Preview** button to see how your item looks in the scanner, and adjust the handles to fit if necessary

6 Click the **Scan** button to import the image into Paint, where you can modify it and save it as an image file

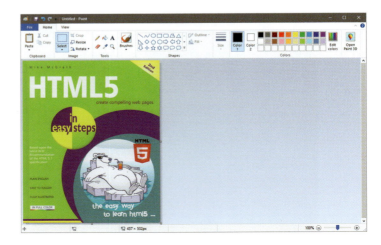

Add Bluetooth

You can connect to an external device that supports Bluetooth wireless technology, such as a Beats Pill speaker, using a Bluetooth USB dongle and the Control Panel in Windows 10:

1 If your PC does not have built-in Bluetooth support you should first insert a Bluetooth dongle into a USB socket

2 Switch on your Bluetooth device and activate it to make it discoverable

3 Open the Control Panel and select **Devices and Printers** then choose to **Add a device** to have Windows 10 search for devices

4 When Windows finds your Bluetooth device, click **Next** to install the drivers for your device

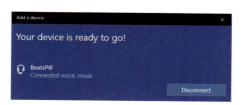

Don't forget

You may see a **notification** in the Action Center to confirm a device has been added.

5 Now, in **Devices and Printers** you see that your Bluetooth device is connected and ready to use

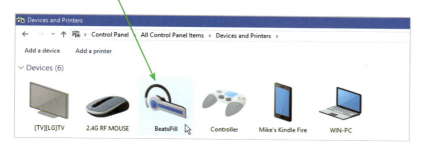

Add a storage device

Adding a storage device to a Windows 10 computer is easy as Windows does the hardware configuration for you – for example, you can add a 2.5" External Hard Disk Drive to the system. As with most current devices, the drive uses a USB connection. If your device uses USB 3.0, connect it to a USB 3.0 socket (if available) rather than USB 2.0. (USB 3.0 is much faster than USB 2.0 so the drive will perform far better.)

1 Connect the device to a USB socket, then switch on the drive if required

2 Windows automatically installs the device (adding any device driver software needed)

3 Go to **Devices and Printers** to see the device is added

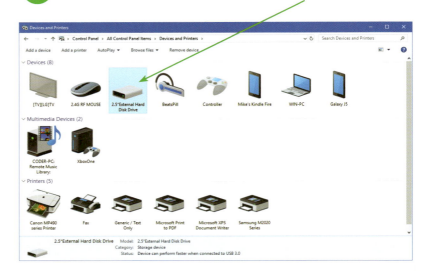

Beware

You can run a USB 3.0 device from a USB 2.0 socket but it will not operate at its **maximum** performance level.

Hot tip

If you are unsure which of your USB sockets are USB 3.0, look for any that are colored **blue** – these are USB 3.0; USB 2.0 are black.

18 Networking Windows

This chapter describes how, if you have more than one computer, you can connect them with cables or wirelessly and share information between them. Windows 10 makes it easy to share files via your network.

Enabling network sharing

Go to Start, Settings, Network & Internet, then click the **Status** item in the left pane and choose **Sharing options**

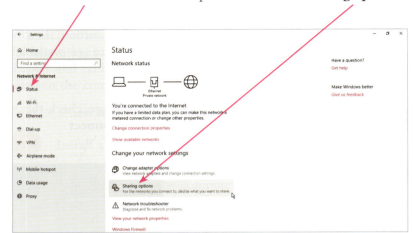

Hot tip

The settings formerly known as network location (Private/Public or Home/Work/Domain) are now called **Sharing options**. You can turn these settings on or off as required.

For your **Private** profile, choose to **Turn on network discovery** to see other devices on the network – and to allow this device to be seen by them

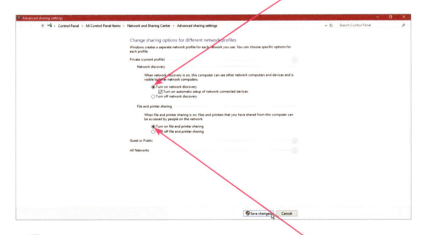

Hot tip

Sharing options automatically set the appropriate firewall and security settings for the network that you are connected to.

For your **Private** profile, also choose to **Turn on file and printer sharing** to allow other devices on the network access to files and printers that share from this device

Click the **Save changes** button to apply your choices

Controlling network settings

Settings related to networking can be found via the Network icon in the System Tray.

1 Place the cursor over the Network icon to see the network name and status

2 Click the Network icon to see connection details. Here the network connection is by Ethernet cable, but there is also a Wi-Fi alternative connection that you can select to switch connections

The button **color** indicates the active state.

3 Next, click the **Airplane mode** button to disable all wireless communication, and see that connection become unavailable

4 Click the **Airplane mode** button again to enable wireless communication once more

Click on the **Network & Internet settings** link in this panel to open the Settings window for the current connection.

5 Now, click the **Wi-Fi** button to disable Wi-Fi connectivity

6 Click the **Wi-Fi** button again to enable Wi-Fi connectivity once more, and choose how you wish to reconnect

Sharing files and folders

If you want to share a file or folder with other users on your network you can use the File Sharing Wizard:

1 Open **File Explorer** and select the folder or the file you would like to share

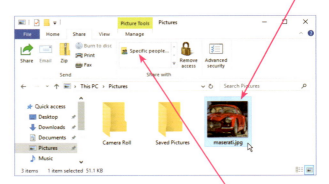

2 Click the **Share** tab and select **Specific people...** to open the "Network access" dialog

3 Choose a network user name from the drop-down list, then click **Add** to include that user

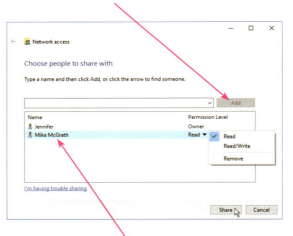

4 Click the user name to change the permission from the default **Read** to **Read/Write** (or **Remove**) as desired

5 Click the **Share** button to assign the permissions and see a confirmation that this item is now shared

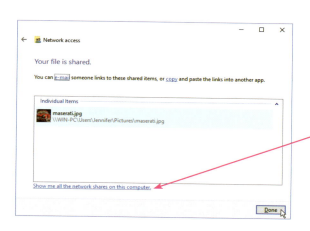

You can click **this link** to see all network shares from this computer.

6 On the chosen user PC, open **Network**, **Users** to see a folder containing items from the sharing network user

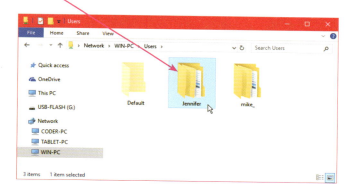

7 Click the sharing user's folder to discover the shared file within its parent **Pictures** folder

maserati.jpg

Only the **selected** file is shared to the chosen user. Other images within the sharing user's Pictures folder are not accessible to the chosen user – unless the entire Picture folder is shared.

Sharing network printers

If you have a printer connected to your PC you can share it with other networked computers on Windows 10, but the option to share the printer is not instantly obvious:

1 Open the Control Panel, then select **Devices & Printers** and right-click on the printer you want to share

2 Next, choose **See what's printing** on the context menu to open the printer's jobs dialog

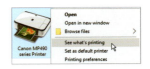

3 Now, select the **Printer, Sharing** menu item to open the "Printer Properties" dialog

4 Choose the "Sharing" tab and check **Share this printer**

You can enter a **new name** for the networked printer on the Sharing tab if you wish.

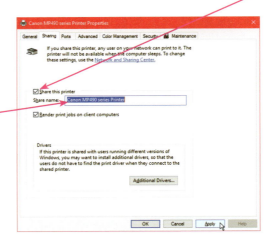

5 Click **Apply**, **OK** to apply the setting so other computers on the network can send print jobs to the shared printer

Sharing to nearby computers

Windows 10 PCs can send files and links to other nearby Windows 10 PCs that have "Nearby sharing" enabled. This feature uses Bluetooth to recognize two nearby devices for file transfer, and may also use Wi-Fi to help transfer files between them. Nearby sharing is particularly useful to share files from the Microsoft Edge web browser and Windows' File Explorer apps:

The option of **Nearby sharing** via a Share dialog is a new feature in Windows 10, and it requires Bluetooth 4.0.

1 Go to Settings, System, and select **Shared experiences** in the left pane, then turn **On** "Nearby sharing"

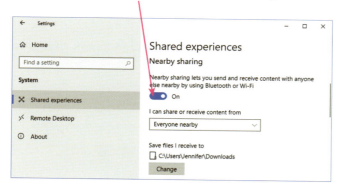

2 Open File Explorer, then right-click on a file and select the **Share** menu option

3 See the "Share" dialog search for nearby devices, then select an available nearby device

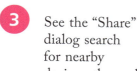

Hot tip

You can also share links to web pages using the **Share button** in the Microsoft Edge web browser to select available nearby devices.

4 See a notification that waits for a response until the selected nearby device accepts the shared file

315

Restricting notifications

When you are connected to a network you can, depending on selected app options, receive frequent Action Center notifications – such as breaking news items and special offers. Often you may find these useful but they can be distracting when you need to concentrate on the task in hand. The **Focus assist** feature in Windows 10 lets you choose which notifications you want to see and hear so you can stay focused on your current task:

The **Focus assist** feature was previously named "Quiet hours". It was renamed and extended to provide more options.

1 Go to Start, Settings, System, then choose the **Focus assist** option in the left pane

2 See that the **Off** (default) option allows all notifications

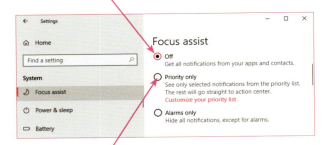

3 Select the **Priority only** option to restrict notifications to only those on your priority list

4 Next, click the **Customize your priority list** link – to open the "Priority list" screen

5 Now, choose how you want to receive **calls**, **texts**, and **reminders** by checking or unchecking the options

Hot tip

You can alternatively select the **Alarms only** option to hide all notifications except important alarms.

6 Scroll down and choose if you want to receive messages from selected contacts

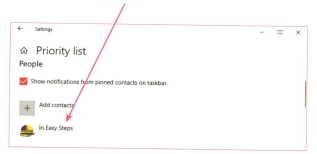

To delete a contact or apps from the "Priority list", select the list item to reveal a **Remove** button that you can click to perform the deletion.

7 Scroll down and choose if you want to receive notifications from selected apps

8 To automate this feature, return to the "Focus assist" screen and scroll down to the "Automatic rules" section

9 Slide the toggle button for "During these times" to **On**, then toggle the other buttons to customize the rules

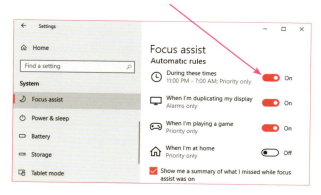

You can also click the **Focus assist** button in the Action Center to quickly switch between "Off", "Priority only", and "Alarms only" mode.

The **Data usage** feature is improved to provide greater control of data.

The **Data usage** detail screen lists how much data has been consumed by each app on your system over the previous 30 days to help identify heavy data usage.

Managing data storage

If you connect to the internet via a metered network connection on a limited data plan, Windows 10 can help you control your data consumption to stay within your agreed limit:

1 Go to Settings, Network & Internet, then choose the **Data usage** option on the left pane

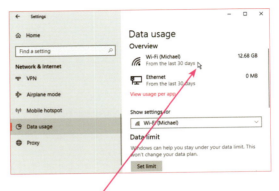

2 Click on a connection in **Overview** to see more detail

3 Return to the Overview screen and click the **Set limit** button

4 Choose the limits that match your data plan, then click the **Save** button to apply the data limit

5 Return to the Overview screen and scroll down to **Background data**

6 Check the **Always** option to "Limit what Store apps and Windows features can do in the background"

Where your device has limited data storage capacity, Windows 10 can help you efficiently manage storage space:

1 Go to Settings, System, then choose the **Storage** option on the left pane to see the "Storage Sense" settings

2 Slide the toggle button to the **On** position for Windows to free up space automatically

The **Storage Sense** feature is improved to delete more temporary files and allow you greater control of when it should run.

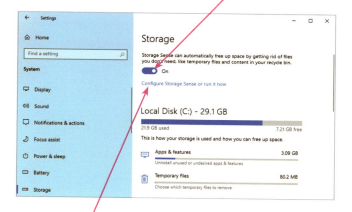

3 Click the **Configure Storage Sense or run it now** link

4 Choose to run Storage Sense **During low free disk space** – or choose a daily, weekly, or monthly schedule

5 Check the option to **Delete temporary files...**

6 Select your preferences for when to empty your **Recycle bin** and **Downloads** folder

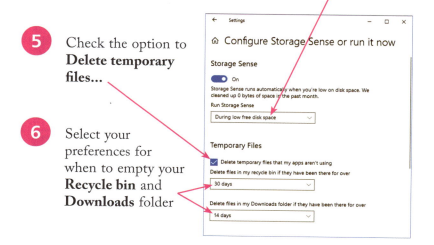

You can scroll down this screen and click a **Clean now** button to free up space at any time.

Monitoring network activity

Windows provides several tools to monitor the activities on your network:

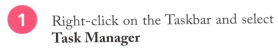

1 Right-click on the Taskbar and select **Task Manager**

2 Select the **More details**, **Performance** tab to see activity charts for the network adapter or adapters (wireless and wired)

3 At the bottom of the window, click **Open Resource Monitor**

4 Comprehensive tables and charts are displayed, giving a real-time view of all networking activity

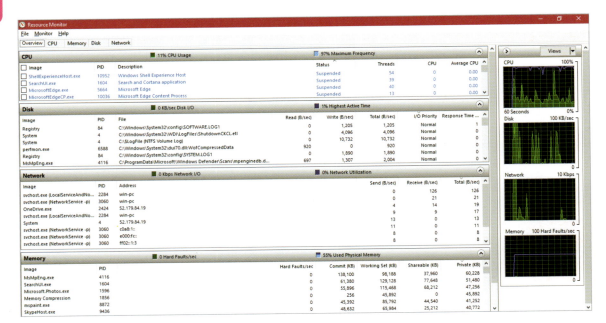

19 Protection and Ease of Access

This chapter demonstrates how Windows 10 protects you and your family. It also describes Ease of Access options and the Windows Mobility Center that is especially useful for portable computer owners.

Guard your privacy

Microsoft recognizes that some users have privacy concerns when using Windows 10, so has provided a Privacy settings page where you can determine what to make public or private. You can also see the information stored about you and delete it if preferred:

1 Go to Start, Settings, **Privacy**, then choose **General**

2 If you prefer not to have your app usage tracked to provide relevant content, move the toggle buttons to **Off** here

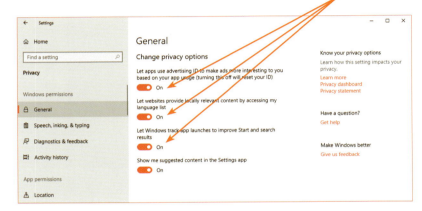

3 Next, choose **Location** in the left-hand pane

4 If you prefer not to reveal your location for local content, click **Change** then move the pop-up toggle button to **Off**

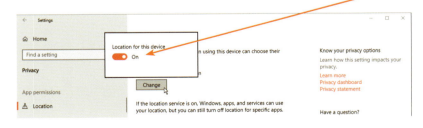

5 Now, choose **Camera** in the left-hand pane

6 If you prefer not to allow apps to use your web camera, move the toggle button to **Off** here

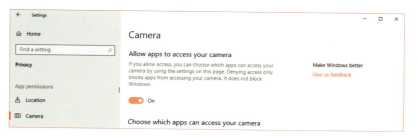

Hot tip

You can leave the toggle button set to **On** for **Camera** and **Location** then scroll down and choose individual apps you want to allow to access your camera.

7 Choose **Microphone** in the left-hand pane

8 If you prefer not to allow apps to use your microphone, move the toggle button to **Off** here

9 Choose **Account info** in the left-hand pane

10 If you prefer not to allow apps to access your name, picture, etc., move the toggle button to **Off** here

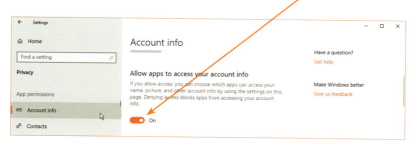

Hot tip

Choose **App diagnostics** in the left-hand pane and set the toggle button to **Off** to deny apps access to other apps on your system.

We suggest you also investigate each of the many other options in the left-hand pane on the **Privacy** page to set each individual option to suit your personal preference. If you want to discover more about any selected option, you can follow the links in the far right-hand pane under the **Know your privacy options** heading.

Account management

When Windows 10 is installed on a computer, an administrator account is created by default. However, the user has the option of creating and using a standard account instead. Let's take a look at both types and see what the pros and cons are:

Administrator account
The administrator account has complete access to the computer and can make any desired changes.

Most people use it for two reasons:

- It's already there.

- It allows them to do whatever they want on the computer.

Note that any program that is run on an administrator account also has complete access to the computer. This is how malware, viruses and rootkits get on to a user's system. It is also possible for the user to cause unintentional damage to their system due to having access to system tools like the Windows Registry and the System Configuration utility.

Standard accounts
Standard accounts are much safer as they do not allow users to make unauthorized changes that affect the system. If a standard account user tries to install a program, for example, they will get a User Account Control (UAC) prompt to provide an administrator password before being allowed to do so.

However, while they may not be able to install programs, make changes to global settings, etc., they will be able to do just about anything else. Therefore, on a day-to-day basis, using a standard account will present no problems to the average user.

The ideal setup, then, is to create a standard account for daily use. This helps protect the user from viruses and malware as they are not allowed to run. Should the user need to make a change that requires administrator permission, they don't even need to log out and then log back in as an administrator – they simply provide the administrator password in the UAC dialog box that appears.

It is also possible to run programs under the administrator account by right-clicking the file to be run and selecting **Run as administrator** from the context menu.

A Windows 10 computer must have at least one **administrator** account.

Doing your day-to-day computing with a **standard** account will help protect your PC from viruses and malware.

You can easily create a standard account by following these steps:

1 Go to the Start menu and open Settings, Accounts, and then click **Family & other users**. In the new window, under "Other users", click **Add someone else to this PC**

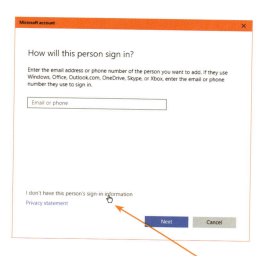

2 Select the option at the bottom **I don't have this person's sign-in information**, then in the next screen, select **Add a user without a Microsoft account**

3 Now, enter the **User name**, **Password** (twice), and answer three **In case you forget your password** questions that may be used to access this account

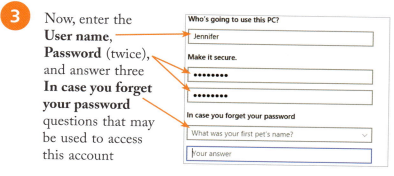

You must complete all fields in the **Who's going to use this PC?** screen.

4 Click **Next** to see a new account is created – by default a standard account

...cont'd

You may at some point wish to change an administrator account to a standard account, or vice versa.

1 Go to Settings, then click Accounts, **Family & other users**

Standard account holders **cannot make changes** to other user accounts.

2 Choose the user account, then click **Change account type**

In this example, "Jennifer" is now an **administrator**.

3 Select **Administrator** from the drop-down menu, then click the **OK** button to apply the change

Set up Family Safety

With Windows 8, child protection was achieved by creating a standard account and then activating the Family Safety utility for that account. Windows 10 simplifies the procedure by offering a Child account option, which is simply a standard account for which the Family Safety utility has already been activated.

Windows 10 makes it easier to **monitor** your children's online activity.

1 Go to Start, Settings, Accounts, then click **Family & other people**. In the new window, click **Add a family member** and select the option to **Add a child**

2 Enter the child's existing email address, then click **Next**, or click **The person I want to add doesn't have an email address**, to create one

Existing standard accounts can be **converted** to Child accounts.

327

3 Now, click **Confirm** to add the child user – and see that an invitation has been sent to the child's email address

4 The new Child account is created, and Family Safety begins monitoring it automatically

You can monitor and control your children's internet activities from the **Manage family settings online** link, or remotely by accessing the Family Safety website at **account.microsoft. com/family**

Defend the system

Windows 10 provides a central location where you can easily manage all your device's security settings:

Windows Security is a convenient new feature in Windows 10.

1 Go to Start, **Windows Security**

2 The status of seven security categories is indicated by check marks over the category icons

Choose **Scan options**, **Windows Defender Offline scan** if you are having difficulty removing malicious software.

3 Click the **Virus & threat protection** icon to see the status and history of your Windows 10 antivirus protection

Below the **Health report** is a **Fresh start** option to start over with a clean installation of Windows 10 – as good as new.

4 Click the **Device performance & health** icon to check for issues and system recommendations

5 Click the **Firewall & network protection** icon to see the status and network, and to troubleshoot network problems

Click **Allow an app through firewall** if you are sure you can trust a blocked app.

6 Click the **App & browser control** icon to control how Windows Defender SmartScreen checks for unrecognized apps and files online

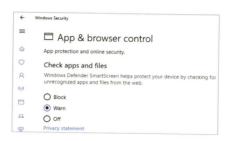

Do not turn SmartScreen to **Off** – it provides better online protection.

7 Click the **Family options** icon to specify **Parental Controls** for your children's online safety and to track their digital lives

You can click the **View family settings** link to visit the Family Safety website at **account. microsoft.com/family**

8 Click the **Account protection** icon to specify security settings for your account and sign-in options

Windows Security was extended by the addition of **Account protection** and **Device Security** features.

9 Click the **Device security** to see details of security features that are built into your device

Ease of Access

Windows 10 provides a number of accessibility options designed to help users see, hear, and use their computers. These options are all available in the **Ease of Access** settings:

1 Go to Start, Settings, and click **Ease of Access**

2 Click **Narrator** and slide the toggle button to the **On** position – to hear the screen reader say "Starting Narrator"

3 Click **Magnifier** and slide the toggle button to the **On** position – choose your zoom level

4 Click **Keyboard** and slide the toggle button to the **On** position – click the on-screen keys to type

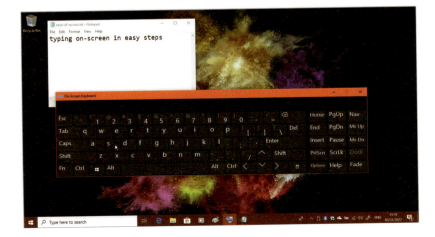

Start Mobility Center

You'll find Windows Mobility Center (WMC) on any portable computer, though not usually on a desktop or all-in-one computer. The utility is basically a control panel that provides all the Windows options specific to portable computers in one easily-accessed location.

There are several ways to open Windows Mobility Center. These include:

- Press **WinKey** + **R** to open the Run box. Type "mblctr", then press **Enter**.

- Go to the Control Panel, Hardware and Sound. Then, click **Windows Mobility Center**.
- You get a link to Windows Mobility Center when you right-click the Battery icon in the System Tray.

When the utility opens, you will see the following window:

The options offered depend on the type of computer and the hardware it is using.

Don't forget

If you are using a desktop PC, Windows Mobility Center may **not** be accessible.

Don't forget

The options in Windows Mobility Center may **differ** from device to device.

Screen management

Windows Mobility Center provides several options related to screen management, via slider controls and icon buttons.

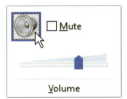

Brightness

The first is Display brightness. This is an important setting with laptops, as the higher it is set, the quicker the battery will run down. The Mobility Center provides a quickly-accessible way of adjusting this setting. If you click on the icon button, you will open the computer's **Power Options** utility, from where you can make changes to various settings including the display brightness.

Volume

As with the brightness setting, the higher the PC's volume level, the greater the load on the battery. You can adjust it with the slider, check the Mute box, or click the icon button to open the **Sound** utility for more options.

External Display

The External Display option allows you to connect your laptop to a different monitor, duplicate the display, or extend the display. Click the icon button to open the **Screen Resolution** utility. If you click **Connect display**, you will open **Project** options in the Windows interface. Both offer the options mentioned above.

Presentation Settings

Laptops are often used in business to give presentations. With this in mind, the **Presentation Settings** option, which is only available in Windows 10 Pro edition, makes it possible to pre-

configure a laptop's settings in terms of volume, screen saver, and background so that they will not detract from the presentation. To do this, click the icon and make your adjustments as shown on the right. Click **OK**, and then click the **Turn on** button. When the presentation is finished, you can revert to the normal settings by clicking the **Turn off** button.

Hot tip

Many people connect their laptops to their **main PC monitor** to take advantage of the larger and usually better displays these offer.

Battery status

The main drawback with portable computers such as laptops is the constant need to conserve battery power. To this end, Windows Mobility Center provides options that help to manage this aspect of portable computing. All the settings described on page 332 affect to some degree the length of time the battery will last. Users looking to conserve battery power will benefit by lowering these settings as far as possible.

A related option provided by Windows Mobility Center is battery power monitoring, or status. This tells the user the percentage of power remaining in the battery.

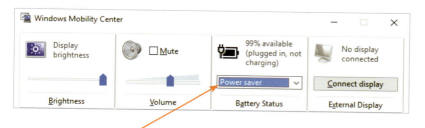

The drop-down menu provides three basic options:

- **Power saver** – this option will extend battery life.

- **High performance** – this option reduces battery life.

- **Balanced** – this option is a compromise between performance and battery life.

Clicking the Battery icon opens the **Power Options** dialog box, which provides settings with which to fine-tune the **Power saver**, **High performance** and **Balanced** options.

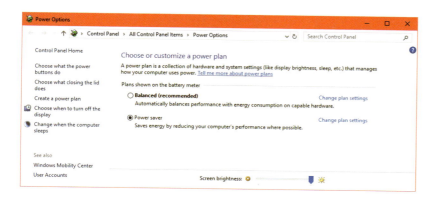

You can also see the battery status from the Battery icon in the System Tray. If the battery is fully charged, the icon will look like this:

If it is running low, it will look like this:

Hover over the icon and you will see the percentage of power remaining:

Power options

This feature is provided for all types of computer, though it takes on particular significance for battery-powered PCs:

1 Go to Start, Settings, System, then click **Power & sleep**

2 You can select when to turn off the PC, and when to send the PC to sleep, when powered by mains or battery

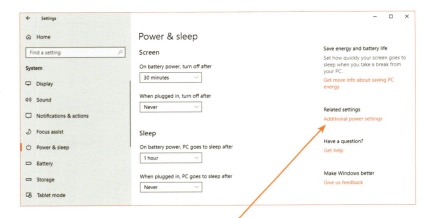

3 Click the **Additional power settings** option, then select **Choose what the power buttons do**

4 From the drop-down menus select **Do nothing**, **Sleep**, **Hibernate**, **Shut down** or **Turn off the display** for when you perform various actions on your computer

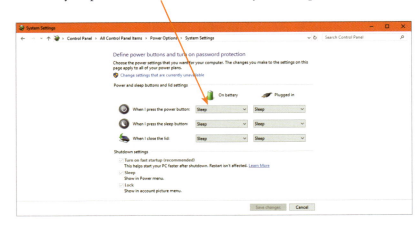

20 Troubleshooting

This chapter describes how Windows 10 attempts to identify issues, and provides a set of troubleshooters and a Steps Recorder. It also demonstrates facilities that allow a friend to remotely connect to your computer and how you could improve program compatibility.

Troubleshooting settings

1 Expand the **Maintenance** section to review the status of the monitoring that is being applied

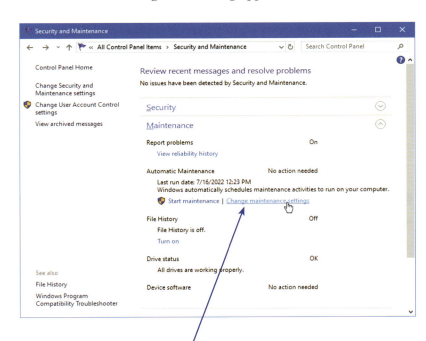

Entries will only appear here when there are problems that Windows has identified and for which **solutions** are available.

2 Click **Change maintenance settings** to specify the scope of problem analysis and maintenance on your system

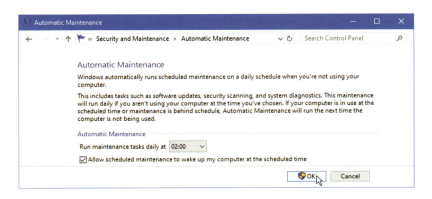

You may want to turn off these options for a system that is being operated by an **inexperienced user**, so they won't have to deal with troubleshooting responses.

3 By default, Windows will remind you when the System Maintenance troubleshooter can help fix problems, and will also allow users to browse for online troubleshooters

Windows troubleshooters

1 Open **Control Panel, Troubleshooting** to see a list of categories and the troubleshooters available within these to handle common problems

339

2 Select a task that appears to match the problem you have, or click the most appropriate category

3 Windows searches online to find any troubleshooting packs in that category

4 The troubleshooters are listed by their sub-categories

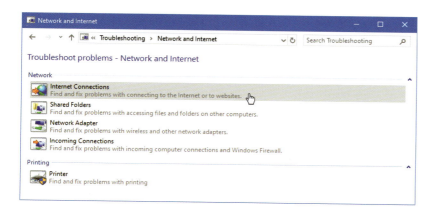

Don't forget

If you encounter a problem, and find no related messages in **Security and Maintenance** you can try the troubleshooters provided by Windows.

Hot tip

Depending on the category you select, you should find one or more troubleshooters **online**, ensuring that you have the latest support for the problem area.

Troubleshooter in action

1 To illustrate, select **Connect to the Internet**, in the **Network and Internet** category

Hot tip

You can also troubleshoot problems by going to Start, Settings, then search for "Troubleshoot" and select this option. Select the problem category then click the **Run the troubleshooter** button that appears.

2 Click **Next** to run the troubleshooter, which carries out a series of checks to detect any internet connection issues

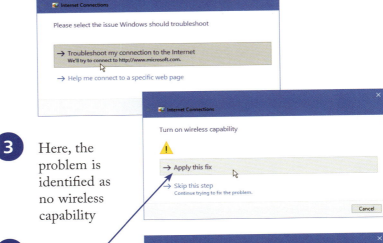

3 Here, the problem is identified as no wireless capability

4 Click **Apply this fix** to try to resolve the problem

5 See a confirmation if the problem is fixed

Steps Recorder

If troubleshooting doesn't help, and you need to report the problem, you can use the Steps Recorder to automatically capture the steps you take, including a text description of where you clicked and a screenshot during each click. You can save the data to a file that can be used by a support professional or a friend helping you with the problem.

To record and save the steps:

1 Go to Start, Windows Accessories, **Steps Recorder**

2 When the Steps Recorder has opened, click its **Start Record** button, then go through the steps to reproduce the problem

3 You will see that the Start Record button label has changed to **Pause Record** – click this to pause recording

4 The Start Record button label has now changed to **Resume Record** – click this to resume recording

5 Click **Add Comment** whenever you want to make notes about any step in the process you are recording

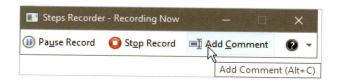

Beware

Some programs – for example, a full-screen game – might not be captured **accurately** or might not provide useful details.

Hot tip

If you want to record any activities that need administrator authority, you must run the **Steps Recorder** as an administrator.

Hot tip

When you record steps, anything you type will not be recorded. If it is relevant to the problem, use the comment option to note what you type.

6 Type your comments in the box that opens at the bottom-right of the screen

7 Click **Stop Record** when you finish all the steps

8 Click **Save**, then choose a name and location for the report – e.g. "MyProblemReport" and your Desktop

9 The report is saved as a compressed Zip file in your chosen location

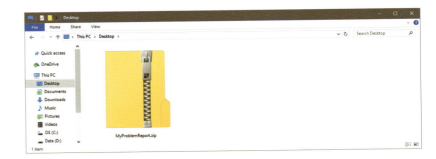

View the report

1 Double-click the compressed Zip file, then double-click the MHTML document (**.mht**) that it contains

2 The report opens in a web browser window

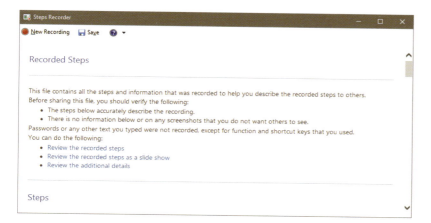

Hot tip

There is a summary of the contents and links to the individual steps, and to additional details that contain technical information intended for advanced users.

3 Each step has a description of the action taken, plus a screenshot of the full screen at that point

Don't forget

You can view the actions and screenshots as a slide show, which proceeds automatically, showing a new step every few seconds.

Send and respond

1 Your helper opens the invitation file and enters the connection password

2 You are notified of the acceptance, and asked to confirm you will allow the helper to connect to your computer

3 Your helper can now see your Desktop on his/her monitor, and observe any actions

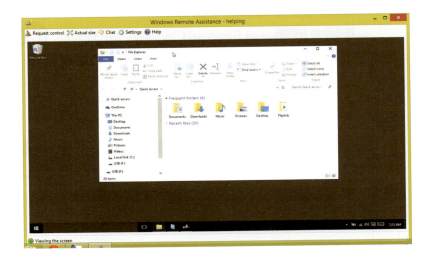

4 Your helper can click **Request control**, asking to

operate your computer using his/her mouse and keyboard

5 When you receive the request, click **Yes** to allow your helper to share control of your Desktop

Click the **Yes** button in Step 5 to allow your helper to respond to User Account Control prompts.

6 Now, either you or your helper can operate the computer using mouse and keyboard

Click **Pause** if you want to temporarily stop the Remote Assistance session – for example, to carry out a separate task.

7 Click **Chat** to communicate via instant messaging, or click **Stop sharing** to return full control to you alone

8 Close Remote Assistance when you have finished

...cont'd

4 Confirm your restore point, then click **Finish**

Beware

If System Restore is being run in Safe Mode or from the System Recovery Options menu, it cannot be undone.

5 Click **Yes** to continue and carry out the System Restore

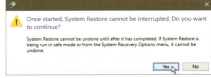

6 Windows will close down and restart, and the system files are restored to the required versions

7 If this does not fix the problem, you can **Undo System Restore**, or **Choose a different restore point**

Don't forget

Once started, you must allow System Restore to complete. You can then Open System Restore and select Undo, if you want to revert to the initial state.

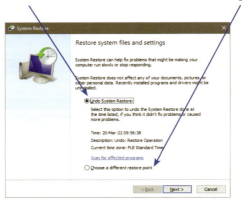

Start in Safe Mode

1 Open Settings, then select **Update & Security**

2 Click **Recovery** on the left-hand pane

3 Under "Advanced start-up" on the right, click **Restart now**

4 The computer will reboot and ask you to "Choose an option" – choose **Troubleshoot**

Troubleshoot
Reset your PC or see advanced options

5 In the "Troubleshoot" screen, choose **Advanced options**

Advanced options

6 Next, choose **See more recovery options**, **Startup Settings**, then click the **Restart** button

Startup Settings
Change Windows startup behavior

7 When the "Startup Settings" screen appears, press the **F4** key or the number 4 key to enable Safe Mode. The computer will now reboot into Safe Mode

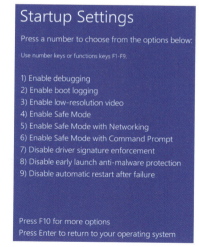

Startup Settings

Press a number to choose from the options below:

Use number keys or functions keys F1-F9.

1) Enable debugging
2) Enable boot logging
3) Enable low-resolution video
4) Enable Safe Mode
5) Enable Safe Mode with Networking
6) Enable Safe Mode with Command Prompt
7) Disable driver signature enforcement
8) Disable early launch anti-malware protection
9) Disable automatic restart after failure

Press F10 for more options
Press Enter to return to your operating system

Note that Startup Settings replaces the Advanced Boot menu found in earlier versions of Windows. Unlike the Advanced Boot menu, Startup Settings cannot be initiated while the PC is booting by pressing the **F8** key. It can only be initiated from within Windows as described above, from a Windows 10 installation disk, or a Windows 10 Recovery drive. Also, the **Startup Settings** options cannot be selected with the mouse or keyboard – a specific key is allocated to each option.

Hot tip

Safe Mode starts Windows with a **limited** set of files and device drivers, **without** the usual startup programs and services. This validates the basic settings.

Don't forget

Safe Mode cannot be initiated by pressing the **F8** key as with previous versions of Windows.

NEW

Startup Settings is a new **feature** in Windows 10.

Program compatibility

When you install programs on your Windows 10 PC, you may come across one or two that refuse to run – this could be due to an incompatibility issue with Windows 10. A possible solution can be sought with the Program Compatibility Troubleshooter. This will recreate the Windows environment for which they were designed and may get them running.

Hot tip

Another way of applying compatibility settings is to right-click the program's executable (setup) file. Click **Properties** and then open the **Compatibility** tab. From here, you can choose an operating system that the program is known to work with.

1 Go to Start, Windows System, Control Panel, (View by: Category), Programs, **Run programs made for previous versions of Windows**

2 Click **Next**, and after a few moments you will see a dialog box showing you a list of all the programs on the PC

Hot tip

If a program won't install at all, the method described on the **right** won't work. In this case, use the method **above**.

3 Select the one you're having trouble with and click **Next**, then select **Troubleshoot program**

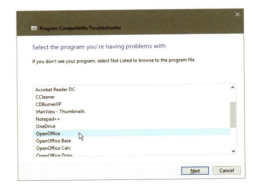

Hot tip

Once a program has been successfully set up, it will use the compatibility settings **every time** it is run.

4 Choose the appropriate problem from the list and click **Next**

5 Windows will try to fix the issue. If the problem hasn't been resolved, click **No, try again** with different settings to repeat the procedure with other possible causes

21 Backup and recovery

You need to keep copies
of your data so you can
recover your system if you
have problems. This chapter
describes how to make
backups and how to restore
your system when necessary.

Sync settings

An important feature in Windows 10 is the ability to synchronize your settings across all your devices. This means that when you change your Desktop background, for example, the change is replicated on all your devices.

Because your settings are stored in the Cloud, not only are they synchronized, they are thus also automatically backed up. Furthermore, the backup is dynamic as it is done in real time.

The synchronization feature is enabled by default, so you may wish to review exactly what is being synchronized, and thus backed up.

1 Open Settings, Accounts, then click **Sync your settings** in the left-hand panel

2 In the right-hand panel, you'll see all the settings on your PC that can be synchronized. At the top, under "Sync your settings" you can turn synchronization on or off altogether

354

With synchronization turned on, your data is **accessible on all the devices** you are logged in to with a Microsoft account. Your settings, such as Wallpaper, can also be replicated on all devices.

In Windows 10, sync settings are found in the **Accounts** category.

If you have **critical** or **confidential** files on OneDrive, you may want to think carefully about synchronizing passwords.

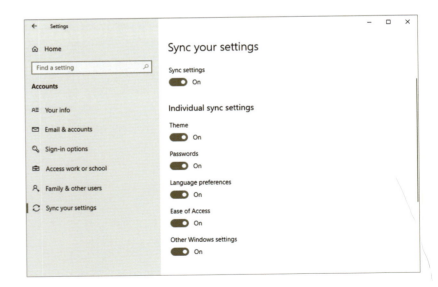

3 You can toggle individual settings on and off by clicking on them

Sync to OneDrive

While the synchronization feature makes it possible to automatically back up your settings, it cannot back up your files and folders. For this, you need the OneDrive feature that is built into Windows 10.

1 Open any File Explorer window, and on the left-hand side you'll see a OneDrive item in the Navigation pane

2 Click on the **OneDrive** item to see all your folders whose contents are stored as duplicates in the Cloud

3 You can keep this selection of folders as they are, add more, delete them, or create your own folder structure

4 To back up a file or folder, just save it within OneDrive – it will be automatically duplicated in the Cloud

5 You can save files to the OneDrive folder from a program's **Save As** menu

The OneDrive **folder** works like any other folder – files can be added, deleted, renamed, etc.

On-Demand Sync lets you see the files stored on OneDrive in File Explorer as **placeholders**. If a copy is not stored locally it will be downloaded automatically when you try to open it. Check the **Files On-Demand** option in the OneDrive settings to enable this feature.

355

Some programs such as Microsoft Office provide a **Save to OneDrive** menu option.

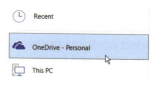

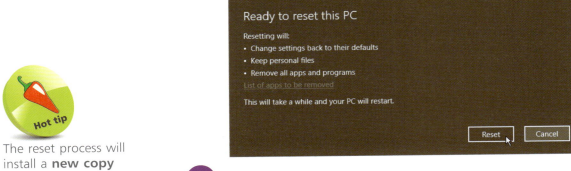

Hot tip

The reset process will install a **new copy** of Windows 10 while retaining the user's Windows apps, data and personalization settings. Everything else will be deleted.

5 Click **Next** on the warning screen, then on the next screen, click **Reset** – the computer will reboot and reset

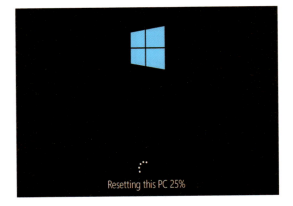

Beware

The big **drawback** is that users will probably have to reinstall/reconfigure most of their software, and reconfigure various Windows settings.

6 When the computer has been reset, Windows begins its setup routine. When that's done, you're back in business

Reinstall your system

The traditional method of completely restoring a Windows PC to its factory settings is to do a clean installation. This wipes the drive clean of all data, after which a new copy of Windows is installed. The procedure is done by booting the PC from the installation disk and is something many will be wary of trying. Windows 10 provides a much simpler method of restoring Windows to its factory settings, courtesy of its Reset utility. You can use the Reset facility like this:

The Reset utility also provides an ideal way of **securely** deleting your data on a computer you are going to sell or scrap.

1 Go to Settings, Update & Security, and choose **Recovery**

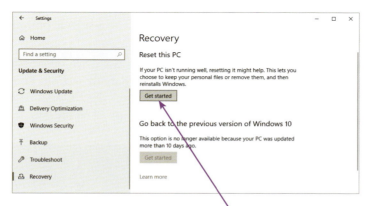

2 Under "Reset this PC", click the **Get started** button

3 When asked to choose an option, choose the option to **Remove everything** to completely reset Windows 10

303

4 Click the **Change settings** link to see your options

5 To remove your files only from the drive where Windows is installed you can accept the default settings and click the **Confirm** button – all data on the PC will be deleted, leaving you with an "as new" copy of Windows

Turn On **Data erasure** to remove files and clean the drive (takes hours). Turn on **Data drives** to remove all files from all drives (for a system that has multiple drives).

6 Now, click the **Reset** button to begin the procedure

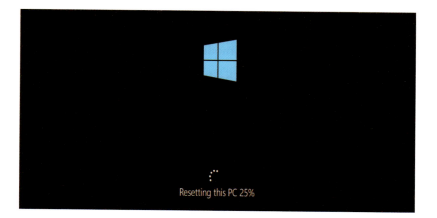

7 The computer will now reboot and you will see the screen above as the Reset procedure begins

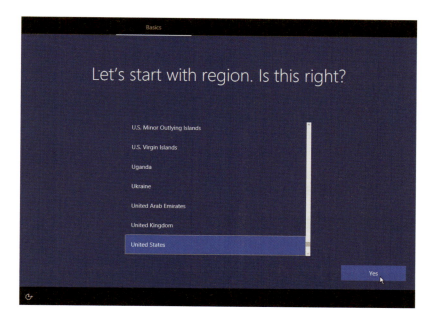

Hot tip

At the end of the Reset, your computer will be exactly how it was when you **first installed** Windows 10.

8 When the Reset is done, Windows goes through its setting-up routine, just like the first time it was installed

…cont'd

Don't forget

By default, backups are made **every hour** and backups are kept forever.

On the "Backup options" page, the **Back up my files** option lets you specify how often your files are backed up – from every 10 minutes to Daily. Consider this option carefully as the more frequent your backups, the more space is used on your backup drive.

The **Keep my backups** option lets you specify how long your backups are kept – from one month to forever, or until space is needed.

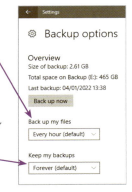

Restoring personal files

To restore a file or folder, scroll down to "Related settings", then click the option to **Restore files from a current backup**. This opens a window showing all your backed-up folders. To restore an entire folder, select that folder, then click the green **Restore** button.

Don't forget

To back up your system by the default settings, or restore personal files, the **backup drive** must be attached.

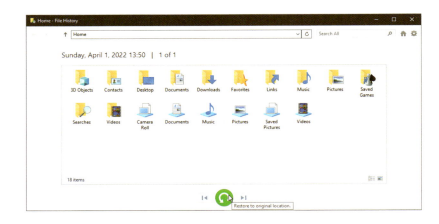

Hot tip

Enable **automatic backups** now – so you won't regret it later.

If you just want to restore a specific file or files within a folder, open the folder, select the file(s), then click the **Restore** button.

Create a system image

A system image is an exact copy of a drive and, by default, it includes the drives required for Windows to run. It includes Windows and your system settings, programs, and files. If desired, it can be configured to include other drives as well.

Should the imaged computer subsequently develop a problem that cannot be repaired, it can be restored from the image.

There are many third-party utilities of this type, such as Acronis True Image, but Windows 10 provides its own.

1 Go to Settings, Update & Security, Backup, then under "Backup using File History" click **More options**

2 Scroll down to "Related settings" and click **See advanced settings** – to open the "File History" dialog:

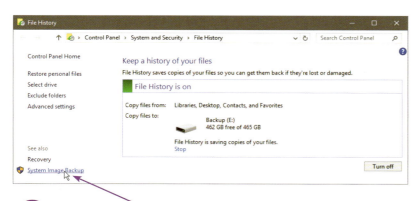

A **system image** will restore the PC to the state it was in when the image was built.

3 Next, click the **System Image Backup** link – to open the "Backup and Restore" dialog

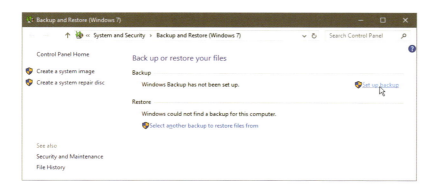

Any type of medium can be used for the image backup. It has to be **separate** to the main system drive, though.

...cont'd

Restoring your system from an image

When you use an image backup to restore your system, be aware that, when done, your system will be exactly the same as when the backup was made. Any changes made to the computer after the backup was made will be lost – this includes files, settings and applications.

How you go about restoring depends on your reason for doing it. If it's because your system is so damaged that you cannot get Windows to start at all, you'll need the aid of a recovery drive, as described on pages 375-376. If it's for some other reason and Windows is working, you can do it within Windows, like this:

1 Go to Settings, **Update & Security**, then choose **Recovery** in the left-hand pane

2 Now, in the right-hand pane, under "Advanced startup", click **Restart now**

If you can't get Windows to start, you'll need a **recovery drive** to restore your system from an image.

Create a system recovery drive **now** – if you leave it until you need it, it will be too late.

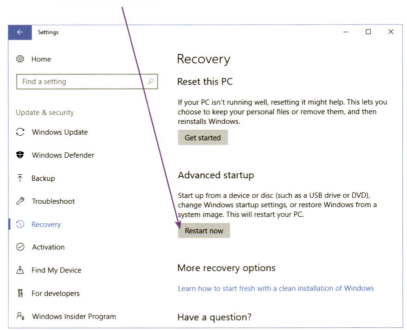

3 When asked to "Choose an option", choose **Troubleshoot**

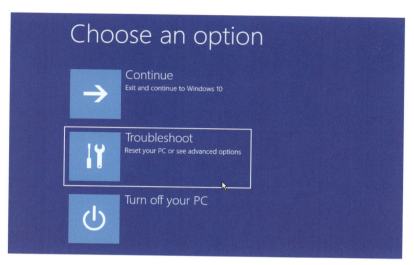

Hot tip

Advanced options also includes **System Restore**, **Start-up Repair**, **Command Prompt** and **Start-up Settings**. These can all be useful, depending on the circumstances.

4 On the "Troubleshoot" page, select **Advanced options**

Beware

The restore procedure **cannot** take place while Windows is running.

…cont'd

5 Now, select **System Image Recovery**. The PC will reboot and the recovery configuration procedure will begin

If you have several image backups, Windows will select **the most recent** one by default.

6 Enter your account password, then select the required image – if you only have one system image, Windows will select it automatically

7 Click **Next**, **Finish** to restore from the image backup

When the image has been restored, the computer will **restart** and boot into your newly-restored Windows.

System recovery drive

There will be occasions when it is impossible to get into Windows for some reason – damaged startup files is a typical example. For this reason, recovery and troubleshooting utilities have to be accessible from outside the Windows environment.

To be able to use the Windows utilities in this type of situation, they have to be first placed on removable media.

1 Go to the Control Panel, (View by: Large icons), and open **File History**

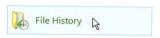

2 In the File History window, click the **Recovery** link at the bottom-left of the window

3 Now, choose the option to **Create a recovery drive**

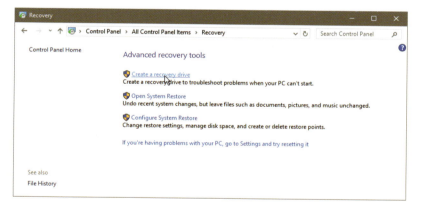

4 Follow the prompts to create a Windows recovery drive

Note that you will need a USB flash drive for this procedure. Also, it will erase anything already stored on the drive. So either use an empty drive or make sure you transfer any important data to another storage device.

Using your recovery drive

The time to use your recovery drive is when you are unable to boot your computer into Windows. When you find yourself in this situation, follow the steps on the next page (page 376).

All the backups in the world are no good to you if you can't get into the system. **Make your recovery drive now**.

1 Connect the recovery drive to your computer

2 Start the PC and go into the BIOS where you need to set the recovery drive as the boot drive – see page 43, where we explain how to do this. The procedure here is the same, apart from the fact that you want to set the recovery drive as the boot drive rather than the CD/DVD drive

3 Restart the computer

4 When the "Choose an option" screen opens, select **Troubleshoot**, then click **Advanced options**

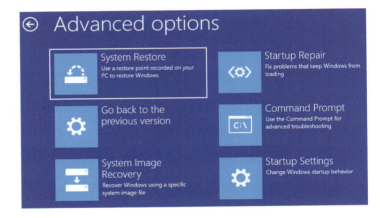

Hot tip

Choosing the **Command Prompt** option restarts the PC in the Windows Recovery Environment that is available before Windows loads. System administrators can enter commands at a prompt to diagnose problems.

Here, you have six troubleshooting and recovery tools that will enable you to resolve most of the issues that are likely to occur. The first option, **System Restore**, will undo any changes made to a system by installing software. So, if you've inadvertently downloaded a virus or malware, System Restore will fix it. You can choose **Go back to the previous version** to return to an earlier installed version of Windows. **System Image Recovery** was explored on pages 372-374, while **Startup Repair** will fix issues that prevent Windows from booting. **Command Prompt** is a troubleshooting tool for advanced users who know diagnostic commands. Finally, **Startup Settings** enables you to start Windows in the various troubleshooting modes illustrated on page 351. These can help you fix a range of problems.

22 Security and encryption

This chapter describes the various encryption facilities that are included in Windows 10 that allow you to protect your sensitive data in the event that your PC is lost or stolen.

Set password to expire

By default, your password can remain the same forever, but you are recommended to change it on a regular basis. Windows can be set to ensure that this happens for Local accounts:

1 Open "Local Users and Groups" (see page 379), select your username and click **More Actions**, **Properties**

You can also double-click the **username** to open Properties.

2 Clear the box for "Password never expires" and click **User must change password at next logon**, then **Apply**, **OK**

Local Security Policy is in Windows 10 Pro and Windows 10 Enterprise editions, but **not** available in the Windows 10 Home edition.

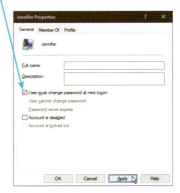

3 Close Local Users and Groups, then open "Local Security Policy" (see page 382) and expand **Account Policies**

You could change the maximum password age to **182 days**, and then you would get a new password twice a year.

4 Select **Password Policy**, then **Maximum password age** to discover the length of password validity

5 When you next sign in to the computer, select your account name as usual and enter your current password

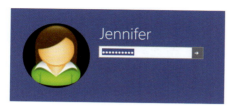

6 Your password needs to be changed. Click **OK**

7 Enter your existing password, then the new password, then confirm the new password and continue

8 Windows changes the password and confirms the change

9 Click **OK** and Windows starts. The password is reset, and future sign-ins will proceed without interruption

When you enter a new password, Windows may remind you that you can create a **password reset disk**. However, it is only needed once, not every time you change your password.

When the specified period has passed, Windows will again notify you that the password has **expired** and require you to provide a new password.

Hide user list

Whenever you start Windows or switch users, the "Sign-in" screen lists all usernames defined for that computer by default.

You'd make changes like this if you had to leave your computer **unattended**. For example, when running a presentation at a meeting or show.

You might feel it would be more secure for the names to remain hidden, especially if you are using your computer in a public area. You can do this using the Local Security Policy.

1 Press **WinKey** + **R** and type "secpol.msc", then click **OK** or press **Enter** to open "Local Security Policy"

2 Expand **Local Policies**, select **Security Options** and locate **Interactive logon: Don't display last signed-in**

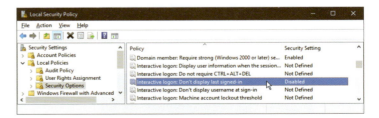

Local Security Policy is in Windows 10 Pro and Windows 10 Enterprise editions, but **not** available in the Windows 10 Home edition.

3 Double-click the entry to display the Properties, select **Enabled**, and then click **OK**

4 The entry will now be shown as Enabled, so click **File, Close** to save the change

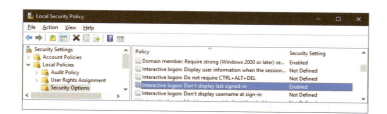

If you have other users on the computer with administrator accounts, they can, of course, view the list of users in **User Accounts**, or make changes to Security Options to reverse the setting.

5 The next time you start Windows or switch users, the "Sign-in" screen is displayed without usernames

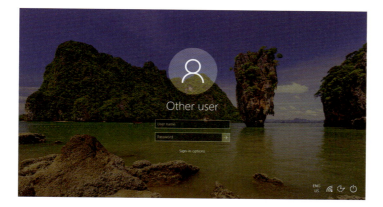

6 Type your username and your password to sign in

There's no user picture, and no **Switch Users** button. If you enter a wrong value, there's no clue and the password reminder is not offered, to preserve the security.

7 If you make a mistake, you are just told the username or password is incorrect, and you must click **OK** and try again

Hot tip

You could use the same device as you used to create a **password reset disk**, since it has the same security requirements.

7 Provide a password, and re-enter it to confirm. Click **Next**

8 Click **Browse...** to choose the destination drive

9 Select the storage device, enter the file name, and click **Save**

Beware

Remove the storage media and **store it in a safe location**, since it can enable anyone to access your encrypted files.

10 Click **Next** to confirm name and location

11 Click **Finish** to complete the Wizard

To restore the certificate, insert the backup media, run **certmgr. msc** to open Certificate Manager, select Personal, Action, All Tasks, Import, then follow the Certificate Import Wizard.

BitLocker To Go

You can encrypt a removable drive with Windows Pro or Enterprise versions, like this:

1 Connect the drive and press **WinKey + X** to open the Power User menu. Select **File Explorer**

2 Right-click the drive icon and select **Turn on BitLocker**

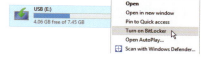

3 Select **Use a password to unlock the drive**, then enter your password twice and click **Next**

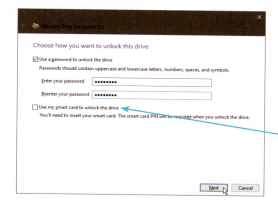

Hot tip

Large organizations use **smart cards** for network authentication and have computers with smart card readers that can access the cards and store information there.

4 Click **Save to a file**, and you will see that a file name is automatically generated

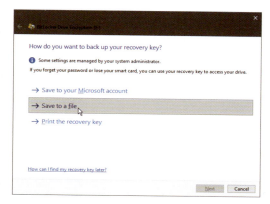

5 Specify the folder and click **Save**

Hot tip

A good choice might be to use the USB flash drive as the **password reset disk** and for your **EFS certificate**.

...cont'd

Hot tip

The **Next** button is grayed out until you save or print the recovery key, then it is enabled and becomes ready to use.

NEW

A more secure encryption mode was introduced in Windows 10 – but this is **not compatible with previous versions** of Windows.

Beware

It can take an hour to encrypt an entire USB drive. If for any reason you need to remove the drive before completion, click **Pause** to interrupt the processing, or else files could be damaged.

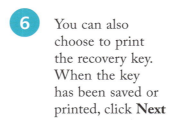

6 You can also choose to print the recovery key. When the key has been saved or printed, click **Next**

7 Choose how much of the drive to encrypt, e.g. the entire drive – then click **Next**

8 Choose your preferred encryption mode, such as Compatible, then click **Next**

9 Click **Start encrypting** and the files on the removable device are processed

10 On completion, a Lock icon is added to the drive to indicate it is now protected by encryption

Access the encrypted drive

You can access an encrypted drive, like this:

1   Insert the removable device and BitLocker will tell you the device is protected

2   Click on the banner to open the password screen

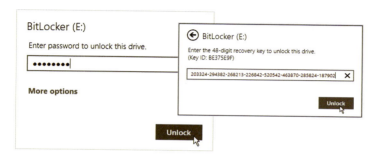

Hot tip

Click **More options** (see Step 3) and you will be able to select **Automatically unlock on this PC** to have Windows remember the password for you.

3   Unlock the drive by entering the password and clicking the **Unlock** button, or if you cannot remember the password click **More options** and enter the recovery key

4   The drive opens. You can open, edit and save files or create new files on this drive, and they will be encrypted

5   Right-click on the drive icon and choose **Manage BitLocker**, then click **Turn off BitLocker** if you want to decrypt the drive back to its original state

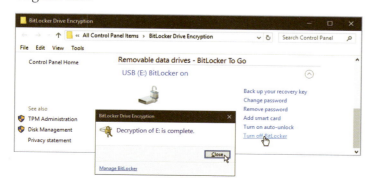

Don't forget

Remember to always use **Safely Remove Hardware** before removing a USB drive.

Whole system encryption

Hot tip

To completely protect your computer and prevent access to your data, you can use BitLocker to **encrypt the Windows boot drive** and internal data drives.

Hot tip

The **TPM Management Console** can also be opened by running a "tpm.msc" command.

Beware

You can enable TPM in the **BIOS**, or you can configure BitLocker to use a **USB drive** instead. However, problems with BitLocker could make your system inaccessible, so only proceed with this if you have adequate technical support.

1 Go to the Control Panel, (View by: Category), **System and Security**, and open **BitLocker Drive Encryption**

2 Select **Turn on BitLocker** for the system or data drive and then follow the prompts to encrypt the drive

3 Any problems with the computer setup will now be detected – for example, you may see this message dialog appear regarding a "Trusted Platform Module" (TPM)

4 Click **Cancel**, then click the **TPM Administration** link back on the BitLocker Drive Encryption screen in Step 2 to discover that the TPM module cannot be found

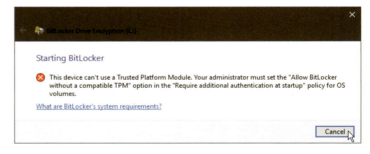

23

Windows PowerShell

This chapter describes the powerful PowerShell command line tool in Windows 10 that can be used to perform administrative tasks.

Opening PowerShell

All editions of Windows 10 include the Windows PowerShell environment, where you can run commands, batch files and applications by typing statements at a console command line.

There are a number of ways to start a PowerShell session:

- Press **WinKey + X** to open the Power User menu. Select **Windows PowerShell**.

- Press **WinKey + R** to open the Run box. Type "powershell", then click **OK**.

- In the Taskbar Search box type "powershell", then hit the **Enter** key.

- On the Apps menu click **Windows PowerShell** in the "Windows PowerShell" group folder.

- Double-click any shortcut to the **powershell.exe** program.

Any method will start a Windows PowerShell session, open at the path location **C:\Users*username*** ready to accept commands.

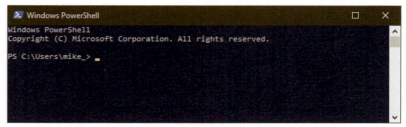

394

● You can open additional independent PowerShell sessions, using the same methods or, from an existing session, type **start powershell** on the command line and press **Enter**.

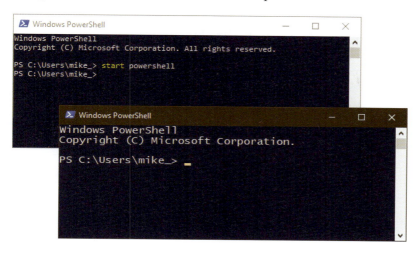

● You can also navigate to **C:\Windows\System32\ WindowsPowerShell\v1.0** and click the **powershell.exe** file icon to open a PowerShell console session.

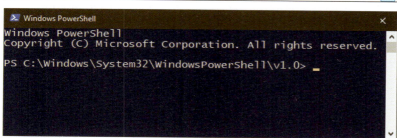

Selecting a folder

You can switch folders in a Windows PowerShell console session using the CD (Change Directory) command. For example, to open the current user's Pictures folder, starting from anywhere:

1 On the Command Line, type these four CD commands, pressing **Enter** after each command:
cd \   cd users   cd "john smith"   cd pictures

Note that **letter case** doesn't matter, but when there are **spaces** in the file or folder names, you should enclose those names within quotation marks.

To avoid problems with long or complex file names, you can open a PowerShell session directly at the required folder.

1 Open File Explorer and use the normal Windows search methods to find the desired folder – from either the Contents pane or the Navigation pane

2 Press and hold **Shift**, then right-click the folder

The PowerShell session is opened and **switched** to the required folder.

3 From the extended right-click menu displayed, select the entry to **Open PowerShell window here**

Running as administrator

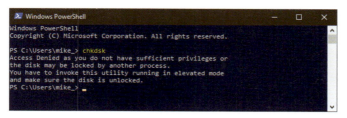

The Windows PowerShell session opened has, by default, the standard user level of privilege. If some commands that you want to run require administrator privilege, you can open an elevated session using the following methods:

- Navigate to **C:\Windows\System32\WindowsPowerShell\ v1.0**, right-click **powershell.exe** and select **Run as Administrator**.

- Enter "powershell" in the Taskbar Search box then right-click on Windows PowerShell and select **Run as Administrator**.

- Right-click on the Start button, or press **WinKey + X**, then choose **Windows PowerShell (Admin)** from the Power User menu.

PowerShell (Admin) from the Power User menu.

- Click **Yes** in the **User Account Control (UAC)** dialog box – to start a Windows PowerShell session with an "Administrator" window title:

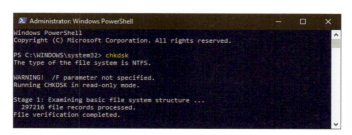

Commands that have a system-wide effect are **restricted** to run only in the elevated administrator mode.

You can also type **start powershell** on the command line of an existing administrator session to get another administrator session – no UAC required.

Notice that each Administrator PowerShell session starts in the **C:\WINDOWS\system32** folder.

Creating shortcuts

You can configure a shortcut to **powershell.exe** to always start in administrator mode:

1 Create a shortcut to the **powershell.exe** program file (at **C:\Windows\System32\ WindowsPowerShell\v1.0\powershell.exe**)

2 Right-click the shortcut and select the **Properties** item

3 Select the **Shortcut** tab and click the **Advanced...** button

4 Check the box **Run as administrator** and click **OK**, then **OK** again

5 Right-click the shortcut icon, select **Rename** and give it a meaningful name – for example, you could rename "Standard Commands" to "Elevated Commands"

6 Double-click the renamed shortcut to start the administrator session

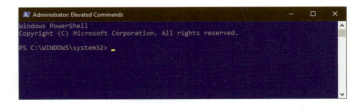

Adjusting appearance

You can adjust the Properties shortcut to control the appearance of the PowerShell window that is launched by that shortcut:

1 Right-click the shortcut icon and click **Properties**

2 Select the **Options** tab

From here, you can adjust the size of the flashing cursor, change how the command history is managed, and change edit options.

3 Select the **Font** tab to choose a different font

4 The recommended font is **Consolas**, since this is a ClearType font that will be more readable in the window

5 Select **Layout** to change the buffer size and screen size

Adjust the width if the default 80 characters is not enough, and change the height (in this case from the default 25 lines to 10 lines). A vertical scrollbar allows you to view the whole buffer of information.

You can also adjust the properties from the Windows PowerShell window – right-click on the title bar then choose **Properties** from the context menu.

As PowerShell provides automatic **syntax coloring**, it is best to avoid changing the default window colors.

The fonts for the Windows PowerShell window must be **fixed-pitch** – i.e. the letters and characters each occupy the same amount of horizontal space.

Using PowerShell

You can use Windows PowerShell to carry out tasks that are not easily achieved using the normal Windows functions. A typical example is to create a text file containing the names of all the files of a particular type in a folder:

1 Open a prompt at the required folder, using the Shift + right-click menu option **Open PowerShell window here**

2 Type this command at the prompt, then press the **Enter** key **dir *.jpg > filelist.txt**

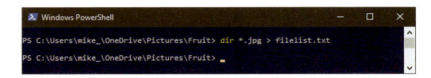

3 Open the folder to see a new file called "filelist.txt", then open that file to see a list of all the JPG files it contains

To list a different type of file, just change **.jpg** to the required file type; e.g. **.doc**. You can also list more than one file type – for example: **dir *.jpg *.tif > filelist.txt**.

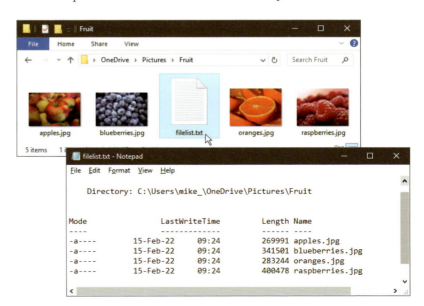

...cont'd

If your Windows PowerShell session is already open, you need to switch directories to get to the required folder. Here, you can use Windows features to assist the PowerShell operation.

1 Open the required folder in File Explorer

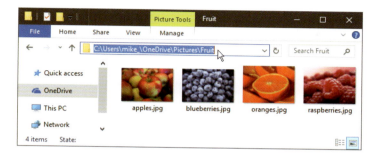

2 Click the Address bar to show the path, and press **Ctrl** + **C**

3 Switch to the Windows PowerShell console and type the command **cd** (followed by a single space)

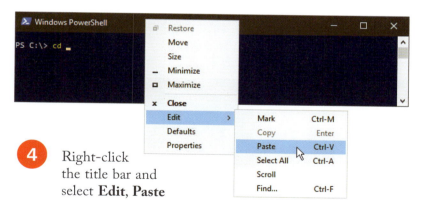

4 Right-click the title bar and select **Edit**, **Paste**

When you select Paste, the contents of the Clipboard are **copied to the command line**, thus completing the CD command already started.

5 Press **Enter** to run the command and switch directories

Discovering cmdlets

The Windows PowerShell console recognizes the familiar DOS commands that are available in the older Command Prompt console, such as **cd**, **dir**, **cp**, **mv**, **rm**, or **cls**, but these are merely aliases to PowerShell "cmdlets" (command-lets). More importantly, Windows PowerShell has many additional cmdlets that make it much more powerful than Command Prompt.

Each cmdlet is named as a hyphenated verb-noun pair. For example, there is a cmdlet named **Get-Alias**. This can be used to discover the name of the cmdlet represented by a DOS alias.

You can see a list of all PowerShell aliases, functions, and cmdlets by typing **Get-Command**. Usefully, every cmdlet has its own individual help file that can be seen by typing **Get-Help** followed by the name of the cmdlet you are seeking help with.

Cmdlets that **Get** return an object that has methods and properties, which you can use to work with PowerShell most effectively. Methods and properties can be listed by "piping" the returned object through to a **Get-Member** cmdlet and can be filtered by adding a **-MemberType** parameter:

1. Open PowerShell, then enter this command to discover the name of the cmdlet representing the **cd** DOS alias
Get-Alias cd

2. Next, enter this command to see a long list of all Windows PowerShell aliases, functions, and cmdlets
Get-Command

3. Scroll through the list to discover a **Get-Date** cmdlet

...cont'd

4 Enter this command to discover more about the cmdlet
Get-Help Get-Date

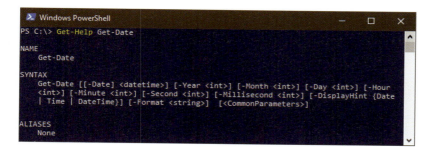

PowerShell is not case-sensitive, so **Get-Help** could be written in lowercase as **get-help** — but mixed case aids readability.

5 Enter this command to discover the cmdlet properties
Get-Date | Get-Member -MemberType Property

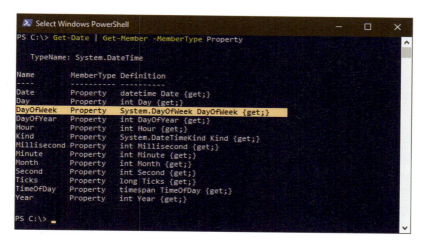

With the piped command, **Get-Date** first returns a Date object, then passes that to the **Get-Member** cmdlet to extract only its properties. Change "Property" to "Method" to see only its methods.

6 Enter these commands in turn to discover the current date and time, and the value of a specific property
Get-Date
(Get-Date).DayOfWeek

The parentheses are required around the cmdlet name to ensure the Date object is first returned before the **DayOfWeek** property value can be extracted.

Combining commands

The true power of Windows PowerShell can be unleashed by combining several commands in a "pipeline". Lines can be broken after each "|" pipe character, and multiple commands can be separated by a ";" semicolon character:

1 Open PowerShell, and type this command, then press Enter
Write-Output "tr:nth-child(even){background:yellow}" |

2 Next, type this command at the >> continuation prompt, then hit Enter to create a style sheet file
Set-Content stripe.css

3 Now, type these commands to create and display a HTML table of date properties styled by the CSS file
Get-Date |
ConvertTo-Html -As List -CssUri stripe.css |
Set-Content date.html ; Invoke-Item date.html

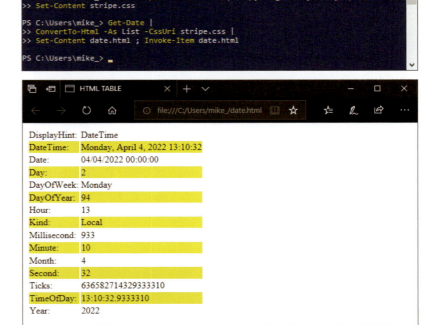

24 Update and maintain

This chapter describes how Windows automatically provides regular updates to the operating system and some apps on your PC to ensure they keep working securely and effectively.

Windows Update

The Windows operating system requires frequent updates to keep it secure and fully operational. Updates are provided on a regular basis for Windows 10 and should be applied when available. You can see what your current update situation is like this:

1 Go to Start, Settings, then click **Update & Security**

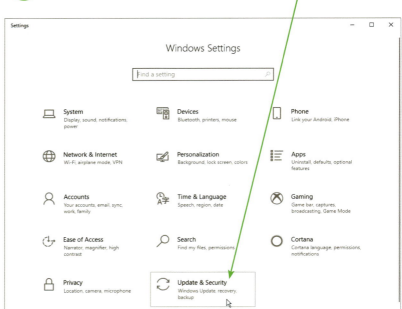

Alternatively, you can type "settings" into the Taskbar Search box, or say "Hey Cortana, open settings", to open the **Settings** window.

2 Next, in the left-hand panel, click **Windows Update**

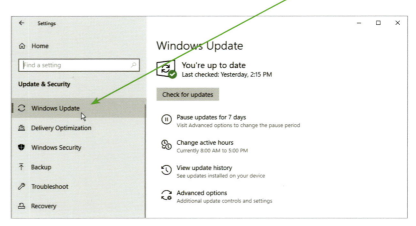

Unlike previous versions of Windows, whose updates only provided **periodical** security patches and bug fixes, the Update model in Windows 10 provides **continuous** security and feature improvements.

3   Now, click the **Check for updates** button

4   Wait to see if any updates are available

5   Any available updates will be downloaded and installed

6   When installation completes, you may be asked to restart the system so that appropriate files can be updated

If Automatic Updating has been set, the indication of updates waiting appears **immediately** when you open Windows Update.

You can selectively apply updates in this manner, but it is much **easier** to let Windows Update do the job automatically.

Update settings

The **active hours** feature is improved to allow you to specify the PC as active up to 18 hours of the day – up from the previous maximum of 12 hours.

1 Open Settings, **Update & Security**, Windows Update, and select the **Change active hours** option

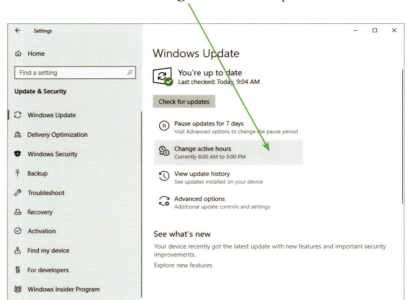

2 Choose to allow automatic adjustment based on activity, or click the **Change** link to open an "Active hours" dialog

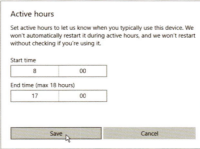

3 Select the **Start time** and **End time** of the period during which you typically use your PC each day

4 Now, click the **Save** button to prevent Windows automatically restarting during the specified period

5 Next, back on the Windows Update screen, select **Advanced options** to configure your update settings

6 To enable the Microsoft Update feature, slide the toggle button for the option to **Receive updates for other Microsoft products when you update Windows** to "On"

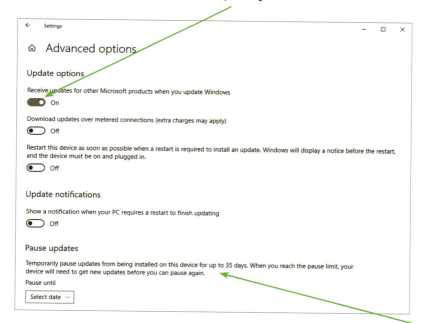

Microsoft **Update** will provide updates for Office, MSN, Windows Defender, and various Windows Server-related products.

The option to schedule update delays for **up to 35 days** can be useful if you want to ensure the reliability of updates before installation.

7 Optionally, also slide the toggle buttons to "On" for the options for **metered connections**, **automatic restarts**, and to **receive a notification** when your PC requires a restart to install an update

Update sources

A new **Unified Update Platform (UUP)** allows much faster downloads and reduced data usage.

Allow updates both from PCs on your **local network** and from the **internet** to be downloaded fastest.

1 Open Settings, Update & Security, Windows Update, and select **Delivery Optimization** on the left pane

2 If you would like to allow updates from multiple sources, slide the toggle button to the **On** position

3 Choose to allow update sources on your local network, or to also allow internet sources

4 Now click the **Advanced options** link on this screen

5 Optionally drag the sliders to choose to limit how much bandwidth to use for downloads

6 Return to the Delivery Optimization screen and click the **Activity monitor** link (below the **Advanced options** link)

7 Here you can examine the **Download statistics** to compare source percentages and average download speeds

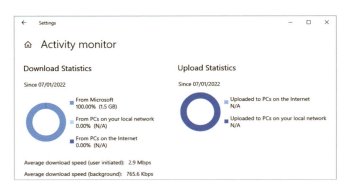

Update history

Updates may be applied automatically in the background, but you can review the activities:

1 Open Settings, Update & Security, Windows Update, and select the **View update history** link

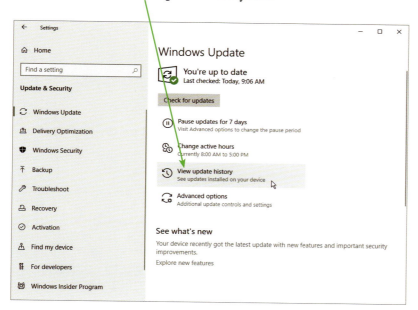

2 Click any > arrow to expand an update category to see installed updates – listed in latest-first order

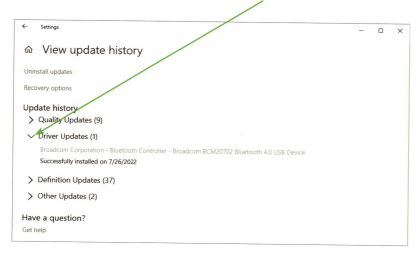

Hot tip

There's an entry for every attempt to apply an update, and results are marked as **Successfully installed** or **Failed to install**. Identify important updates that have failed, and check to ensure that a subsequent update attempt succeeded.

...cont'd

You can review the Windows and other updates that have been installed on your computer, and remove any that may be causing problems.

Hot tip

There are some updates that cannot be removed this way. If that is the case, there will be no **Uninstall** button shown when you select the update.

1 On the "Update history" screen, select the **Uninstall updates** link

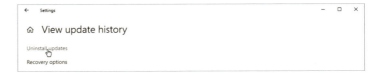

2 Select an update and click **Uninstall** on the toolbar to remove that update

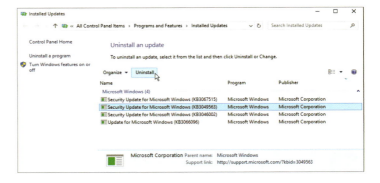

Hot tip

You can switch back and forth between the Updates and the Programs list, using the **Uninstall a program** or **View installed updates** links in the left-hand pane.

3 You can also change the appearance of the update items using the **More options** button on the toolbar – for example, from the Details view above, to Tiles view below

More options button

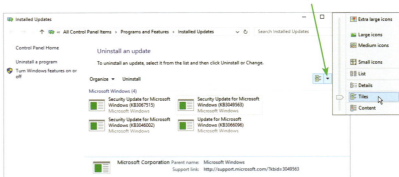

412

Installed updates

Installed updates can also be managed via the Control Panel:

1 Go to Start, Windows System, Control Panel, Programs, then select **Programs and Features**

2 In the left-hand pane, click View installed updates

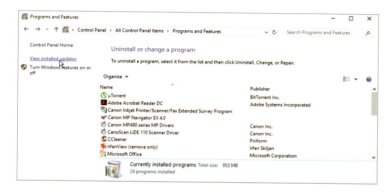

3 To expand or collapse the list of updates for each category, and to view details, click the arrow buttons to the right of each category heading

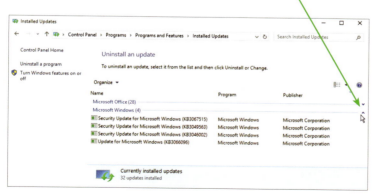

Click the **Uninstall a program** link in the left-hand pane to manage installed programs.

4 Select an update and click Uninstall on the toolbar to remove that update

Upgrading Windows

Sometimes, adding updates isn't enough – you need to upgrade your edition of Windows to an edition that has the extra functions you need. Alternatively, you may want to upgrade from 32-bit Windows to 64-bit Windows, so your computer can take advantage of the larger amounts of memory that 64-bit systems can utilize.

32-bit to 64-bit

This isn't an upgrade in the usual sense – you cannot install the new operating system and retain existing folders and data files. Instead, you create a completely new system, replacing the existing setup, then install your applications and apply Windows updates. You can back up your data files and folders before you make the change and afterwards restore the backup to your revised system. However, you will have to re-install all of your apps, and may need to install 64-bit versions of drivers for devices unless Windows has them.

Upgrading editions

Changing editions can be carried out as a true upgrade. You update the operating system files, but leave your data files and folders unaffected. The application programs that you have installed will continue to operate.

Upgrade paths

With Windows 7 and 8, there were a number of upgrade paths possible between the various versions. Windows 10 provides only one – if you currently have the entry version, Windows 10 Home, you can upgrade it to Windows 10 Pro. To implement this upgrade you will need to buy the Windows 10 Pro Pack from the Microsoft Store – open Settings, **Update & Security**, Activation, then press the **Go to the Store** button:

You can see a **comparison of features** in each edition of Windows 10 on pages 16-17.

You can install **any** edition of 64-bit Windows on your computer if it is 64-bit capable and has enough memory to make the transition worthwhile – ideally 4GB of memory.

Resetting your PC

If you want to return your system to its initial state (if, for example, you are disposing of a PC), Windows 10 provides an easy way to reset the system. This procedure provides three options of how thoroughly the reset should clean the system:

- **Reset Windows only** – this restores the Windows system files and keeps your personal files and apps intact.

- **Reset Windows to new** – this restores the Windows system files and deletes your personal files and apps.

- **Reset Windows and clean** – this restores the Windows system files and completely removes your personal files and apps from the hard disk drive.

You may just want to reset Windows 10 to its original pristine state if you have, over time, installed many apps or if you feel the system has become sluggish. OneDrive proves invaluable for this, as you can simply access your personal files there.

1 Open Settings, Update & Security, then select the **Recovery** option on the left-hand pane

2 Under "Reset this PC", click the **Get started** button

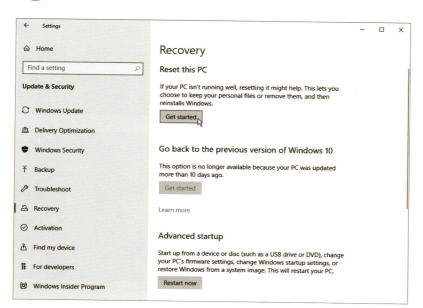

Resetting Windows 10 is **like re-installing** the operating system, so it does take quite a while.

Notice that you may also have an option here to **revert** to the previously-installed version of Windows if you recently upgraded the PC to Windows 10.

...cont'd

3 Choose to keep or remove your personal files – e.g. click **Remove everything**

4 Review the current settings then click **Next** to proceed, or click the **Change settings** link

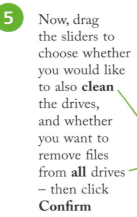

5 Now, drag the sliders to choose whether you would like to also **clean** the drives, and whether you want to remove files from **all** drives – then click **Confirm**

6 Carefully review the actions to be performed by the reset and, if you are happy with these, click the **Reset** button to begin

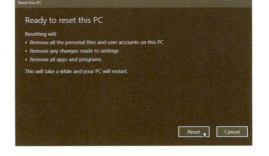

Hot tip

If you are selling the PC you should choose to set **Data erasure** and **Data drives** to "On" to perform the most thorough system reset.

Beware

The **reset** process will require you to enter certain information, such as your location and your Wi-Fi key – just like installing Windows 10 for the very first time.

Disk Cleanup

For everyday tasks, you can use the tools found in drive Properties.

1 Press **WinKey + X**, select File Explorer, This PC, then expand **Devices and drives** in the right-hand pane

2 Next, right-click on a drive and click **Properties** from the context menu – to open the drive's "Properties" dialog box

3 In the Properties dialog box, select the **General** tab

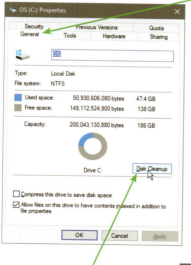

41/

You could also select Disk Cleanup from the list of **Administrative Tools** via Control Panel, or search for it in the Taskbar Search box.

4 Next, click the **Disk Cleanup** button to calculate the disk space that can be released

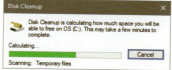

...cont'd

Some categories of file are suggested, but you can select others – e.g. **Recycle Bin** or **Temporary Files** – to increase the amount of space that will be made available.

Click **Cancel** if you change your mind and want to look again at the categories and files selected.

5 Select or clear file categories and click the **View Files** button to see what will be deleted for each category

6 When you are happy with your selection, click **OK** to proceed with Disk Cleanup

7 Click **Delete Files** to confirm that you want to permanently delete the selected files

8 Disk Cleanup now proceeds to free the space used by those files on the selected drive

Note that you may be prompted for administrator permission to remove certain types of file. If so, you'll see a box that lets you extend the permission to all the files of that type. Make sure this box is checked, and then click **Continue**.

Clean up system files

If you need more free space, there will almost certainly be some system files that are not really necessary and can be removed safely. Old system restore files are a typical example (these can occupy gigabytes of disk space).

1 Open the Disk Cleanup dialog, then click the **Clean up system files** button to calculate the disk space that can be released by removing old system files

2 Temporary files can also use a lot of disk space. System error memory dump files are also good candidates for deletion

When you choose **Clean up system files** you'll get the More Options tab where you can, additionally, remove programs that you do not use, or remove older restore points, shadow copies and backups.

Defragmentation

Defragmentation optimizes your file system for faster performance by rearranging files stored on a disk to occupy contiguous storage.

1 For any drive, from the Properties dialog, Tools tab, click the **Optimize** button

2 All drives that can be defragmented are listed, with the latest information about their fragmentation status

Don't forget

The larger the drive, the **longer** the optimization process takes.

3 Select a drive and click the **Analyze** button to see the current state of the drive

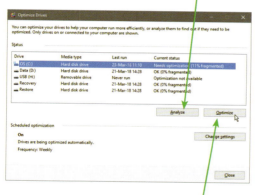

4 Select the drive and click the **Optimize** button to analyze then defragment the drive by relocating files

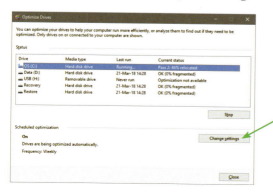

Hot tip

With the schedule turned on, you can still run an immediate defragment. Click **Change settings** to change the frequency or to turn off scheduled optimization entirely.

...cont'd

Windows automates the defragmentation process so that it happens in the background on a regular basis. However, you may wish to change the default settings:

1 If it is not already done, click the **Turn on** button

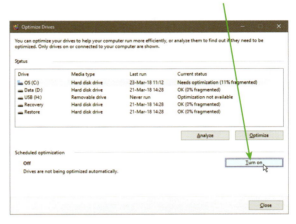

Don't forget

You could also select **Defragment and Optimize Drives** from the Administrative Tools via the Control Panel.

2 Check Run on a schedule. Then, set the desired schedule from the drop-down boxes

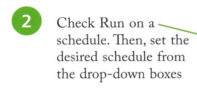

3 Click the **Choose** button and select the drives to be optimized

Hot tip

You can choose **any** drive to defragment, even if you start from Properties for a different drive.

4 Click OK. Your drives will now be defragmented according to the settings specified. Click the **Close** button

25

Windows performance

This chapter describes the Windows 10 tools that measure the performance of your PC and identify issues affecting its performance. It also demonstrates how Windows 10 can even help you speed up the system by using USB flash drives to act as a cache for system files.

System Properties

Windows provides a number of ways for displaying properties of your system. You can see the **Device specifications** and **Windows specifications** on an "About" screen using any of these methods:

- Go to Start, Settings, System, **About**.

- Open the Power User menu by pressing **WinKey** + **X** and selecting **System**.

- Open **File Explorer, This PC** then on the ribbon toolbar select the **Computer** tab and click **System properties**.

The **About** screen displays system properties as part of the modern Settings feature, whereas the alternative described on the opposite page displays system properties as part of the older Control Panel feature.

...cont'd

You can also discover **System Properties** using these two methods:

- Go to Start, Windows System, Control Panel, (View by: Category), **System and Security**, and click on the **System** icon link.

- Press the **WinKey** **Pause/Break** keys.

  +

You can also type "about system" in the Taskbar **Search box** to display System Properties.

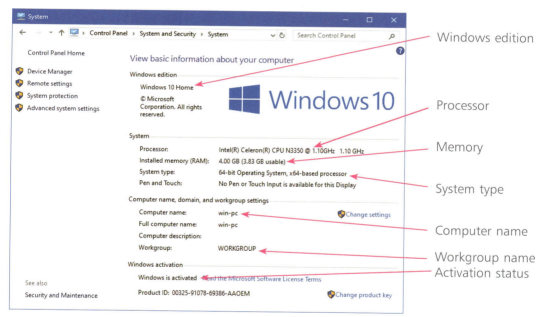

Windows edition

Processor

Memory

System type

Computer name

Workgroup name
Activation status

The pane on the left above provides various useful links, including:

- Device Manager
- Remote settings
- System protection
- Advanced system settings

On the right, you'll find details of the operating system. This tells you the edition of Windows installed on the PC and basic details about the hardware in the PC – processor manufacturer, processor speed, amount of memory and type of system.

Device Manager provides details of the system components. **Advanced system settings** provides the full System Properties.

353

Device Manager

As we saw on page 423, System Properties provides a link to the Device Manager, and you can also access Device Manager from the Power User menu and from the Control Panel.

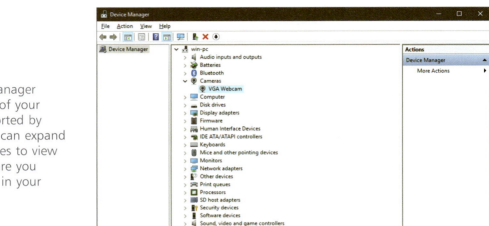

The Device Manager displays a list of your **hardware**, sorted by category. You can expand these categories to view which hardware you have installed in your computer.

So what is it, and what does it do? Essentially, the Device Manager is an extension of the Microsoft Management Console that provides a central and organized view of all the hardware installed in the computer. Its purpose is to provide a means of managing this hardware. For example: hard drives, keyboards, sound cards, USB devices, etc.

Some of the things you can do with the Device Manager include:

- Change hardware configuration.

- Manage hardware drivers.

- Enable and disable hardware.

- Identify and resolve conflicts between hardware devices.

- View a device's status.

- View a device's technical properties.

Click the arrow to the left of the device categories to see what **devices** are in the category.

We'll take a look at how you can troubleshoot malfunctioning devices with the Device Manager on the next page.

Troubleshooting with the Device Manager

When a device in your computer has a problem, it is flagged as such in the Device Manager. Different symbols indicate specific types of problem. For example:

● A black exclamation point (!) on a yellow field indicates the device has a problem – although it may still be functioning.

To see what the issue is, right-click on the device icon and select **Properties**. On the **General** tab under Device Status you may see a message that says "The drivers for this device are not installed". Note that this can also indicate that the driver is present but has been corrupted. To resolve the issue, click the **Update driver** button, or right-click the device icon and choose **Update driver**. Windows will now try to locate the correct driver for the device, and download and install it.

Other symbols indicate other issues that may require attention, for example:

● A down-arrow indicates a disabled device. Note that while the device may be disabled, it is still consuming system resources and is thus reducing the performance of the system.

Right-click on the device icon and select **Properties**. On the **General** tab under Device status you may see a message that says "The device is disabled". To resolve the issue, click the **Enable Device** button, or right-click the device icon and choose **Enable**. Windows will now enable the device ready for use. Click Finish to exit the process.

When you open the Device Manager, take note of any **symbols** you see. These indicate issues that will need to be resolved.

The **Driver** tab in a device's Properties offers options to roll back to a previous driver (i.e. one that works properly), to disable the device, and to uninstall the device.

Improving performance

1 Go to Windows System, Control Panel, (View by: Category), **System and Security**, **System**. Click **Advanced system settings**, and then **Settings...** under "Performance"

2 The default **Let Windows choose what's best for my computer** will have most of the effects selected

You don't need to change hardware; you can use **Performance Options** to make changes to the settings to get more efficient operation.

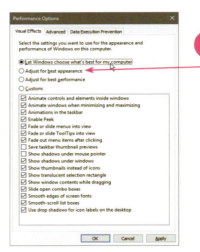

3 Choosing **Adjust for best appearance** means <u>all</u> of the effects will be selected

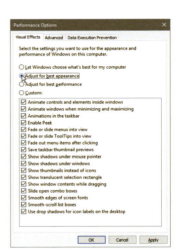

4 You get <u>no</u> effects if you choose **Adjust for best performance**

5 The best balance is to select **Let Windows choose what's best for my computer**, click **Apply**, then deselect effects you can manage without

6 Click **OK**, then **Apply**, and your choices of effects become the Custom setting

Processor scheduling

1 Click the **Advanced** tab, and you can choose to prioritize **Programs** or **Background services**

The usual choice is Programs, but you might choose Background services for a computer that acts as a print server or provides backups.

You should only consider changing the processor scheduling on computers that are mainly used for **background** tasks.

Virtual memory

Windows creates a Paging file to supplement system memory. To review or change the settings:

1 From the Advanced tab, click the Virtual memory **Change...** button

By default, Windows will automatically manage the paging file for your drive or drives. To choose the values yourself:

1 Uncheck **Automatically manage paging file size for all drives**

2 Click **Custom size** and choose sizes, then click the **Set** button to apply

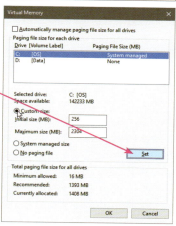

Setting the initial size the same as the maximum will avoid the need for Windows to adjust the size of the paging file, though this may not necessarily improve performance. With multiple drives, choose the one with most space available.

Make sure you always have **at least one drive** with a paging file, even on a large-memory PC, since some programs rely on the paging file.

Data Execution Prevention

The third tab in the Performance Options is for Data Execution Prevention or DEP. This is a security feature intended to prevent damage to your computer from viruses and other security threats, by monitoring programs to make sure they use system memory safely. If a program tries executing code from memory in an incorrect way, DEP closes the program.

If you add a program to the **exception list**, but decide that you do want it to be monitored by DEP, you can clear the box next to the program.

1 By default, Windows will turn on DEP for essential programs and services only

2 You can choose to **Turn on DEP for all programs and services except those I select**

3 Click **Add...** to select programs for which you want to turn DEP off

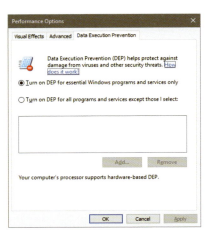

If DEP keeps closing a particular program that you trust, and your antivirus software does not detect a threat, the program might not run correctly when DEP is turned on. You should check for a DEP-compatible version of the program, or an update from the software publisher, before you choose to turn off DEP for that program.

If DEP closes a program that is part of Windows, the cause could be **a program you have recently installed** that operates inside Windows. Check for a DEP-compatible version.

Hardware-based DEP

Some processors use hardware technology to prevent programs from running code in protected memory locations. In this case, you will be told that your processor supports hardware-based DEP. If your processor does not support hardware-based DEP, your computer will still be protected because Windows will use software-based DEP.

Advanced system settings

Windows provides another way to display the Performance Options:

1   Open **Control Panel**, **System**, **Advanced system settings**

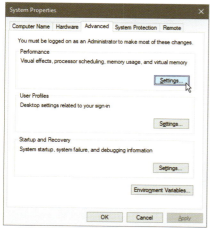

2   In the Performance section click the **Settings...** button

3   Performance Options is displayed, with **Visual Effects** selected

4   Select a tab and adjust settings to your liking

System Properties also gives access to the Device Manager:

1   Click the **Hardware** tab, then click the **Device Manager** button (or click the **Device Manager** link in the System panel)

The Device Manager lists all the **hardware devices** installed on your computer, and allows you to change their properties.

Task Manager

Windows Task Manager is a very useful utility that is still available in Windows 10. To access the Task Manager, right-click on the Taskbar and select **Task Manager**. Another way is to press **Ctrl + Alt + Delete** on the keyboard, then select the **Task Manager** option. When the Task Manager opens, click **More details** at the bottom for an extended view.

Your hardware is just one part of your PC that can be monitored with the Task Manager. You can also keep a close eye on your software in the **Processes**, **App history** and **Startup** tabs.

Windows 10 now has an **alternative** way to control which programs run when the system starts up. Go to Start, Settings, Apps, Startup to set your preferences.

The Task Manager allows you to do a number of things. These include viewing each of the tasks currently running on the computer, each of the **Processes**, your **App history**, **Services** and **Startup** programs. It also allows you to monitor the performance of the PC's hardware. Click the **Performance** tab, and on the left you will see entries for the major hardware in the system – CPU, Memory, Disk (hard drive), Ethernet, and Wi-Fi. These let you see how these devices are functioning and show any problems as they arise. For example, click **Disk** and on the right you'll see two graphs showing disk activity over the past 60-second period. The top graph shows the level of disk access, and the lower graph shows the speed of transfer to the disk in kilobytes per second:

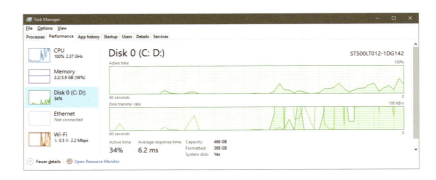

Event Viewer

Another useful tool provided by Windows with which to monitor your system in regard to performance and troubleshooting is the Event Viewer.

1   Go to Windows System, Control Panel, (View by: Category), **System and Security**, then click the **Administrative Tools** icon link

2   Now, click **Event Viewer** then expand **Windows Logs**

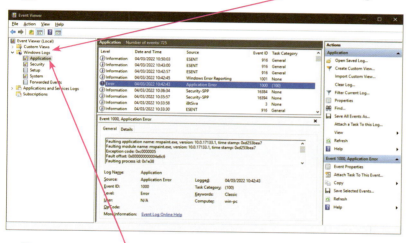

451

Advanced users might find the information helpful when **troubleshooting problems** with Windows or other programs. For most users, the Event Viewer will only be used when directed by technical support staff.

3   Select **Application**, and Windows identifies significant app events on your computer – for example: when a program encounters an error or a user logs on. The details are recorded in event logs that you can read using the Event Viewer. Windows keeps the following useful Logs:

System Log – this Log records events logged by Windows' system components, for example, the failure of a driver or other system component to load during startup is recorded in the System Log.

Application Log – the Application Log records events logged by programs, for example, a database program might record a file error in the Application Log.

Security Log – the Security Log records security events, such as valid and invalid logon attempts, and events related to resource use such as creating, opening, or deleting files or other objects. The Security Log helps track and identify possible breaches to security.

Windows monitors

Open the Performance Monitor by going to Windows System, Control Panel, (View by: Category), **System and Security**, **Administrative Tools**, **Performance Monitor**.

The program starts with an overview and a system summary. There's also a link to open the **Resource Monitor** program.

Use the **Performance Monitor** and **Resource Monitor** to view performance data either in real time or from a Log file.

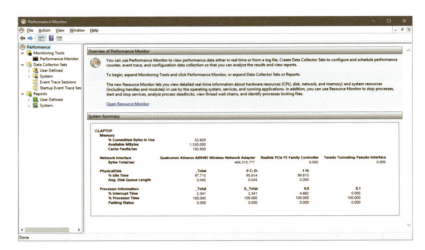

1 Expand **Data Collector Sets** or **Reports** to see Log details

2 Expand **Monitoring Tools** and click **Performance Monitor** to display the graph of processor activity

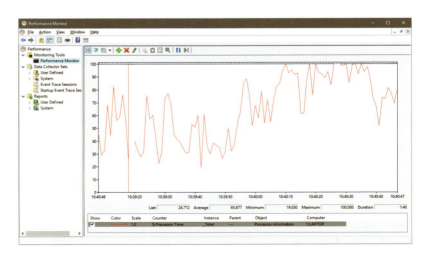

3 Back in **Administrative Tools**, open the **Resource Monitor**

Tabs in the Resource Monitor let you view systems resource usage in real time, and manage the active applications and services:

4 Click **Overview** for a summary of computer activity

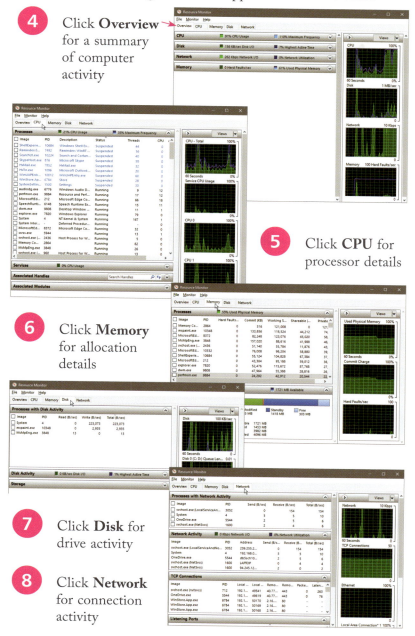

5 Click **CPU** for processor details

6 Click **Memory** for allocation details

7 Click **Disk** for drive activity

8 Click **Network** for connection activity

You can open the **Resource Monitor** utility from Advanced Tools, Performance Monitor or from the Task Manager.

The Resource Monitor also includes graphs for **network data transfer** activity.

Information on the system

1 Open the **Task Manager** to get information about the programs and processes now running on the computer

2 Click **Processes** for a list of all open applications and background processes for the current user

Don't forget

You can also open the Task Manager by pressing the keyboard shortcut **Ctrl** + **Shift** + **Esc**, or by right-clicking an empty area on the Taskbar and then selecting Task Manager.

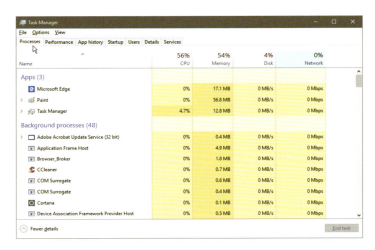

3 Click **Performance** for graphs of the CPU, memory, disk and network usage

4 Click **App history** to see how each of your apps has used the CPU and the network

Hot tip

Note that the Task Manager provides a **link** to open the Resource Monitor (on the Performance tab).

5 Press **WinKey + R**, then type "msinfo32" in the Run box to launch the System Information window

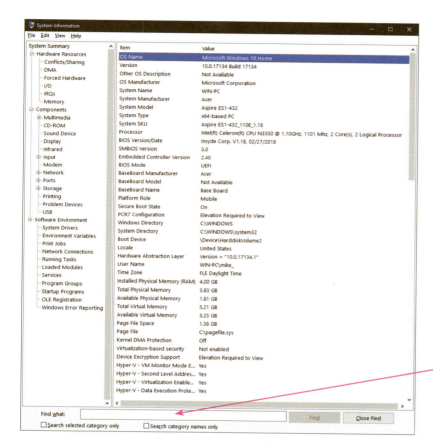

You could also enter "msinfo32" in the Taskbar **Search box** to open System Information.

To find a specific detail, type keywords in the **Find what:** box, choose **Search selected category only** (if appropriate), then click the **Find** button.

System Information opens, showing a **System Summary** listing details of your computer – operating system, computer name, type of BIOS, boot device, username, amount of memory, etc. There are further subcategories in listed under three group headings:

- **Hardware Resources** – technical details of the computer's hardware, intended for IT professionals.

- **Components** – details of disk drives, sound devices, modems and other devices.

- **Software Environment** – shows information about drivers, network connections, and other program-related details.

Reliability Monitor

1 Go to Windows System, Control Panel (View by: Large icons), **Security and Maintenance,** then expand the **Maintenance** section

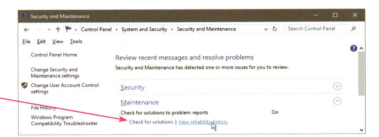

Click the **Check for solutions** *link for help with any problem.*

2 Next, click the **View reliability history** link to launch the Reliability Monitor that records system problems

Security and Maintenance provides links to several useful Windows tools.

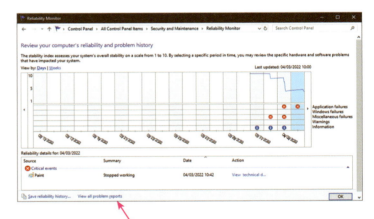

3 Now, click the **View all problem reports** link to see details of each problem encountered

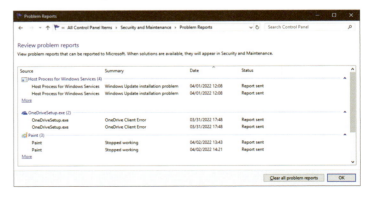

Boosting performance

There's another way to boost the performance of your computer, without having to make major upgrades to the hardware. You can add USB components such as an external drive or a flash drive.

1 Connect a second hard drive – for example, the external Hard Disk Drive (HDD) shown here:

2 The first time you do this, Windows installs the device driver software automatically

3 Windows assigns a drive letter to the drive

The HDD drive is listed under **This PC** in the **Devices and drives** category.

First connect the drive to the **mains supply** via its power adapter (if required), then connect the USB cable to a **USB port** on the computer.

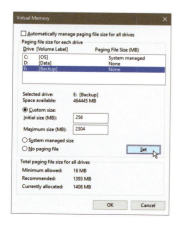

4 Open **Virtual memory** (see page 427) to assign the HDD drive a page file

5 Restart the system to apply

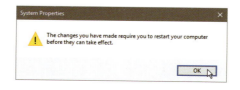

Avoid **removing** the drive while the system is active, if you have created a page file on it.

If you add a USB flash drive to your computer, you may be able to use ReadyBoost to improve the overall performance.

1 Connect the USB drive, then right-click its icon in File Explorer and select **Properties** from the context menu

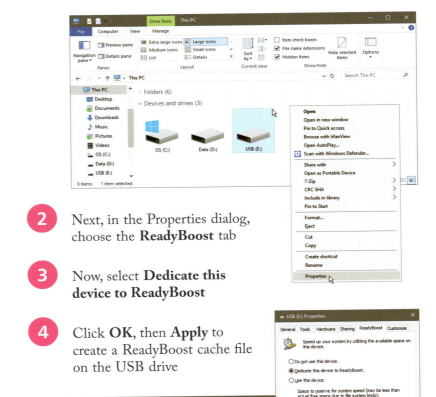

2 Next, in the Properties dialog, choose the **ReadyBoost** tab

3 Now, select **Dedicate this device to ReadyBoost**

4 Click **OK**, then **Apply** to create a ReadyBoost cache file on the USB drive

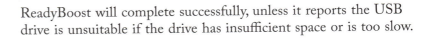

ReadyBoost will complete successfully, unless it reports the USB drive is unsuitable if the drive has insufficient space or is too slow.

32-bit versus 64-bit

Windows 10 editions are available as either 32-bit or 64-bit. This refers to the addressing structure used by the processor. Desktop computers generally have a 64-bit processor that can run either version of Windows. Some laptop and Netbook computers have 32-bit processors, and so can only run the 32-bit Windows. To check the processor level and the current operating system, open System Information (**WinKey + R** and type "msinfo32").

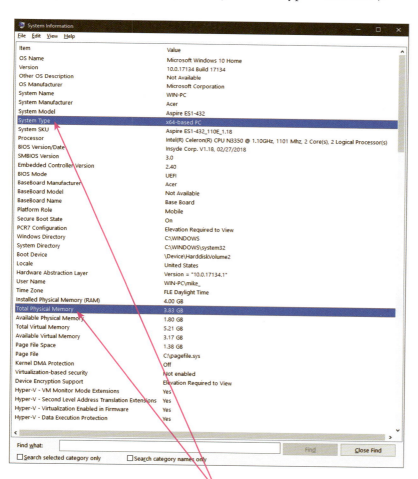

You should note the amount of **memory** as well as **64-bit** capability. You need at least 2GB memory to benefit from the 64-bit version of Windows 10.

If the System Type is an **x86-based** PC it is a 32-bit system that cannot run 64-bit Windows 10.

Here, the System Type is a x64-based PC, which means it has a 64-bit processor and can run both 32-bit and 64-bit editions of Windows, and has Total Physical Memory of 3.83GB.

...cont'd

It may improve the performance of your 64-bit-capable computer if you install the 64-bit operating system, but only if there is sufficient memory to make this worthwhile. You'll need at least 2GB – and more if possible.

There's no information report to tell you how much memory you can add to your computer, but you can find free memory scanner tools online to check your system.

Beware

You **cannot** upgrade from 32-bit to 64-bit – you must install a fresh system, completely replacing the existing system. So make sure you back up your data first. You also need 64-bit versions of drivers for all of your devices.

1 Go to **crucial.com**, then agree the terms and click the **Scan Computer** button

2 When prompted, click **Run** to check your system

Don't forget

With 64-bit Windows installed, you will find **two** Program File folders – one for 32-bit (often called x86) and one for 64-bit applications.

Program Files

Program Files (x86)

Here, the installed memory is 4GB and the maximum possible memory is 8GB. If this system was running 32-bit Windows switching to 64-bit Windows is possible, but would be only be of marginal benefit. 32-bit Windows can use a maximum of 4GB memory, whereas 64-bit Windows can use up to 192GB memory.

26

Windows Registry

This chapter describes the Windows Registry that is at the heart of the Windows operating system. It demonstrates how editing the Registry may let you perform tasks that are not otherwise supported. However, do be aware that errors in making such changes could leave your system unusable.

The Windows Registry

The Windows Registry was introduced in the early versions of Windows as a way of **organizing** and **centralizing** information that was originally stored in separate INI (initialization) files.

From time to time you may encounter Windows **tips** that are designed to make your system better, faster or easier to use, and such tips often rely on making changes to the Registry.

Change the Registry **with care**. Only use trusted sources when you do make changes. And make sure you have a Registry backup before you make any changes.

Arguably the most important component in the Windows system, since it records everything about your hardware and software, the Windows Registry is something that in normal circumstances you never need to deal with directly.

The Registry is a structured database that stores the configuration settings and options for applications, device drivers, user interface, services, and all kinds of operating system components. It also stores all the counters that are used to provide the performance reports and charts.

Installation programs, applications and device software all deal directly with the Registry, so all the updates happen in the background. However, the Registry stores user-based settings in a user-specific location, thus allowing multiple users to share the same machine, yet have their own personal details and preferences. The Registry also makes it possible to establish levels of privilege, to control what actions a particular user is permitted to carry out.

Changes to the Registry Editor

When you make changes to the setup for your user account, Windows writes the necessary updates to the Registry for you. Similarly, when you install new programs or hardware devices, many Registry modifications will be applied. Normally, you won't need to know the details.

Registry Editor

There will be times, however, when the developers have failed to provide a necessary change, and the only way (or the quickest way) to make the adjustment is by working directly with the Registry. Windows includes a Registry Editor that you can use, with caution since the Registry is a crucial part of your system, to browse and edit the Registry.

The Registry is made of a number of separate files, but you never need to be concerned with the physical structure since the Registry Editor gives you access to the full Registry, displaying the logical structure and taking care of the specifics of updates.

Before you browse or edit the Registry, you should have an understanding of the structure and how changes get applied, and especially how the original values can be saved – just in case changes get applied that have unwelcome effects.

The structure of the Registry

The data in the Windows Registry is organized in a hierarchical (or tree) format. The nodes in the tree are called keys. Each key can contain subkeys and entries. An entry consists of a name, a data type and a value, and it is referenced by the sequence of subkeys that lead to that particular entry.

There are five top level keys:

- **HKEY_CLASSES_ROOT**   **HKCR**
  Information about file types, shortcuts and interface items (alias for parts of **HKLM** and **HKCU**).

- **HKEY_CURRENT_USER**   **HKCU**
  Contains the user profile for the currently logged on user, with Desktop, network, printers, and program preferences (alias for part of **HKU**).

- **HKEY_LOCAL_MACHINE**   **HKLM**
  Information about the computer system, including hardware and operating system data such as bus type, system memory, device drivers, and startup control data.

- **HKEY_USERS**   **HKU**
  Contains information about actively loaded user profiles and the default profile.

- **HKEY_CURRENT_CONFIG**   **HKCC**
  The hardware profile used at startup; for example to configure device drivers and display resolution (alias for part of **HKLM**).

Sections of the Registry are stored in the System32 and User folders, each subtree having a single file plus a Log file – for example, Sam and **Sam.log**, or System and **System.log**. Subtrees associated with files are known as Registry hives. They include:

HKEY_LOCAL_MACHINE\SAM	Sam
HKEY_LOCAL_MACHINE\SECURITY	Security
HKEY_LOCAL_MACHINE\SOFTWARE	Software
HKEY_LOCAL_MACHINE\SYSTEM	System
HKEY_CURRENT_CONFIG	System
HKEY_CURRENT_USER	System
HKEY_USERS\.DEFAULT	Default

Beware

Some products available on the internet suggest the Registry needs regular maintenance or cleaning. Although problems can arise, in general the Registry is **self-sufficient** and such products are not really necessary.

Hot tip

Applications read the Registry to check that a specific **key** exists, or to open a key and select entry **values** that are included.

Don't forget

The tree, subtree, alias, hive, and file structure can be very **complex**, but the view taken via the Registry Editor is fortunately more straightforward.

Registry backup

Before using the Registry Editor you should create a restore point using System Restore. The restore point will contain information about the Registry, and you can use it to undo changes to your system. Follow these steps to create a manual restore point:

1 Go to Start, Windows System, Control Panel, (View by: Large icons), System, and click the **System protection** link

2 Choose the **System Protection** tab and click **Configure**, then select **Turn on system protection** and click the **Apply** button

3 Next select the drive you want to protect and click the **Create...** button to create a restore point immediately

4 Type a description of your new restore point

5 When the restore point is created, click **Close**

6 On the **System Protection** tab, click the **System Restore** button, then click **Next** – to see your new restore point

You can also back up **individual** parts of the Registry, just before you make changes to them (see page 449).

This shows that System Restore had made its **daily restore point**, so this could be used instead of a manual restore point, unless you've already made some changes during the current session.

444

Open Registry Editor

The Registry Editor is not accessible via the Control Panel, Administrative Tools or through any shortcuts. You must run the program **regedit.exe** by name.

1 Press **WinKey + R** to open the Run box. Enter "regedit", and click **OK**

2 Assuming you have an administrator account, click **Yes** to start the Registry Editor with full administrator privileges

3 The Registry Editor starts, and the first time it runs you'll see the five main subtrees, with all their branches collapsed

4 Select a key – e.g. **HKEY_LOCAL_MACHINE** (**HKLM**) – and double-click to expand to the next level

This is an **advanced** program, which will usually be run via an administrator account, though it can be run using a standard account.

Registry Editor will save the **last key** referenced in the session, and open at that point the next time you run the program.

The right-hand pane displays the **entries** and data **values** for the selected key. You can also click the arrow buttons to extend or collapse the branches of the subtrees.

Example Registry change

Before exploring the Registry further, it will be useful to look at a typical Registry update, used to make changes for which Windows has no formal method included.

One such requirement is to change the registered organization and registered owner for the computer. These names will have been set up when Windows was installed. The names chosen may no longer be appropriate, perhaps because you've changed companies, or because the computer was passed on or purchased from another user.

You can see the registration details, like this:

You'll find many such suggested changes on the internet, usually in lists of Windows **hints and tips**. These are often referred to as Registry "hacks".

1 Press **WinKey + R** and type "winver"

2 The details of the installed version of Windows are shown, along with the registered owner and organization

3 Assume that these details need to be revised to "Jennifer" and "In Easy Steps"

Do make sure that the sites you use as sources for Registry changes are **reliable**, and check the details carefully to ensure the change does **exactly** what it claims.

You will find that this particular change is included in a number of Windows hints and tips lists. You'll even find a solution at the Microsoft website **microsoft.com**

All the suggestions follow a similar pattern. They advise you to run **regedit.exe** and find the Registry key named **HKEY_LOCAL_ MACHINE\SOFTWARE\Microsoft\Windows NT\CurrentVersion**, where you can change the owner and organization. Some of the websites also discuss the need for administrator authority, and they usually warn about taking backups before making changes.

1 Locate the subkey **SOFTWARE** and double-click

To locate the key you can step through the path, subkey by subkey, double-clicking each one in turn.

2 Scroll down to subkey **Microsoft** and double-click

3 Scroll down to subkey **Windows NT** and double-click

Although the subkeys are shown in capitals or mixed case, as displayed in the Registry, they are in fact not case-sensitive.

4 Select subkey **CurrentVersion** and scroll through the list of entries to select **RegisteredOrganization**

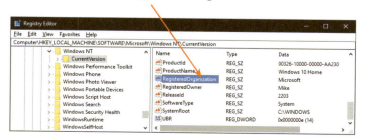

If the **RegisteredOrganization** and **RegisteredOwner** keys are absent, you can create them. Right-click on CurrentVersion, then choose New, String Value to create a new key. Right-click the key and choose Modify, then enter Name and Data values and click OK.

Finding a key

1 Select the highest level key **Computer**, then click **Edit**, **Find...** (or press **Ctrl** + **F**)

2 Check **Keys**, then type the required subkey "CurrentVersion" and click **Find Next**

3 The search may find an entry that is not the one you are looking for – for example, in **HKEY_CLASSES_ROOT** – press **F3** to continue searching

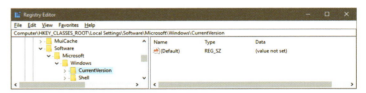

4 The search may then find another entry that is, again, not the one you are looking for – let's try a different approach

5 Check **Values**, then type the required value "RegisteredOrganization" and click **Find Next**

Back up before changes

1 Select the subkey, or a value entry within the subkey, and then click **File**, **Export...**

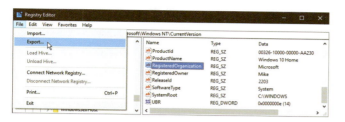

You should **make a backup** of the branch at the subkey within which changes are required.

2 Your Documents folder will be selected by default, but you can choose a different folder if desired

You can create a backup of the whole Registry, but it is sufficient to back up **just the branches being changed**.

3 Provide a file name for the Registration File (**.reg**) that is being created, and choose **Selected branch**

4 The Registration file is written to the selected folder

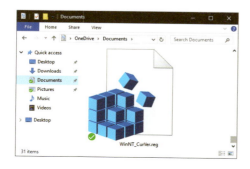

The **.reg** file will have all the subkeys, value entries and data contents for everything within the subkey selected for Export.

Change a Value entry

1 Select the **Value** entry to be changed, and double-click

This entry has text data. The value data for other entries could be binary or numbers. You must replace existing contents with the same type of data values.

2 The Value entry is opened with Value data displayed, ready for editing

3 Replace the existing contents with the required information

4 Click **OK** to apply and save the change. It is immediately in effect

If you change your mind part way through, you cannot just close Registry Editor – you must restore the original values using the branch backup, or else reverse the changes individually.

5 Repeat for any other values to be changed – for example, add a surname for the "Registered Owner"

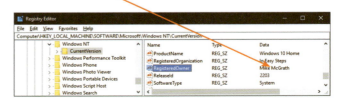

6 Close the Registry Editor when you have finished – no Save is required, since changes are dynamically applied

Using a standard account

Log off and switch to a standard user account (with no administrator privileges), making sure no other accounts are active.

1 Press **WinKey + R** to open the Run box. Enter "regedit" and click **OK**

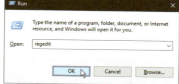

2 There's no UAC interception; Registry Editor starts up at **Computer** (or at the last key referenced by this account)

When you run Regedit from a standard user account, it operates at a **lower** privilege level.

3 Locate the Value entry **RegisteredOrganization** in the **Windows NT** subkey, and double-click the name

4 The current value is shown

5 Change the value to the required text and click **OK**

6 Registry Editor displays an error message to say it is unable to edit the entry

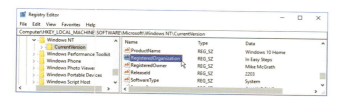

The standard account can edit and create Registry keys under **HKEY_CURRENT_USER**, but not entries under **HKEY_LOCAL_MACHINE**. Some Registry entries are even blocked for reading.

...cont'd

If there are several administrator accounts, they'll be listed, and you can **choose the appropriate** account.

There's **no obvious visual difference** between the full Regedit session and the previous limited session, but you can now make the changes.

If you are signed in with a standard user account but you need full Registry Editor access, you must run Regedit as an administrator.

1 Type "regedit" in the Taskbar Search box and press **Enter**

2 Right-click the Regedit search result and select **Run as administrator**

3 Provide the password or PIN for the administrator account displayed, to allow the Registry Editor to start with full administrator privileges

As an alternative, you can open the Windows PowerShell as an administrator, and start **regedit.exe** from there.

The Windows PowerShell is flagged as Administrator, and running **regedit.exe** from here starts the full session without further UAC prompts.

1 Press **WinKey** + **X** and click **Windows PowerShell (Admin)**

2 Respond to the UAC prompt, then type "regedit" and press **Enter**. The full Registry Editor will start

Scripted updates

You'll find that some websites offer scripted versions of Registry updates that you can download and run. These are similar to the Registration files that you create when you back up a branch of the Registry. To illustrate this method, you can create your own script to update the RegisteredOwner details.

1 Open **Notepad** and type the Registry Editor header, the subkey path and the Value entries required

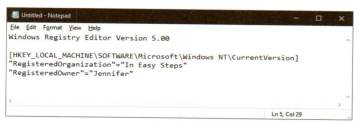

Using scripts that are provided can make it easier to apply updates, as long as you **trust** the source websites.

2 Select **File**, **Save** and choose a folder if required, or accept the default – normally this will be the Documents folder

3 Type the file name and file type; e.g. **Reg_Org_Own.reg**

4 Click **Save**, and the Registration file will be added to the specified folder

This **.reg** file automates the process followed to find the subkey and amend the Value entries for Organization and Owner.

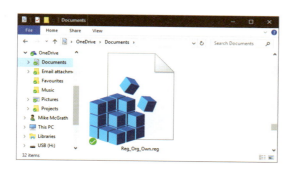

Applying an update

You use this same process to apply the backup Registration file, if you decide to **reverse** the changes you have made.

The update is applied **without** any requirement to run Regedit or open the Registry.

It is well worth repeating that **you must change the Registry with care**. Only use trusted sources when you do make changes. And make sure you have a Registry backup before you make any change.

1 To apply an update, double-click the Registration file

2 There will be a UAC prompt, and then you will be warned of the potential dangers of updates

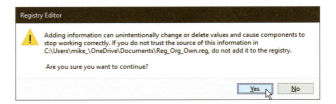

3 If you are happy with the update, click **Yes** then click **OK** to continue

4 The keys and values included are added to the Registry

5 Confirm the update by running **Winver**

6 You can also open the Registry and check the subkey and its Value entries

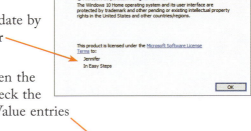

Resize Taskbar thumbnails

When you move the mouse cursor over a Windows 10 Taskbar button, you'll see a small version of the application window.

To make this larger in size:

1 Open Regedit.exe, and locate the subkey **HKEY_ CURRENT_USER\Software\Microsoft\Windows\ CurrentVersion\Explorer\Taskband**

2 Right-click the right-hand pane and select **New, DWORD (32-bit) Value,** then name the value "MinThumbSizePx"

An **address bar** was added to the Registry Editor in the Windows 10 so you can search by typing or pasting a registry path – character case is not sensitive.

3 Double-click the value, then set the **Decimal** value to "350"

Registry updates require you to change hexadecimal or decimal **number values,** or create **keys** or change **text values**.

4 Log out and log in again to put the change into effect

5 View a Taskbar thumbnail to see the enlarged thumbnail results

Adjust the value again to fine-tune the results, or **delete** the value entry to return to the default thumbnail.

Remove shortcut suffix

When you create a shortcut on the Desktop, Windows insists on adding the word "Shortcut" to the name, like this:

1 Locate the Notepad.exe program file, which is usually found in **C:\Windows\System32**

The shortcut **suffix** and **arrow icon** help identify links that can safely be deleted. Removing the suffix and arrow icon allows shortcuts to look just like the file to which they point – those that you probably do not want to delete.

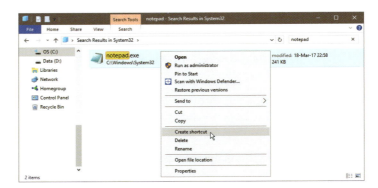

2 Right-click the program icon and select **Create shortcut**

3 The shortcut cannot be added to the program folder, so click **Yes** to place it on the Desktop

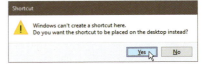

4 The shortcut is created and given the program name followed by - **Shortcut**

If you often find yourself editing the name to remove this addition, you might like to edit the Registry to avoid the suffix for all future shortcuts you create (this change won't affect existing shortcuts).

1 Run **regedit.exe** and find the key **HKEY_CURRENT_USER\ Software\Microsoft\Windows\CurrentVersion\Explorer**

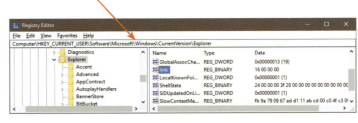

2 Right-click the "link" entry, then select **Modify...** from the context menu

3 Change the first part of the number (e.g. 18) to 00 to give a value of **00 00 00 00**

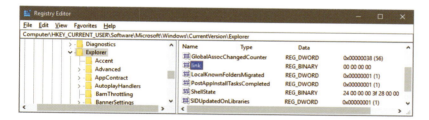

4 Click **OK** to update the value, then close **regedit.exe**

You must log out and log in again for the change to take effect. Now, when you create a shortcut, it will just display the program name with no suffix.

Remove shortcut arrows

You can also use Registry updates to change the shortcut icons, avoiding the shortcut arrow overlay, or using a different (perhaps smaller) arrow to overlay the shortcut icons.

There are a number of different methods suggested for this. They involve adding a reference to an alternative icon file in a value entry in the key **HKEY_LOCAL_MACHINE\SOFTWARE\Microsoft\Windows\CurrentVersion\Explorer\Shell Icons**.

You can search the internet for relevant articles using a search term such as "Windows remove shortcut arrow" and choose your preferred website. Note that the instructions provided may differ for Windows 32-bit versus Windows 64-bit systems.

As with all Registry updates, make sure that you back up first, before making any changes.

*Sometimes changes such as these have **unexpected side effects**, so a backup or restore point will be particularly important.*

Adjust Desktop Peek

You can change the time delay before Desktop Peek reduces the screen to the Desktop.

Don't forget

When the mouse moves over the Peek button at the bottom-right of the screen, all open windows are replaced by empty frames. This can be distracting when you are just moving the mouse to a corner to help locate the pointer.

Hot tip

The **default** is 500 (half a second), 1000 is one second, and 0 is instant. To return to the default, set the value to 500 or delete the Value entry.

1 Run **regedit.exe** and find the key **HKEY_CURRENT_USER\ Software\Microsoft\Windows\CurrentVersion\Explorer\ Advanced**

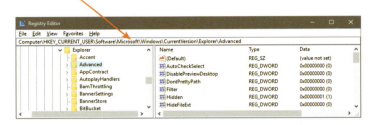

2 Right-click the right-hand pane and select **New, DWORD (32-bit) Value** (see page 455) and name the value "DesktopLivePreviewHoverTime"

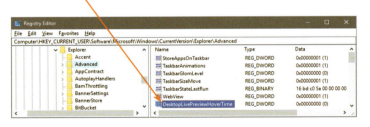

3 Double-click to edit, select **Decimal** and enter a value in milliseconds, for example "2000" (two seconds), then click **OK** to apply the new value

4 Now, log out, then log in again to put this Registry update into effect and try the change to Desktop Peek

27 Extending Windows

This chapter describes how Windows 10 provides great extensibility for remote connection, portability, virtual system hosting, and connection to other devices.

Remote Desktop connection

The "Remote Desktop" feature is available on Windows 10 Pro editions and is used to access one computer from another remotely, for example, connecting to your work computer from home. You will have access to all of your programs, files, and network resources, as if you were sitting in front of your computer at work.

On the Remote Computer

Before the Remote Desktop feature can be used it needs to be enabled on the computer that is to be remotely accessed:

1 Go to Start, Settings, System, and click the **Remote Desktop** item in the left pane

2 Next slide the "Enable Remote Desktop" toggle button to the **On** position

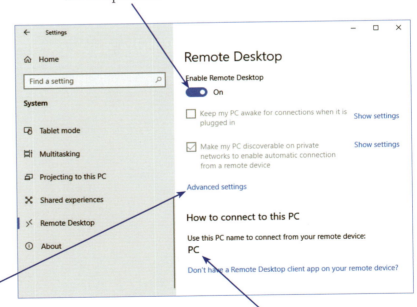

3 Now, make a note of the remote computer's name as you will need it to connect from the accessing computer – it's simply named "PC" in the example above

On the Accessing Computer

You now have to open the Remote Desktop Connection:

1 Type "Remote Desktop" in the Taskbar Search box, then click the **Remote Desktop Connection** result

2 Enter the name of the remote computer (type "PC" in our example), then click the **Connect** button

Click **Show Options** to reveal a range of settings with which to enhance the remote connection.

3 Next, enter the user name and password for the account you wish to log into on the remote computer

4 Now, click the **OK** button to load the remote computer's desktop onto the accessing computer's screen

Once the connection is made and authenticated, **everything** on the remote PC is open to, and can be controlled by, the accessing computer.

Windows To Go

Windows To Go is a feature found in Windows 10 Enterprise that enables a fully-functional copy of Windows 10 to be created on a USB drive. The procedure makes the drive bootable in the same way that Windows installation disks are.

Not just any USB drive can be used with Windows To Go. Microsoft has specified certain requirements that manufacturers must meet in order for their USB drives to qualify as a supported Windows To Go device. One such USB drive is the Kingston DataTraveler shown below:

External **USB drives** can be used, as well as flash drives.

The minimum storage space required by Windows To Go is 32GB. This is enough for Windows 10 itself, but if you also need to transport applications such as Microsoft Office, plus files, a larger USB drive will be required. Currently, flash drives up to 512GB are readily available.

A Windows To Go drive can be plugged into a USB socket on any computer and, because it is bootable, a Windows 10 session can be loaded on that computer. Once booted, it functions and is controlled by standard enterprise management tools such as System Center Configuration Manager (SCCM) and Active Directory group policies.

Windows To Go will only work on USB drives built **specifically** for it.

Windows To Go provides an ideal solution for anyone who needs mobile computer access, for example, business representatives out in the field will be able to work from any computer. Also, it's more cost-effective for IT departments to replace a faulty USB drive than it is to deal with the downtime and expense of returning a laptop to the office, repairing it, and returning it to the field.

Windows To Go is also ideal for trying out Windows 10 (or other software) on a machine, without affecting that machine.

Virtual machine

A virtual computer is one that is created by and run within a computer virtualization program. It is a fully-functional replica of a physical computer and can run programs, access the internet, etc.

Popular programs of this type include VMware and VirtualBox – the latter being a free download from **www.virtualbox.org** However, with some versions of Windows 10 there is no need for third-party virtualization software – one, called Hyper-V, is supplied with Windows 10 Pro edition. It does need to be installed first, though, like this:

Client Hyper-V has very **stringent hardware requirements**. Not every PC will be able to run it.

1 Click Start, Settings then type "Windows features" into the Search box

2 Select the **Turn Windows features on or off** result to open the Windows Features dialog box

3 Check the boxes next to **Hyper-V**, then click **OK**

4 Restart the computer when prompted, to launch Hyper-V

5 Now, in the Taskbar Search box, type "hyper" and press **Enter**. The Hyper-V Manager opens, as shown below

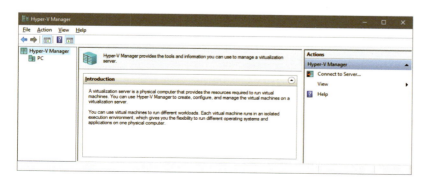

Install guest system

To try Hyper-V you can create a Windows 7 virtual PC, like this:

1 At the top-left of the Hyper-V Manager, select the computer name, then click **Action**, **New**, **Virtual Machine** – to open the New Virtual Machine Wizard

This example demonstrates how to create a **Windows 7** guest system, but you can create guest systems for other operating systems too.

2 Click the **Next** button, then name the new virtual machine "Windows 7" and click **Next** again

3 Choose **Generation 1**, click **Next** and assign a valid startup memory allocation, then click **Finish**

Hyper-V's **Hardware options** provide a range of settings for all the hardware components found in a computer.

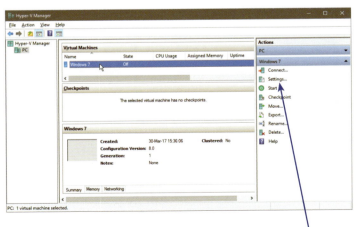

4 Expand "Windows 7" in the Actions pane, then click **Settings...**

5 Next, select **Legacy Network Adapter**, then click **Add**

6 Select **DVD Drive** under "IDE Controller 1". Here, you can specify an image file (ISO) or optical drive for installation of the operating system. To use an installation disk, select **Physical CD/DVD drive**, then click **Apply**

7 Insert the Windows 7 installation disk in the DVD drive, then return to the Actions pane and click **Connect...**

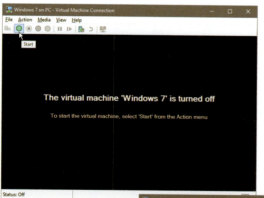

8 Now, click **Start** to begin building the Virtual Machine within Hyper-V

9 Proceed to install Windows 7 inside the Virtual Machine

Hot tip

Potential uses for virtual PCs include sandboxed **software evaluation**, other **operating systems**, and **safe web browsing**.

Hot tip

Hyper-V has a feature called **Snapshots**. These let you save the state of a virtual PC, so you can revert back in much the same way as a system backup lets you roll back to the point when the backup was made.

Android devices

Windows 10 lets you easily copy music, photos, videos, and documents between your computer and an Android smartphone or tablet device.

1 Turn **On** and **connect** a device to your Windows 10 computer via a USB cable connection – for example, connect a tablet running the Android operating system

2 A notification invites you to choose what happens with this device – click on the notification

3 From the pop-up menu that appears, choose the option to "Open device to view files" – to launch File Explorer where you can copy and paste files between your device and Windows 10 PC

Windows 10 remembers the **AutoPlay** option you select when you connect a new device, and will automatically perform the same action each time you reconnect that device. You can change the preferred action for a device on the Settings, AutoPlay screen.

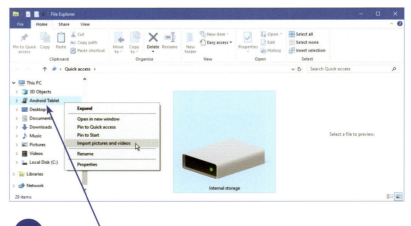

4 Right-click the connected device icon in File Explorer, then choose the **Import pictures and videos** option

5 After Windows 10 completes the search of your Android tablet device, click the **More options** link

Optionally you can click the **Next** button to use existing import settings – skipping Steps 6 and 7.

6 Choose where imported items should be placed, and naming formats

7 Check the option to **Open File Explorer after import**, then click the **OK** button

8 Select and name items to be imported, then click the **Import** button

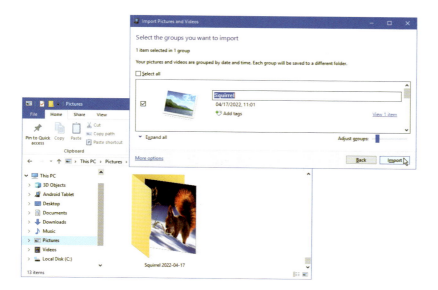

Always use the **Safely Remove Hardware** feature to disconnect USB devices from your computer.

Kindle devices

Windows 10 lets you easily sync music, photos, and videos between your computer and a Kindle Fire tablet device.

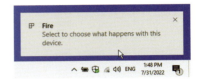

1 Turn **On** and **connect** a Kindle Fire device to your Windows 10 computer via a USB cable connection

2 A notification invites you to choose what happens with this device – click on the notification

3 From the pop-up menu that appears, choose the option to "Sync digital media files to this device" – to launch Windows Media Player, where you can create a list of picture, audio, and video files to sync between your Kindle Fire device and your Windows 10 PC

Hot tip

Once your Kindle Fire is connected you can find it in File Explorer and access its folder contents.

4 Select Music, Videos, and Pictures folders in turn, then drag and drop items onto the **Sync list** area

5 When your list is done, click the **Start sync** button

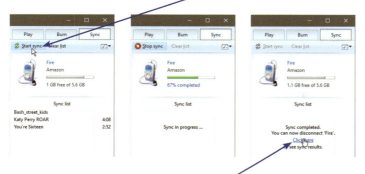

6 To see the sync results, click this link on completion

Don't forget

You can reconnect your Kindle Fire at any time and edit your chosen sync files list to change what is copied into the Kindle folders.

7 Copies of the selected media files appear in their respective folders on your Kindle Fire device

8 You can now disconnect your Kindle Fire device from the PC and play the media files on your Kindle Fire whenever you like

You're Sixteen (You're Beautiful And You're Mine)
Ringo Starr

Windows news

Microsoft introduces new features into Windows 10 as it evolves. You can follow development of the latest features by regularly visiting the Windows blog at **blogs.windows.com**

You can join the **Windows Insider Program** to receive new feature updates before they are made available for general release.

Sometimes you can learn of new features for Windows 10 before their official announcement, from websites that claim to have inside knowledge. There are several of these, such as the "Windows Central" at **windowscentral.com**

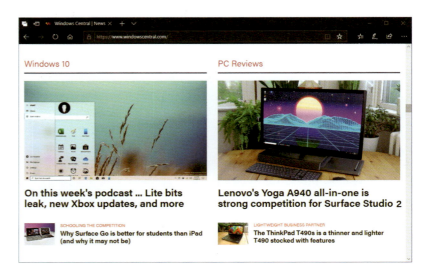

Windows 10 continues to be developed in Microsoft's battle against Android and Apple. Time will tell who will dominate.

Index

U

V

W

X

Y

Z